The Return
Of The Repressed

SUNY series in Psychoanalysis and Culture
Henry Sussman, editor

THE RETURN OF THE REPRESSED

Gothic Horror from *The Castle of Otranto* to *Alien*

VALDINE CLEMENS

STATE UNIVERSITY OF NEW YORK PRESS

COVER ART: Francisco de Goya y Lucientes' *Las Resultas* (*The Consequences*), Etching Working Proof, Plate 72, of *The Disasters of War* series (1814–20). I wish to thank the Norton Simon Art Foundation, Pasadena, CA.

Quotes from *The Shining* by Stephen King, copyright © 1977 by Stephen King, used by permission of Doubleday, a division of Bantam Doubleday Dell Publishing Group, Inc., and Hodder and Stoughton Limited.

Quotes from "The Virtue of Love: Lord Hardwick's Marriage Act" by Erica Harth. In *Cultural Critique*, 9 (Spring 1988) pp. 123–54. Used by permission of the University of Minnesota Press.

For information, address State University of New York Press, State University Plaza, Albany, N.Y., 12246

Production by Marilyn P. Semerad
Marketing by Fran Keneston

Library of Congress Cataloging-in-Publication Data

Clemens, Valdine, 1948–
    The return of the repressed : gothic horror from the Castle of Otranto to Alien / Valdine Clemens.
        p.   cm.—(SUNY series in psychoanalysis and culture)
    Includes bibliographical references and index.
    ISBN 0-7914-4327-2 (alk. paper). —ISBN 0-7914-4328-0 (pbk. : alk. paper)
    1. Horror tales, English—History and criticism.   2. Psychological fiction,   English—History and criticism.   3. Psychoanalysis and literature—England—History.   4. Gothic revival (Literature)—Great Britain.   5. Gothic revival (Literature)— United States.   6. Horror films—History and criticism.   7. Psychoanalysis and motion pictures.   I. Title.   II. Series.
PR830.T3C59   1999
823'.0873809—dc21
                                                                                    98-52055
                                                                                    CIP

10   9   8   7   6   5   4   3   2   1

This book is dedicated to the memory of my mother, Mabel Clemens.

CONTENTS

ACKNOWLEDGMENTS

I would like to thank Evelyn J. Hinz for her invaluable, generous assistance and advice. Her intelligence, insight, and keen interest are deeply appreciated.

For their helpful comments and suggestions, I would like to thank Judith Flynn, W. Ross Hartsough, Richard P. Sugg, and John J. Teunissen. Judith Flynn kindly saved me time and trouble by sharing some hard-to-get material needed for the *Dr Jekyll and Mr Hyde* chapter. Particular thanks go to John Teunissen, for persuading me that Stephen King's *Shining* is necessary reading in any study of the Gothic tradition.

Jeffrey Berman's encouragement and thoughtful criticism are also much appreciated, as is David Ketterer's close and careful reading of the manuscript.

The sometimes onerous task of obtaining materials unavailable in Winnipeg was made much easier by the cheerful, helpful women who work in Document Delivery at the University of Manitoba.

For his support, which included sharing his excellent library, reading and commenting on drafts, working on the index, and repeatedly solving my computer problems, I am very grateful to Maurice Mierau. Our son, Jeremy, also deserves thanks for his patience and willingness to let Mom work, and his interesting observations on the subjects of Frankenstein, Dracula, and many other matters. He has taught me much.

Introduction: What Gothic Nightmares Do

The bulk of readers, the only kind to which we moderns devote our lucubrations, seem now much more pleased to be frightened out of their wits than to be assisted in making a proper use of them.

—Isaac d'Israeli, *V*

*T*his study is based on the premise that literature provides what Kenneth Burke calls "equipment for living" (253). The question that remains, of course, is what *kind* of equipment Gothic fiction provides. Burke suggests that a "sociological" approach to literature entails evaluating particular art forms according to their "bearing on human welfare" (253). He uses proverbs to illustrate his point, showing how they "size up situations in various ways" corresponding to the proverbs' different aims, such as "promise, admonition, solace, vengeance, foretelling, instruction, charting" (262, 255). Because the primary impulse of Gothic tales is the arousal of fear, they might at first appear to have little in common with the tradition of proverbial wisdom, yet they too "size up situations" in particular ways, according to particular aims. Not only do Gothic stories convey admonitory, prophetic, and instructional messages, but also they perform a literary (or cinematic) type of psychosocial therapy. That is, in frightening us out of our habitual "wits," Gothic fiction can actually shock us into using them in more viable ways.

The Gothic tale is generally most effective when it is most affective. The reader usually judges the story's success by his or her own immediate

1

visceral response—whether the hairs stand on end, the skin is all goose bumps, the nerves are stretched to the limit, the spine tingles, and above all, whether one feels riveted, completely and utterly focused on the fear and suspense of the unfolding events. The early Gothic novelists understood, however dimly, the importance of this effect. In 1797, for example, one writer enthusiastically promised his readers that his tale would "chill—... make the sensitive soul thrill with horror—... make the very hair stand perched on its native habitual roost, where so long it had lain recumbent" (qtd. in J. M. S. Tompkins 222).[1]

In evolutionary terms, such symptoms can be understood as vestiges of the early human, or even prehuman, fight-or-flight response. Reading Gothic fiction is an atavistic experience. In its stimulation of an intense physical and emotional reaction, such fiction provides an antidote for the excessively cerebral consciousness, the de-vitalized state that Thomas Hardy called the "ache of modernism" and to which D. H. Lawrence referred— anticipating modern media jargon—with the term "talking heads."[2]

The scenes of physical degradation that permeate Gothic novels also draw the reader into an ambience of psychological regression. C. G. Jung says of individual regression that "[what it] brings to the surface certainly seems at first sight to be slime from the depths; but ... this 'slime' contains not merely incompatible and rejected remnants of everyday life, or inconvenient and objectionable animal tendencies, but also germs of new life and vital possibilities for the future" (*Structure* 34–35).

Through this process, Jung argues, one becomes re-acquainted with the inner world of the psyche. Although one momentarily forgoes the problem of outward adaptation (which is one reason that Gothic tales often have been dismissed as self-indulgent, excessive, and childish), the eventual result may be re-orientation to a more viable relation with the outer world.

The ghostly element in Gothic tales offers a similar opportunity for the most rational, enlightened, and skeptical reader to regress to an exhilarating state of "daemonic dread." As a number of critics have pointed out, the preoccupation with primordial fear in late-eighteenth-century fiction signified a reaction against the increasing secularism of the postenlightenment era. Devendra P. Varma, for example, writes that the Gothic novels "met the need of their times, which had not been met by the polished intellectualism of the Augustan age. These novels answered to a demand for something wild and primitive, exciting the primordial emotions" (228–29). In a similar vein, Joel Porte has suggested that Gothic mystery can be seen "as a substitute for discredited religious mystery" and that "Gothic fiction [is] the expression of a fundamentally Protestant theological or religious disquietude" (43).[3] When Reason and Science usurped God, Gothic rushed in to fill the resulting vacuum with the daemonic. The feeling most consistently evoked in Gothic tales is the terror of the life-threatened creature, wholly at the mercy of forces that are neither controllable nor understandable; a terror that at its most elemental level makes little distinction between "natural" and "supernatural" causes.

According to Rudolf Otto, this feeling, "emerging in the mind of primeval man, forms the starting-point for the entire religious development in history. 'Daemons' and 'gods' alike spring from this root" (14). Otto suggests that "even when the higher and purer mode of expression" of the numinous experience has been attained,

> it is possible for the primitive types of excitation that were formerly a part of it to break out in the soul in all their original naïvete and so to be experienced afresh. That this is so is shown by the potent attraction again and again exercised by the element of horror and 'shudder' in ghost stories, even among persons of high all-round education. It is a remarkable fact that the physical reaction to which this unique 'dread' of the uncanny gives rise is also unique, and is not found in the case of any 'natural' fear or terror. We say: 'my blood ran icy cold', and 'my flesh crept'. The 'cold blood' feeling may be a symptom of ordinary, natural fear, but there is something nonnatural or supernatural about the symptom of 'creeping flesh'. (16)

As S. L. Varnado has shown, Otto's analysis provides valuable insights into the way that the supernatural in Gothic fiction creates an effect of numinosity. More than that, however—and central to an understanding of the dynamics of Gothic horror—is Otto's argument that a sense of the numinous involves an element of atavism.

Specifically, it is through the evocation of intense creature-terror that Gothic stories achieve their critical ends of admonishing, foretelling, and instructing. In this respect, they are comparable to certain types of nightmares, which serve as alarming reminders that things are not as they should be or not what they appear to be. For the person who pays attention to the dream life, the nightmare is a message from the unconscious, often arising when a given attitude is proving inadequate to a current life situation. This type of nightmare vividly predicts the potentially disastrous consequences of persisting in a particular attitude or mode of action. It may also simultaneously reveal something that has been previously rejected or unacknowledged by consciousness, and so indirectly indicate the means of readjusting one's attitude.[4]

This "return of the repressed," or emergence of whatever has been previously rejected by consciousness, is a fundamental dynamism of Gothic narratives. Something—some entity, knowledge, emotion, or feeling—which has been submerged or held at bay because it threatens the established order of things, develops a cumulative energy that demands its release and forces it to the realm of visibility where it must be acknowledged. The approach and the appearance of the repressed create an aura of menace and "uncanniness," both in Freud's sense of "*unheimlich*"—something that becomes apparent although one feels it "ought" to remain hidden (17: 224, 241)—and in the Jungian sense of something possessing an awesome or transpersonal, numinous quality.

It is commonly thought that the backward-looking Gothic novel, with its oneiric landscapes, is less socially responsible than the "realistic" novel, which pays closer attention to the surface textures of daily life; but such a view underestimates both the critical import of these seemingly escapist fictions and the extent to which many of them do provide realistic social detail. Growing out of the ancient tradition of the ghost story, Gothic novels emerged with the development of the urban-industrial world; they serve as a kind of anthropological time-line, suggesting how young this type of social organization is, how long the more dangerous, precarious hunting and gathering life lasted, and how the past continues to shape the psychic realities of the present. They stress the fragility of civilized constraints on human behavior and demonstrate that the world is much older and less anthropocentric than we would like to think.

As Julia Briggs has noted, later Gothic fiction is haunted by the Darwinian revelation of the world as "infinitely older, larger, wilder and less anthropocentric" than had previously been supposed. According to Briggs, however, Gothic operates as a reaction against the materialism of Darwinian science: the ghost tale (which she sees as having declined since the 1920s) set up "counter-suggestions that provided reassurance, beneath its more obvious terrors: undermining the apparent predictability of the material world, it gave comforting proof that there *was* something beyond" (24). Thus, Briggs accepts Freud's idea (as I do not) that the ghost story "depends upon the existence of a tension between an outmoded, but not entirely abandoned belief and an enlightened scepticism" (16). My view is that the capacity for superstitious fear can never be entirely "abandoned"; the ghosts just take on different forms.

From its inception, Gothic fiction has presented a challenge to enlightened skepticism. Early Gothic fiction revealed the one-sidedness of the Age of Reason and tended to unsettle prevailing assumptions about civilized superiority, the march of progress, and the powers of the rational mind. Goya's eighteenth-century dictum that "the sleep of reason breeds monsters" could be rephrased into the Gothic recognition that reason (or excessive rationality) itself is a form of sleep or unawareness, which breeds monsters. Thus, the tension in Gothic narratives often takes the form of a widening gap between the reader's growing understanding of a lurking horror, and a more rationally inclined protagonist's resistance to the truth.

Gothic fiction also addresses the cultural rootlessness that characterizes contemporary Western society. To live in a world of accelerating technological change can be both a blessing and an affliction; on the one hand there is greater immediate safety and comfort, but on the other hand there is an increasing sense of temporal fragmentation and consequent anxiety about the future. The past, present, and future, the dead and the living, are no longer felt to be vitally connected as they formerly were in less technologically advanced societies.[5] Gothic fiction helps to correct this condition of psychological short-sightedness by forging an imaginative connection with the archaic past.

Gothic's cultural critique often involves a more historically specific political concern as well. Rosemary Jackson has argued that fantastic literature, of which Gothic is one expression, "emerges in periods of relative 'stability' (mid-eighteenth-century, late nineteenth-century, mid-twentieth century)" and that this fact "points to a direct relation between cultural repression and its generation of oppositional energies which are expressed through various forms of fantasy in art" (179). While I agree with Jackson that Gothic introduces "oppositional energies" into a given social order, I hope to show that the "order" into which those energies are introduced is already showing signs of accelerating destabilization.

A "national brand" of Gothic fiction seems to proliferate whenever the political and economic dominance that a given country has acquired appears to be passing its peak and about to decline: England in the late eighteenth, as well as early and late nineteenth centuries, and America in the late twentieth century. Although writers have been producing Gothic fiction fairly continuously for the last two centuries, the readership for Gothic horror has expanded significantly in such crisis periods, when the public mood becomes uneasy and pessimistic, and when re-evaluation of the national identity seems to take on a particular urgency.

The "appetite for the . . . horrible" that Sir Walter Scott disparagingly noted in his own day (*Heart* 13) is actually a quite natural response to the perceived weakening of the social fabric on which people have come to rely. In descending imaginatively into the darker and "lower" realms of human experience, where one realizes in a fairly visceral way both the precariousness of life and the existence of powers greater than oneself, one temporarily abdicates accustomed social attitudes and constraints, as well as personal desires and concerns, attaining thereby a heightened sense of their relative, historically conditioned nature.

The usual interpretation of the historical connection between Gothic horror and periods of social unrest is that Gothic registers or reflects these moments of radical cultural shift. Jack Sullivan, for example, suggests that people develop a "fetish for disaster . . . when things appear to be falling apart, [and] supernatural horror stories provide their authors and readers with a masochistic, but relatively safe means of fantasizing the worst" (3). This type of fiction does more than simply reflect popular attitudes, however; it also influences them. In both its literary and cinematic forms, Gothic horror can actually facilitate a process of cultural change.

Not infrequently, the Gothic protagonists' struggles with hidden guilt, transgression, and retribution point to a larger societal need to confront similar issues of social and moral responsibility. Their stories identify a gap between official ideology and actual reality. "Admonitory and prophetic," Gothic narratives often portray the consequences of the Seven Deadly Sins in grotesque imagery that has a grimly medieval vividness. By such means they become agents of social and psychological transformation, reaching into the collective past, reviving awareness of the "ancestral . . . body" (Bakhtin 323), and thereby revealing fresh "possibilities for the future" (Jung, *Structure* 34–35)

The taste for Gothic horror also may be stimulated when social havoc occurring somewhere else is near enough to be noticeable but not near enough to directly affect the average daily life. It is not difficult to see a parallel between the effect of the news from France on English citizens in the 1790s after the Reign of Terror began, and the effect of media glimpses of world-wide human atrocities (or serial cannibal-rapist killers at home) on citizens in the Western industrial world today. To experience fear, calamity, and human savagery, however vicariously, is also to gain some appreciation of their reality.

The historical specificity of Gothic tales helps to explain why their power to shock readers tends to weaken over time, despite the evident consistency in narrative movement and in certain recurring images and themes. What is dreadful to one generation of Gothic readers does not remain dreadful to the next because there is a continual historical alteration in the precise characteristics of what is being repressed. The threshold separating the admissible and the inadmissible is a constantly shifting cultural ground because psychic readjustment, individually and collectively, is an on-going process.

This power to facilitate self-re-evaluation is not the only way in which the Gothic story and the nightmare resemble each other, for their manner of doing so is also similar; both rely largely on images to convey their messages. As David Punter observes, "Gothic fiction becomes a process of cultural self-analysis, and the images which it throws up become the dream-figures of a troubled social group" (425). It is a mistake to assume, however, that because the visual image seems to demand a more emotional or less intellectually rigorous response, it does not invite judgement or reflection. Objecting to such notions about archetypal psychology, James Hillman emphasizes the importance of intellectual concentration: the image-making activity of the mind does "invite judgement as a further precision of the image, judgement arising from the image itself as an effect of the image's own presentation of a claim for response" (8–9); the "multiplicity of psychic phenomena" that appear in the form of images can then be perceived "with precision and particularity rather than generalized" as abstract verbal formulations (52).

The ease of transition from literary to cinematic forms of the Gothic is partly due to the importance of the image, particularly the originating image of the ancient castle as bastion of personal or cultural identity under assault. From Walpole's collapsing Castle of Otranto, to King's burning Overlook Hotel in *The Shining*, to Ridley Scott's exploding spaceship in *Alien*, Gothic tales enact a confrontation with a haunting and/or imprisoning past. The castle is a multivalent symbol; it may be associated with the maternal or the sexual body, the human psyche, or the patriarchal social order. The dark tunnels and underground passages of Gothic edifices represent descent into the unconscious, away from the socially constructed self and toward the uncivilized, the primitive. Violence, pursuit, and rape occur in these lower depths, yet they are also the realms where valuable discoveries are made.

Architectural imagery frequently serves to signify the forceful incursion of the unconscious life into the conscious (which may be one reason that opponents of both Gothic fiction and architecture have at times described them in terms of "invasion, infection, and degeneracy" [Lyndenberg 104]). Eve Kosofsky Sedgwick has focused on surfaces and interfaces in Gothic fiction, noting that moments of crisis inevitably involve a violent breaking, disruption, or transgression of boundaries: doors, walls, locked drawers, taboos drawn on speech and action, and so forth. The folktale "Bluebeard" appeared in print at the beginning of the eighteenth century, providing an important literary paradigm for this motif. In this tale, first set down by Charles Perrault, Bluebeard's young wife unlocks a forbidden door and discovers the bloody remains of all the former wives he has murdered.

Another set of doors that Gothic unlocks is that which segregates our different mental and emotional capacities. Contemporary neurophysiologists investigating the model of the tripartite human brain (reptilian, mammalian, and specifically human areas) have described it in terms of a structural division of labor, which they argue is necessary for psychological stability.[6] Gothic antiheroes such as the "ape-like" Mr. Hyde and the reptilian Dracula cross the thresholds that separate these domains, thereby disturbing the complacency of civilized consciousness.

Jung argues that "[w]hatever we persistently exclude from conscious training and adaptation necessarily remains in an untrained, undeveloped, infantile, archaic condition" (*Structure* 124); or in the words of Sir Francis Bacon, "All passions flourish and acquire vigour by being forbidden"—and the repressed that returns in Gothic fiction is often remarkably vigorous and disruptive. Violent sexuality, especially male sexuality, is a continuing preoccupation of Gothic fiction. The Gothic presentation of sex is extremely unromantic and anti-idealistic (except in the case of sentimental Female Gothic). Gothic stories highlight the tremendous power and sometimes "irresistible" (a Gothic by-word) force of the instincts. The atavistic antihero, typically an aspiring rapist, compels our attention as a vital yet self-destructive figure to a greater degree than he invites our moral condemnation. His presence demonstrates the danger of underestimating the force of the instinctual life.

Similarly, the female figures fleeing through dark passages and hiding or being imprisoned in the underground vaults of Gothic castles and monasteries generally emerge at some climactic point in the story to reveal the full extent of their creative or destructive powers. Rather than appearing as fully rounded characters, these figures function as manifestations of the feminine principle in life, which a post-Reformation, post-Enlightenment and urban-industrial world has consistently undervalued. During the late-eighteenth-century Gothic vogue, many staunchly Protestant writers found access to the feminine realm by reverting imaginatively to a medieval Catholic world, which still venerated the Mother Goddess in the form of the Virgin Mary.

The lack of "realistic" characterization in Gothic fiction has been regarded by some critics as one of the genre's characteristic deficiencies. Elizabeth Napier, for example, asserts that the early Gothic novels suffer from a "systematic failure" in that they "seldom . . . lead to the profound realizations about human consciousness that some critics have asserted that they do" (7). Napier feels that the "subordination of character in Gothic fiction recurs frequently enough to cast doubt on recent critical celebrations of the Gothic as psychologically exploratory" (34). Napier's underlying assumption, however, seems to be that characters' "depth of personality" (34) can be the only index of a story's psychological insight. Although it is true that Gothic narratives tend to be concerned with the ego-personality only insofar as it places itself in opposition to the instinctual or transpersonal elements of the psyche, this also means that characters in Gothic stories are like the figures in our dreams; they embody and act out conflicting, subconscious psychic energies.

The connection between Gothic fiction and the unconscious also pertains to the genesis of these novels, which in turn helps to explain their impact. Although artistic craft must not be discounted, it is nevertheless remarkable how many outstanding Gothic tales have been written in a kind of "white heat" and inspired by disturbing, somehow unforgettable dreams. Four of the most influential works in the tradition are said to have begun in this fashion: *The Castle of Otranto, Frankenstein, Dr. Jekyll and Mr. Hyde,* and *Dracula.* It is also apparent that novels such as Bram Stoker's *Dracula,* which is somewhat flawed aesthetically, have made a deeper impression on the popular imagination than works of considerably greater elegance and finesse, such as Henry James's *The Turn of the Screw.* My own explanation for the lower voltage of James's tales is that they create a sense of mystification, intrigue, and perplexity, but little sense of the awesome, the mysterious, the "superstitious dread."[7]

If writers of Gothic fiction tend to be unconsciously empowered, however, they nevertheless seem to share a strong awareness of belonging to a particular tradition, and they often draw attention to their literary lineage through various allusions within their stories. Gothic fiction writers appear to be "very conscious of the main current" that both directs them and is redirected by them (to borrow T. S. Eliot's phrase from his "Tradition and the Individual Talent" [785]). My study of Gothic fiction is similarly designed to participate in and further this alternative to what F. R. Leavis has called "The Great Tradition."

The earliest twentieth-century studies of Gothic and supernatural fiction, such as Dorothy Scarborough's *The Supernatural in Modern English Fiction* (1917), Edith Birkhead's *The Tale of Terror* (1921), and Eino Railo's *The Haunted Castle* (1927), awakened a long-dormant scholarly interest in

Gothic fiction, but their critical value is limited by their tendency to survey a great deal of material without offering any in-depth analysis of the texts and their cultural climate. Montague Summers's *The Gothic Quest,* a wide-ranging if somewhat eccentric and unreliable work, appeared in 1938. Although an advocate of Gothic in general, Summers is wholly unsympathetic to the element of political subversiveness in Gothic fiction: "it cannot be denied that particularly during the last decade of the eighteenth century vicious and subversive ideology had begun to infiltrate and poison fiction. Fortunately the mischief was soon stamped out and squashed, in no small part through the admirable energies of *The Anti-Jacobin Review*" (400–01). As he sees it, however, Walpole, Radcliffe, Lewis, and Charles Maturin were free from this taint of "socialism."

At midcentury, the critic who perhaps did more than any other to stimulate academic interest in Gothic fiction was Devendra P. Varma, whose *Gothic Flame* appeared in 1957 and who supervised the Arno Press editions of doctoral dissertations on Gothic novels that appeared in the late 1970s. Two more recent promising studies are Elizabeth MacAndrew's *The Gothic Tradition in Fiction* (1979), which stresses the "properties of dream symbolism" in Gothic fiction (4) with a view to suggesting the general moral and psychological value of the genre, and William Patrick Day's *In the Circles of Fear and Desire* (1985), which examines some of the ways the genre "validated and formalized" the literary technique of incorporating certain features of the dream life into fiction (31).

Other recent critics of Gothic have addressed its social relevance, but mainly in terms of particular political agendas. Since Ellen Moers's seminal discussion of "Female Gothic" in 1976, in which she argued for the existence of a specifically female line of Gothic writers, including Mary Shelley, Charlotte Brontë, and Carson McCullers, feminist critics have focused on the struggle of women readers and writers to interrogate patriarchal values and to establish their own literary territory apart from the dominant masculine tradition. A large quantity and variety of feminist criticism of Gothic literature has appeared since Moers's essay, most of it taking a sociological or social/psychological perspective. Claire Kahane, for example, has argued that twentieth-century women writers such as Flannery O'Connor have transformed the Gothic mode "into a profound articulation of both their revolt against the cultural order and their sense of helplessness within it" ("Maternal" 256).[8]

Marxist critics have emphasized the potential subversiveness of Gothic fiction, as do those who follow structuralist and semiotic theory. David Punter, for example, cites Herbert Read as saying that "[r]ealism is a bourgeois prejudice," and he argues that Gothic fiction, in its recourse to the supernatural and its concern with cultural taboos, is antagonistic to that prejudice (19–20). Conversely, but with a similar political interest, Terry Lovell has stated that early Gothic fiction written and read by women simply "reproduced the middle-class woman's relationship to patriarchal capitalism," although this response was a "deeply ambivalent one, which protested while it submitted" (71). Chris Baldick examines how the Frankenstein myth refers to "genuine causes for alarm" in modern industrial capitalism (9).

Gothic fiction also has become a focus for those involved in the "problematization" of our epistemological and ontological assumptions, and here Tzvetan Todorov's structuralist approach in *The Fantastic* has been very influential. Todorov charts (literally) different varieties of nonrealistic fiction as conceptual puzzles that either remain unresolved (pure-fantastic) or else are resolved by verifying the supernatural (fantastic-marvelous) or by revealing a natural cause (fantastic-uncanny). Margaret L. Carter (1987) uses the Todorovian formula to investigate multiplicity of interpretation of the supernatural in Gothic fiction. Another critic concerned with representational and linguistic problems is George E. Haggerty (1988), who cites the work of Roman Jakobson to argue that the "problem of the Gothic novel . . . is fundamentally a problem of language" (1).

Although the history of Gothic criticism has been characterized increasingly by interchange between certain of these various perspectives,[9] there still remains the need for a more multidisciplinary approach, and particularly for one which brings together two disciplinary orientations that are often assumed to be antithetical: psychology and sociopolitical history. As I hope to demonstrate, the conjunction of these approaches is necessitated by the psychopolitical nature of Gothic fiction and is also in keeping with the controlling theme of this fiction: the danger of compartmentalization.

In order to bring the two fields together, however, what is also needed is a different psychological approach than has hitherto been employed in the study of Gothic. That is, most psychoanalytic criticism of Gothic has tended to employ Freudian theory[10] and to view Gothic as a conservative form that offers the reader a safe opportunity for the exorcism of fear, as well as an opportunity for the "id's night out"—a temporary release from civilized constrictions that neither challenges nor alters the essential nature of those constrictions.

While Freudian theory can be useful in diagnosing the psychological aberrations, sexual neuroses, and oedipal conflicts found so frequently in Gothic tales, it does not provide an adequate basis for assessing the therapeutic potential of the Gothic experience; for this, we need Jung, along with a wider range of cultural and psychological theory. My study, therefore, utilizes a broader, more multidisciplinary approach and in the spirit of Gothic fiction is also designed to transgress some of the traditional boundaries of literary criticism[11] (incorporating, for example, contemporary reviews of the work in question and pertinent biographical information about the author, as well as utilizing recent neuroscientific theories about the biological evolution of consciousness). Similarly, Gothic narratives tend to suggest the dangers of rigidly compartmentalizing social, psychological, and physical domains and demonstrate the need to cross the boundaries between them.

My study also involves close textual analysis, which in turn expands the parameters of New Criticism through the use of insights from depth psychology. They help to explain both the symbolic and archetypal nature of Gothic imagery, and how it identifies, at an emotional level, contemporary religious, moral, social, and psychological issues. The Gothic reiteration of the "unspeakable" stresses a world of felt experience existing beyond the threshold of consciousness signified by words.

Because this study is concerned with tracing Gothic fiction's changing signature,[12] I will begin by examining the roots of Gothic in the medieval/Renaissance periods and deal with subsequent "mainstream" works in chronological order. In selecting these major texts, I have chosen those that have appeared at different periods of crisis and that reflect different national concerns. Additionally, the texts chosen are those that are generally recognized as having exerted considerable influence on both the Gothic literary tradition and the popular imagination.

In the analysis of these works, a major focus will be on the depiction of violence within and against the family and on the related interrogation of the place of women (and children) in society. It is at this point that Gothic's sociological and psychological concerns intersect, for these novels not only tend to emphasize the destructive potential of uncontrolled masculine aggression and repressed feminine energy, they also challenge their societies' privileging of "masculine" values, such as purposiveness, activity, and reason, over "feminine" values, such as relatedness, receptivity, and feeling.

Finally, this study is designed to explore Gothic fiction's involvement in the process of cultural change. As I hope to show, at certain times and places, this seemingly "escapist" form of literature can play an active part in the transformation of collective attitudes. Thus, I also hope that this study will help to explain why, in our own time, horror writers and film makers have found such a large and receptive audience eager for the experience of being "scared half to death."

CHAPTER ONE

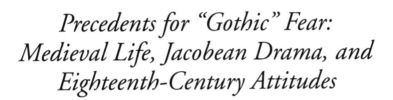

Precedents for "Gothic" Fear:
Medieval Life, Jacobean Drama, and
Eighteenth-Century Attitudes

The first Gothic novels, whose vogue reached its crest in the 1790s, appeared at a time when Enlightenment contempt for the barbarity of the Middle Ages was giving way to a sense of nostalgia, of looking back with longing to a time when the miraculous and the daemonic were experienced as actual events in everyday life. Alfred E. Longueil has demonstrated how the meaning of the word Gothic shifted over the course of the eighteenth century, from a pejorative term suggesting the barbaric and unenlightened, to a neutral term denoting the medieval period, to a literary term indicating the presence of the supernatural in a given work, whether or not it featured a medieval setting.

Eighteenth-century writers' notions about the Middle Ages were actually rather fuzzy, especially in comparison to seventeenth-century scholarship on that era. During the seventeenth century, the term Gothic "came into extensive use . . . as an epithet employed by the Parliamentary leaders to defend the prerogatives of Parliament against the pretensions of the King to absolute right to govern England. To this end the parliamentarians searched the ancient records of English civilization for precedent and authority against the principle of monarchical absolutism" (Kliger 1). Seventeenth-century antiquarians were more interested in medieval social and political institutions than in medieval art, and partly because their intent was to use their research as legal evidence, they were exceptionally meticulous: "Textual accuracy was valued highly, and close study of the lexicon was promoted by a pressing concern with minutiae" (Donatelli 436).

Eighteenth-century writers and readers, however, evinced little interest in these ponderous tomes, and their somewhat less precise notions about medieval life were based primarily on two bodies of evidence—medieval cathedrals and castles (or what was left of them in Protestant England) and heroic romances, usually as transcribed and modified by antiquarians such as Thomas Warton.[1] Thus, most early fictional reconstructions of medieval life were makeshift efforts, to say the least. Pseudomedievalism became the vogue, first in architecture and then in literature,[2] and with a few exceptions no-one seemed particularly concerned about historical accuracy. What mattered in Gothic fiction was not historical reconstruction but the evocation of intense emotional states, especially that of superstitious fear.

The early Gothic writers' sense of this "medieval" emotional component actually accords well with what some researchers have argued about life in the Middle Ages: it was characterized by high-pitched emotionalism, acceptance of supernatural and magical intervention, intense fear of the daemonic, and a strong sense of the grotesque. The first chapter of J. Huizinga's *The Waning of the Middle Ages* is titled "The Violent Tenor of Life." He paints a picture of a widespread vehement, high-strung emotionalism in a culture "overcharged with religious images and concepts" (164). The age was "crowded" with "ghost-seeing, signs, spectres and apparitions" (167). Medieval superstition extended into political and military life: "The custom of princes, in the fifteenth century, frequently to seek counsel in political matters from ecstatic preachers and great visionaries, maintained a kind of religious tension in state affairs which at any moment might manifest itself in decisions of a totally unexpected character" (17). The fear of the supernatural was also prevalent in earlier, pre-urban medieval culture, as Aron Gurevich describes it in his study, *Medieval popular culture: Problems of belief and perception*. Gurevich documents many lively accounts of encounters with divine and daemonic figures, and his evidence forcefully illustrates his argument that the people of this era lived in a constant state of fear for the welfare of their souls: "The individual . . . [was] the object of the devil's ceaseless assaults. Like a fortress situated in enemy territory, he remain[ed] under constant siege" (186).

According to Gurevich, it was not usually the devil himself whom people encountered, but his emissaries in the form of trickster demons who bore a strong relation to pre-Christian elves and sprites; "the people's attitude towards them was ambivalent, vacillating between fear and hatred and good-natured humour" (194). Gurevich suggests that the grotesquerie in these accounts, which combines so many paradoxical elements and which is so difficult for the modern reader to comprehend, is partly due to the medieval belief that laughter and ridicule were effective weapons in the battle against the forces of evil; in "this psychological context laughter becomes the means of overcoming *fear, the intensity of which is difficult for us even to imagine*" (184, 192; my emphasis). In one such story,

> [o]ne nun eagerly wanted lettuce, and she ate a leaf of it, forgetting to make the sign of the cross over the food. She was straightway possessed by a demon. The abbot Ecvitius was summoned, and he began to pray for her healing. As soon as the abbot appeared in the garden, where the possessed nun was in convulsions, the frightened demon, 'as if justifying himself', cried out, 'What have I done wrong? I was sitting on a leaf of lettuce, and she came and ate me'. The abbot indignantly ordered him to abandon the unfortunate nun, and immediately the demon withdrew. (188)

Gurevich suggests that the medieval fusion of the frightful and the humorous was part of a dualistic world view in which "heaven [and presumably hell] and earth stood face to face. . . . The earthly world in itself was taken completely for granted; the other world . . . was perceived as part of the same universe as the earth, and presented no riddle to medieval people. It was the meeting of the two that struck a note of marvel" (183). The eternal conflict between the sacred and the daemonic was the point of collision between the mundane and supermundane worlds, although even here some interesting ambiguities can be found, in stories about "good" demons (190–91). Demons had a playful aspect, demonstrated partly through their unlimited "capability for metamorphosis," which allowed them to appear as "handsome men and beautiful women, priests, monkeys, pigs, cats, dogs or reptiles" (188). But their horrific aspect, according to Gurevich, was often stronger: "In Gregory the Great's depiction demons are extremely monstrous: black repulsive spirits, terrifying dragons enveloping men with their tails, swallowing their heads or shoving their snouts into their mouths and sucking out their souls, etc. Other authors have similar depictions, as do church sculptures and carvings" (188). Succubae and incubi could seduce or attack the unguarded soul of the unwary sleeper;[3] the boundaries of self were continually susceptible to violation, and the physical body was felt to be a terribly weak and fallible defender of the soul.

Mikhail Bakhtin in *Rabelais and His World* focuses on medieval carnival, in which, he argues, an antityrannical impulse found expression in the form of the grotesque. Because Bakhtin wrote his treatise on Rabelais and late medieval society in Stalinist Russia, it is perhaps understandable that he sees the grotesque and carnivalesque elements in the Rabelaisian fictional world as a psychological balancing of the Catholic Church's oppressive, monolithic regime. Whereas Gurevich sees medieval laughter as defensive, Bakhtin regards it as derisive. "Festive" carnivalesque laughter especially has, in his view, a subversive function: the emphasis on bodily degradation in carnival antics serves as "a bodily and popular corrective to individual idealistic and spiritual pretense" (22).

Bakhtin argues that the ritual of degradation is regenerative because it hurls "the object down into the lower zone," the area of "defecation, copulation, conception, pregnancy, birth," and "digs a bodily grave for a new birth" (21). The effect of this descent is liberation "from the prevailing view of the world, conventions, established truths, clichés, all that is humdrum and universally accepted" and a revelation of "the relative nature of all that exists" (34). He states that "in the medieval mysteries, the devil is a gay ambivalent figure expressing the unofficial point of view" and insists that "there is nothing terrifying or alien in him" (41). He depicts medieval carnival as a metamorphic force undermining stasis.

Bakhtin's distinction between the grotesque and the classical body associates the grotesque with the "cosmic, ancestral element of the body": blood as seed buried in the earth, dung as a link between body and earth, urine as a link between body and sea (323, 327, 335). His ideas about medieval "cosmic terror" are based on materialist suppositions and clearly reflect his antitotalitarian stance:

> An obscure memory of cosmic perturbations and the dim terror of human catastrophes form the very basis of human thought, speech, and images. This cosmic terror is not mystic in the strict sense of the word; rather it is the fear of that which is materially huge and cannot be overcome by force. It is used by all religious systems to oppress man and his consciousness. . . . The struggle against cosmic terror in all its forms and manifestations did not rely on abstract hope or on the eternal spirit, but on the material principle in man himself. Man assimilated the cosmic elements: earth, water, air, and fire. . . . He became aware of the cosmos within himself. (335–36)

He adds in a footnote:

> This cosmic terror is more essential and stronger than individual bodily fear of destruction. . . . Cosmic terror is the heritage of man's impotence in the presence of nature. Folk culture did not know this fear and overcame it through laughter . . . [with] indestructible confidence in the might and final victory of man. Official culture, on the contrary, often used and even cultivated this fear in order to humiliate and oppress man. (336 n.9)

Bakhtin's contention that for the medieval person pleasure and confidence outweighed terror is perhaps the weakest part of his argument, as Gurevich's later work suggests. Obviously, one cannot overcome a fear that one does not "know" in some way.

In an attempt to assert some individual control over a universe charged with both hostile and beneficent supernatural forces, people in the Middle Ages apparently resorted frequently to magic. As Keith Thomas demonstrates, the early Church in Europe condoned and even appropriated the rituals of pagan religions in order to win converts by convincing them that its new magic was more powerful than the old (27–28, 54). Thomas argues that magic was a psychologically efficacious means of overcoming fear and helplessness in a time when technological control over the elements was relatively weak.

The Church leaders distinguished between divine intervention through prayer and manipulation by magic, and leaders such as St. Augustine (354–430) warned against "'any perverted knowledge . . . sought by arts magical'" (qtd. in Steiner 394); yet as Thomas shows, "the distinction was repeatedly blurred in the popular mind" (46). Thus many Catholic rituals became mingled with pagan ones aimed at propitiating divine favor in matters of health and fertility, whether human, animal, or agricultural. Pagan festivals were incorporated into the Church year; holy water when poured down the throat of a bewitched cow would cure it; the Host could be sprinkled over the garden as a protection against caterpillars; the Mass could be a means of foretelling the future; images of local or patron saints possessed miraculous curative powers (Thomas 29–56).

The Church's magical power could also be used for maleficent purposes, even by the clergy itself, so that the "Lateran Council of 1215 had ruled that the eucharist and holy oil should be kept under lock and key" (Thomas 39). Shortly after England's break with the Catholic Church, the first Edwardian Prayer Book "insisted that the bread should be placed by the officiating minister direct in the communicant's mouth, because in past times people had often carried the sacrament away and 'kept it with them and diversely abused it, to superstition and wickedness'" (Thomas 38–39).

The church building itself was believed to be consecrated ground and to constitute a sacred and timeless space, "haunted," in a sense, by the holy spirit.[4] The building of the cathedral was often associated with some incident of miraculous intercession (Frankl 207–10). This was another element based on pagan magic and popish superstition, which the early Protestant reformers attacked as idolatrous; the Elizabethan Prayer Book included no ceremony for the consecration of churches, although the principle was revived near the end of the sixteenth century (Thomas 66, 67).

Along with medieval architecture and romance, perhaps the major source for the Gothic novelists' ideas about life in the Middle Ages was Jacobean drama, to which innumerable allusions can be found throughout late-eighteenth-century Gothic fiction.[5] Although this drama took place in a post-Reformation society, a great deal of it was very "medieval" in spirit.

The "theatricality" of church ritual and decoration that the reformers set out to eliminate (Thomas 87) found a new channel of expression in the secular drama of the Elizabethan-Jacobean period. Initially, the theatre celebrated England's new sense of religious and political independence. In the words of U. M. Ellis-Fermor, the drama of the Elizabethan age proper in which the early works of Shakespeare appeared was "characterized by its faith in vitality, its worship of the glorious processes of life, an expansion and elation of mind which corresponds directly to the upward movement of a prosperous and expanding society" (1).

The only exception to this rule was Christopher Marlowe, whose *Tragical History of Doctor Faustus* (1588) influenced many Gothic novels and whose "keen spiritual sense sees through the delusion of prosperity that intoxicates his contemporaries as a whole and anticipates that mood of spiritual despair which is its necessary result and becomes the centre of the later tragic mood" (Ellis-Fermor 1–2). Ellis-Fermor sees Marlowe as "a thinker coming at the climax of a movement . . . [whose beginnings] may be traced in the separation of drama from the medieval Church. . . . It was at the hands of Marlowe that the Church finally lost the drama" (7).

In *Doctor Faustus*, Marlowe revives the old mystery and morality plays, incorporating them with the Germanic Faust legend and infusing them with a more modern philosophical ambiguity in a tragedy that itself ambiguously verges on farce. Faustus discovers his human limitations and his need for divine grace too late, when he realizes he has sold his soul for a mess of pottage. His diabolical powers amount to little more than a series of jokes (one aimed at the Catholic Church) and literal leg-pullings. The enhancement of earthly powers bestowed upon him by the devil becomes pathetic in the light of Faustus's recognition that he too is "but a man condemned to die" (scene 12) and that he has forfeited all hope of spiritual life. Despite the farcical elements in the play, the final scene of Faustus's approaching death and eternal damnation would likely have struck Marlowe's Protestant audience as impressively horrific, in the light of their new belief that purgatory was no longer a possibility. Faustus cries:

> O God,
> If thou wilt not have mercy on my soul,
> Yet for Christ's sake, whose blood hath ransom'd me,
> Impose some end to my incessant pain;
> Let Faustus live in hell a thousand years,
> A hundred thousand, and at last be sav'd!
> O, no end is limited to damned souls! (Scene 16)

Faustus epitomizes the self-conscious and self-absorbed nature of the Renaissance questing spirit, and his psychological and spiritual alienation is signified by the fact that throughout the play he repeatedly addresses himself in the second person. The general undercurrent of anxiety about Elizabethan society's rupture with the Catholic past is registered when Faustus views the Seven Deadly Sins, in an entertainment given by Lucifer: Pride appears first, declaring "I disdain to have any parents" (scene 6). Marlowe's satirical criticism derides not only corrupt Catholicism but also extremist Protestantism, for the play presents a remarkably vivid reminder of Protestantism's own Catholic parentage.[6]

At the end of the sixteenth century, when the spirit of uneasiness and disillusionment became more widespread, drama no longer registered the sense of confidence and celebration that dominated the earlier era. Like Marlowe's prophetic work, late Elizabethan and early Jacobean tragedy took on a strong medieval flavor, many of its "backward-looking" themes and motifs anticipating those of later Gothic fiction. The fictional ghosts, daemons, and witches of the Jacobean stage, however, would have been somewhat more familiar to their audience than those in the eighteenth-century novel would have been to their readers, since popular belief in these super-mundane beings and activities was still strong in the late Renaissance.

The late Renaissance mood of anxiety, apprehension, disillusionment, and weariness of spirit was an effect of both the new intellectual freedom from dogmatic theology, and the political uncertainties of the day. The queen was aging, and there was no sure heir-apparent; after her death in 1603 the accession of King James brought momentary relief, but the dissatisfaction felt by diverse groups about his monarchial style, so different from Elizabeth's, also raised the spectre of political instability and insecurity.

As well, with the loss of the medieval world view, the spiritual world was experienced no longer as "circumambient and interpenetrating" but as a theoretical supposition (Ellis-Fermor 8). In the conviction that he has lost the power to discern any spiritual significance in daily life without having gained any significant measure of control over events, the late Renaissance dramatist begins to deflate the optimism of the earlier phase. Man is no noble "piece of work," no "paragon of animals," but merely a "quintessence of dust" (*Hamlet* 2.3): "unaccommodated . . . a poor, bare, forked animal" (*King Lear* 3.4). Life's "petty pace" creeps on to "the last syllable of recorded time, / . . . . And then is heard no more: it is a tale / Told by an idiot, full of sound and fury, / Signifying nothing" (*Macbeth* 5.5).

Into this atmosphere of disappointment and futility come some very "Gothic" shocks to the system. A world of medieval horrors and frights emerges: "ghost-seeing, signs, spectres and apparitions," plus witches, compacts with the devil, and eternal damnation. Although the dramatic commentary surrounding the staged appearance of Renaissance ghosts is usually speculative, partly because the new theology disallowed the possibility of ghosts returning from purgatory (Thomas 703), the stress remains on all that is undreamt of in Protestant philosophy. The sense of cultural breakdown is registered in high-pitched feeling, mental and emotional disorders, obsessions, suggestions of incest, and even child murder. The bodily degradation Bakhtin analyzes so well is also part of the dramatic ritual enacted at this cultural/historical nadir. Rankness, corruption, dung, and worms devouring decomposing bodies are repeated motifs.

In John Webster's *Duchess of Malfi* (first produced ca. 1612) the cynical Bosola declares,

> Man stands amazed to see his deformity
> In any other creature but himself.
> But in our own flesh, though we bear diseases
> Which have their true names only ta'en from beasts,—
> As the most ulcerous wolf and swinish measle,—
> Though we are eaten up of lice and worms,

And though continually we bear about us
A rotten and dead body, we delight
To hide it in rich tissue. (2.1)

In the same play, the antihero, Ferdinand, loses his mind out of guilt for having ordered his sister's death by strangulation; he suffers from "lycan-thropia," imagining himself to have been transformed into a wolf. Exhibiting behavior that is supposedly common to this disorder, he begins to haunt churchyards in the dead of night, where he digs up dead bodies. The doctor reports that one night Ferdinand was found,

Behind Saint Mark's church, with the leg of a man
Upon his shoulder; and he howled fearfully;
Said he was a wolf, only the difference
Was, a wolf's skin was hairy on the outside,
His on the inside; bade them take their swords,
Rip up his flesh, and try. (5.3)

This profanation of the sacred and the degeneration of the human into the bestial, which also appears in much subsequent Gothic fiction, evokes the medieval carnivalesque degradation described by Bakhtin, which in his view served to stimulate feeling and awareness and to vitalize the social world. At the end of Elizabeth's forty-five-year reign, the almost universal sense of triumph over England's break with the Catholic Church began to dissipate, and the shock and anxiety that are part of any major social upheaval set in. It was at this point that Renaissance tragedy began to dig up the "dead" past, which Reformation zeal was still violently repudiating.

Another major factor in the drama's mood of anxiety was the awareness that the Puritans, "who regarded the theatre as an abomination in the sight of the Lord" (Gassner 324), were steadily becoming consolidated into a powerful, strident, and divisive faction. Contempt for the puritanical attitude and fear of its consequences finds expression in grotesque humor: "Shall my pothecary out-go me because I am a cuckold? I have found out his roguery; he makes alum of his wife's urine, and sells it to Puritans that have sore throats with overstraining" (*The Duchess of Malfi* 4.3); "for young Charbon the puritan and old Polysam the papist, howsome'er their hearts are severed in religion, their heads are both one: they may jowl horns together like any deer i' the herd" (*All's Well That Ends Well* 1.3.55–59).

The dark period of Jacobean drama was relatively brief. Ellis-Fermor comments that when "the Stuart dynasty seemed to be settled upon the

throne securely enough to avoid civil war, invasion and economic ruin . . .
the dark world of tragedy [in drama could] be skirted without *that tight-
ening of the nerves, that sickening sense of impending doom*, inseparable from
the major drama of the first decade" (25, 26; my emphasis). The stage gave
way to Shakespeare's triumphant romance as well as to Beaumont and
Fletcher's "flaccid romanticism" (Gassner 324), and with the exception
of John Webster, the horror was, for the moment, "resolutely put aside"
(Ellis-Fermor 25).

A feature common to both Jacobean drama and Gothic fiction is
their emphasis on modes of awareness and apprehension that no longer
enjoy widespread public sanction. The Renaissance, however, was a more
transitional period, in which many of the learned elite rejected this "archaic" sensibility while the illiterate populace maintained it,[7] whereas in
the late eighteenth century, rational skepticism was more widespread.
Elizabethan and Jacobean drama emerged within fifty years after the Reformation had rid England of a corrupt Catholic Church and in the process
deprived the country of many of its traditional religious and social rituals.
Gothic fiction arose at the next major stage of this desacralizing movement,
when people were beginning to feel dissatisfied with the imaginative
and emotional constriction of neoclassical aesthetics and Enlightenment
rationalism.

Additionally, both Jacobean drama and Gothic fiction arose in periods of heightened social anxiety: the former at the end of Elizabeth's and
the beginning of James I's reigns, and the latter (mainly) after the American and during the French and Industrial Revolutions. Both forms evoke
superstitious dread, presenting tales of calamity (or near-calamity) and
seemingly inexplicable ghostly visitations that reflect a social mood of fear,
fragility, and uncertainty.

Just as the dark period of Jacobean drama was relatively brief, so was
the "heyday" of Gothic horror. The deluge of Gothic novels that began in
the 1790s dwindled into a trickle near the end of the Regency period.[8]
When the expansion of the voters' franchise in 1832 and the ascension of
the popular Queen Victoria in 1837 ushered in a new sense of forward-
looking prosperity, Gothic horror took second place to what has been
called the "realistic" school of fiction.[9]

Social conditions in the earlier part of the eighteenth century were fairly stable, compared to those of the late Renaissance and later eighteenth century, and the literature of this period reflected a more confident attitude. The social upheavals of the seventeenth century were followed by a period of consolidation and economic development, and the novel appeared as a new and energetic literary form in the works of Defoe, Fielding, Richardson, Smollett, Swift, and later Sterne.[10] The traces of the past had been nullified in much seventeenth-century philosophical inquiry: Cartesian dualism posited the thinking self as the *sine qua non* of human existence, and Lockean rationalism envisioned individual experience as beginning at birth from zero.

In the opinion of Lancelot Whyte, it was ironically Descartes's insistence on awareness as the defining characteristic of "mind" that necessitated the development of the idea of the unconscious (27–28); "within fifty years of the publication of Descartes' first essay, at the very moment when the Cartesian doctrine emphasizing man's consciousness attained its greatest influence, the process of correction was already at work" (37). Whyte sees the German romantic movement as the first exploration of the idea that "in the unconscious mind lies the contact of the individual with the universal powers of nature. The springs of human nature lie in the unconscious, for it links the individual with the universal, or at least the organic" (69–70). He points out that throughout western European society

> [f]rom the eighteenth century onward growing interest was shown not only in the normal rhythms of consciousness (sleep, dreams, reveries, etc.) but also in unusual or pathological states (fainting, ecstasy, hypnosis, hallucinations, dissociation, drugged conditions, epilepsy, forgetfulness, etc.) and in processes underlying ordinary thought (imagination, judgement, selection, diagnosis, interest, sympathy, etc.). (70)

This renewed interest in nonrational experience was also shown in a wider acceptance of the supernatural; as early as "the time of Addison's *Spectator* [1711–12, 1714] it had become more respectable to believe in ghosts than to be a total sceptic. . . . [T]he possibility of ghosts was a reality . . . for many educated men, however much the rationalists laughed at them" (Thomas 706).

In English literature, self-confidence and the satirical spirit were expressed via the neoclassical aesthetics of the Augustan poets led by Pope, but dissatisfaction with the limited and prescriptive nature of the Augustan vision set in fairly quickly. Around midcentury, when novelistic activity seemed to be coming to an impasse, English poetry entered the "Age of

Sensibility."[11] The melancholy "graveyard poets" began to brood on life's transience, and a growing public interest in the Middle Ages was seen in the popularity of folk ballads and heroic romances, promulgated by writers such as Thomas Warton. All this work provided fuel for the imagination of the Gothic novelists. But what seems to have been even more influential than this poetic ambience of gloom and romance was the growing interest in theoretical speculation about the meaning and function of fear.

Following Longinus (first century A.D.), Edmund Burke in his influential 1757 essay on the sublime suggested that "pleasure follows the will. . . . But pain is always inflicted by a power in some way superior, because we never submit to pain willingly. . . . So that strength, violence, pain, terror, are ideas that rush upon the mind together" (65). The power of the sublime "hurries us on by an irresistible force" (57). Burke's emphasis on the importance of obscurity as an element in sublime terror was heeded by many later Gothic writers: "[H]ardly any thing can strike the mind with its greatness, which does not make some sort of approach towards infinity; which nothing can do whilst we are able to perceive its bounds." To illustrate his point he quotes a passage from the Book of Job, 4.13–17, with the comment that its

> sublimity is principally due to the terrible uncertainty of the thing described. *In thoughts from the visions of the night, when deep sleep falleth upon men, fear came upon me and trembling, which make all my bones to shake. Then a spirit passed before my face. The hair of my flesh stood up. It stood still,* but I could not discern the form thereof; *an image was before mine eyes; there was silence; and I heard a voice,—Shall mortal man be more just than God?* (63; Burke's emphasis)

In 1773 John and Anna Laetitia (Barbauld) Aiken made the similar observation that a "well-wrought [scene] of artificial terror awakens the mind, and keeps it on the stretch; and where the agency of invisible beings is introduced, of 'forms unseen, and mightier far than we,' our imagination, darting forth, explores with rapture the new world which is laid open to its view, and rejoices in the expansion of its powers. . . . [P]ain and terror is lost in amazement" (125). The newly awakened appreciation of Gothic architecture was similarly stimulated by the appeal of its "alarming" power. Richard Hurd's 1762 *Letters on Chivalry and Romance* developed the analogy (first suggested by John Hughes in 1715) between Gothic architecture and Spenser's poetic technique in *The Faerie Queene.* Hurd argued that Spenser's art, like Gothic architecture, cannot be judged adequately by neoclassical aesthetic rules (61). His study marks one of the major shifts traced by Longueil in the connotations of the word *Gothic*. Hurd associates 'Gothic' with the quality of power, as opposed to the grace and beauty of classical symmetry: "[F]or the more solemn fancies of witchcraft and incantation, the horrors of the Gothic were above measure striking and terrible. The mummeries of the pagan [i.e., hellenic] priests were childish, but the Gothic [i.e. northern Germanic] Enchanters shook and alarmed all nature" (48–49). Hurd's allegiance to the "dawn of reason" in his own age does seem somewhat ambivalent; he quotes Addison as saying "'[O]ur forefathers looked on nature with reverence and horror before the world was enlightened by learning and philosophy'" (53–54). Yet the longing for the lost world of "Gothic" enchantment, with which he identifies both Spenser's "land of faery" and the old latinate chivalric romances, permeates Hurd's speculations. He argues that when Milton and Shakespeare resort to "Gothic" touches in their works, the effect is "more sublime, more terrible, more alarming than those of the classic fablers"—and hence "more poetical" (54–55).

Hurd concludes that his age has "gained a great deal of good sense [but] lost . . . a world of fine fabling" (120). It should be noted, however, that Hurd was referring to the state of affairs in his own literate and literary world, whereas an oral tradition of "fine fabling" was apparently still being carried on by the largely illiterate lower classes. With increasing literacy, however, and wider distribution of popular novels via the circulating libraries during the later decades of the century, it would not be long before "[t]he winter evening pastime of story-telling by the fire had gone out of use, and the older generation listened while their sons and daughters read [popular] romances" (J. M. S. Tompkins 2).[12]

In the same year that Hurd's study appeared, the "Cock Lane Ghost" caused a sensation in London, and the social uproar it provoked says much about the ambivalent status of the supernatural at this time. The public reaction to newspaper accounts of the ghost ranged from credulity to ridicule, but skeptical or not, people were clearly fascinated. The ghost was said to be that of a woman named Fanny Lynes, who (again it was said) "had been lured to London, and then imprisoned and murdered by poisoning" (Clery 13). Fanny supposedly had returned from the dead to accuse her murderer by means of knocking and scratching sounds, for which she had earned the name of "Scratching Fanny." Large crowds visited the house where the hauntings were said to occur, and neighborhood taverns profited from sightseers who could not get into the house and were content to quench their thirst in the vicinity (Clery 14). The house was visited by high and low: Samuel Johnson conscientiously tried to ascertain the validity of the ghost, without success (Clery 14), and Horace Walpole went there after a night at the opera in the company of the Duke of York, Lady Northumberland, and others. Walpole wrote about the visit in a tone of urbane amusement, yet as E. J. Clery has pointed out, the fact that the group ventured out in pouring rain and stayed in the crowded, dirty house until 1:30 A.M. suggests that the visit meant more to them than simply a pleasant diversion to round off the evening's entertainment (24–25).

In the end, it came out that the skeptics were justified when the wooden block used to produce the knocking and scratching sounds was discovered. The original diagnosis of Fanny's death from smallpox was confirmed, and the whole episode was revealed to have been a hoax engineered by a man who for personal and financial reasons wished to discredit the man "accused" of murdering Fanny. The crowd that later came to watch the perpetrator of the hoax stand in the pillory "made a collection on his behalf" (Clery 32), perhaps in appreciation of the excitement and entertainment his fiction had provided. As Clery observes, it is clear that at this time the "question of belief appeared to make little or no difference to the intensity of response" to the possibility of the supernatural (32).[13]

That year as well, another important study concerning the marvelous in literature appeared: Thomas Warton's *Observations on the Fairy Queen*. Like Hurd, Warton admired the "magic and enchantment" of the chivalric romances, and in this work he stresses the emotional appeal of *The Faerie Queene* as something "which more powerfully attracts us, which engages the affections the feelings of the heart (*sic*), rather than the cold approbation of the head" (1: 16). Warton also suggests the stimulating power of fear: the old romancers' "fictions and fablings . . . contribute, in a wonderful degree to rouse and invigorate all the powers of the imagination: to store the fancy with those sublime and *alarming* images which true poetry best delights to display" (2: 268; my emphasis).

The desire was growing for more "alarming," "terrible," and "invigorating" stories than had appeared thus far in eighteenth-century fiction. Clearly, the cultural climate was moving toward a wider acceptance of the nonrational modes of perception that were vaguely associated with medieval life, with its "ghost-seeing, signs, spectres and apparitions." Two years after the appearance of Hurd's and Warton's studies, this symbolic language of the unconscious would find expression in the first Gothic novel.

CHAPTER TWO

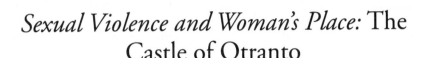

Sexual Violence and Woman's Place: The Castle of Otranto

*T*he *Castle of Otranto* is a story about family violence, published at a time when the institution of marriage was receiving considerable public attention. The villain of *Otranto*, Prince Manfred, seeks to dispose of his devoted wife, Hippolita, in order to marry the lovely young Isabella. Isabella had been betrothed to Conrad, the son of Manfred and Hippolita, before the young man had been mysteriously killed by being crushed under a giant helmet shortly before their wedding day. Most of the story is devoted to Manfred's frenzied pursuit of Isabella through the halls and underground passages of the Castle, a chase which is punctuated by mysterious supernatural events and culminates in his murdering his own daughter, Matilda. He stabs her to death, under the mistaken impression that she is Isabella. Isabella ends up marrying the noble young Theodore, who has been assisting the maidens in their troubles and who at the end of the story assumes his rightful place as heir of Otranto. Manfred, sufficiently chastised by both natural and supernatural events (which include the collapse of the castle walls), willingly gives up the throne, which his grandfather had usurped; he and Hippolita both retire to nearby convents.

When Horace Walpole's melodramatic tale appeared in 1764, it received a mixed response, even from the friends to whom he sent copies. Thomas Gray wrote him from Cambridge that "it engages our attention here, makes some of us cry a little, and all in general afraid to go to bed o'nights" (Sabor 14, 25 n. 25).[1] Gilly Williams, in contrast, felt that the effect of *Otranto* was soporific: that "no boarding-school Miss of thirteen could get half through [*Otranto*] without yawning. It consists of ghosts and enchantments . . . helmets drop from the moon, and cover half a family. He says it was a dream, and I fancy one when he had some feverish disposition in him" (Sabor 66).[2] The reviews similarly treated *Otranto* "none too kindly" (Mehrota 24). When the first edition appeared under the guise of being a recovered medieval manuscript, an anonymous writer in the *Critical Review* pointed out that the scene in which "a picture comes out of its panel" seemed to indicate that the work might be "a modern fabrick; for we doubt whether pictures were fixed in pannels before the year 1243." This reviewer stated that "[t]he publication of any work, at this time, in England composed of such rotten materials, is a phenomenon we cannot account for" and complained about the story's many absurdities and "monstrosities," while grudgingly allowing that the narrative was lively, the characters "well marked," and "the catastrophe . . . most wretched" (Sabor 68–69).

After the second edition revealed that the author was a member of Parliament, whose father had formerly been prime minister of England (for twenty years, until 1742), the same reviewer responded somewhat less vehemently, but still skeptically, especially with regard to Walpole's attempt to explain in his new preface his reasons for combining romantic with realistic and high with low styles in *Otranto*. The critic objected to Walpole's use of Shakespeare as a literary precedent, stating that "if Shakespear[*sic*] had possessed the critical knowledge of modern times, he would have kept these two kinds of writing distinct" (Sabor 69).[3]

The *Monthly's* review of the first edition was more favorable, stating that for "[t]hose who can digest the absurdities of Gothic fiction" *Otranto* offered "considerable entertainment" (Sabor 71). As K. K. Mehrota comments, this reviewer "obviously seems to have enjoyed reading *The Castle of Otranto,* though he is half ashamed to confess it" (24). But when the authorship was revealed a few months later, the same reviewer wrote a second piece in which he strongly disapproved of the novel, on the grounds that the "indulgence we afforded to the foibles of a supposed antiquity, we can by no means extend to the singularity of a false taste in a cultivated period of learning." The critic was appalled that an author of Walpole's "refined and polished genius, should be an advocate for re-establishing the barbarous superstitions of Gothic devilism!" (Sabor 72).[4]

However, the general readership appeared to be less concerned than the critics were with upholding the superior taste and wisdom of their more "cultivated period." Walpole, who had self-published the first edition, brought out two more in quick succession to meet the demand; the second edition appeared just three months after the first printing of five hundred copies, and the third was printed about one year later. Moreover, as Mehrota notes, "[s]till better evidence of its popularity is afforded by its publication as a serial in a slightly abridged form, in *The Universal Magazine*" in April 1765 (22–23). That *Otranto* did in fact provide for many readers the *frisson* that is indispensable to a good Gothic tale is suggested by Friedrich M. Grimm's comments on its French translation a couple of years later: "[A]ll these things make the hair of the sage stand on end, as much as that of the child and his nurse; so much are the sources of the marvellous the same to all men" (Sabor 73).

Judging by such reviews, one would conclude that what captured readers' immediate *conscious* attention was not the sexual violence with which *Otranto* abounds, but the evocation of the supernatural. Some readers evidently also were affected by the plot's "wretched catastrophe," as well as by the sexually charged imagery. For Grimm, some of the things that make the hair stand on end are "that enormous helmet, that monstrous sword, the portrait which starts from its frame and walks away, the skeleton of the hermit praying in the oratory, the vaults, the subterranean passages, the moonshine" (Sabor 73).[5] For a reader in the post-Freudian era, the phallic symbolism in the gigantic sword and helmet, along with the vaginal and uterine symbolism in the vaults and subterranean passages, would be difficult to miss, but Walpole's audience appeared to apprehend the psychological import of this imagery in a subliminal rather than a conscious manner.

Whereas *Otranto*'s manifest content of supernatural "Gothic" apparatus was apparently an admissible subject for discussion, the latent content of domestic and sexual violence was not—a discrepancy that can be explained partly by the fact that cultural conditions at this time were highly repressive for women. The supernatural element could be held responsible, so to speak, for the atmosphere of terror and psychic turmoil that also arises from familial abuse. The fact that *Otranto* captivated as many readers as it did suggests that they were indeed "haunted" by this taboo topic and that the novel offered emotional confirmation of a social problem that, even within the context of the marriage debate, was still being denied conscious public recognition.

Walpole's use of a nonrealistic or "romantic" historical setting established one of the most important conventions of Gothic fiction, which would be taken up by later writers: the strategy of displacement, whereby readers can distance themselves from their immediate social world, with its particular biases and constraints. Suspending the rules of realism allows the entry of normally inadmissible material that, while it reflects actual social conditions, does so in a somewhat disguised or muted form. This may be one reason why *Otranto's* medievalism also seemed to deflect readers' attention from the novel's concern with the questions of marriage, property, and legitimate inheritance, which had already become controversial public issues.

Ten years before the publication of *Otranto,* after a lengthy period of heated parliamentary and public debate, Lord Hardwicke's Marriage Act prohibiting clandestine marriages had become law: clandestine marriages being those that fulfilled the Church's legal requirements of free consent and no legal impediments (in consanguinity, affinity, and age of consent) but did not satisfy the other requirements of being publicly announced and conducted. Such marriages had nevertheless been upheld by the Church as valid and indissoluble unions. Sometimes called "Fleet Marriages," after one of the major centers in London where they took place, they were very popular and gave rise to a highly competitive, organized business. From 1694 to 1754 "between two and three hundred thousand marriages were solemnized with the Fleet prison and its rules" (Brown 117; also 118, 128).

Erica Harth points out that parliamentary debate on the issue centered on questions of property and interest: "With the accumulation of commercial wealth in the first half of the eighteenth century, there was a considerable increase in the incidence of the 'marriage à la mode,' which united money and status" (127). Whether they were for or against the bill, everyone recognized that it would strengthen parental (i.e., paternal) control over the children's choice of marriage partners. "Opponents viewed the bill as endorsing a type of class endogamy that would allow the aristocracy to strengthen its power by monopolizing England's new wealth" (Harth 128). Harth also notes that during this period there had been "a sharp increase in the transfer of property through heiresses," a fact that lends support to her argument that the act was a victory for "patriarchal power" rather than, as other historians have suggested, for "affective individualism" (Stone, *Family* 241) or romantic love (Harth 130). Walpole himself, who had been an M.P. since 1742, opposed the bill. In Martin Kallich's words, Walpole regarded it "as an unjust and inhumane law . . . [one that] undermined individual liberty and, as it protected families with large fortunes, encouraged pride and aristocracy, 'that bane of society, that golden grate that separates the nobility from the plebeians'" (46).[6]

Harth suggests that the Hardwicke Act was an attempt to control two anarchic forces: sexuality (especially female sexuality), and the newly circulating capital which "cut across the lines of status, blurring social distinctions" (136). Her metaphorical depiction of the situation inadvertently provides a clue to Walpole's concerns in *The Castle of Otranto:*

> [F]emale virtue [was] a cornerstone of the social edifice. The eighteenth-century edifice seemed especially insecure. The mortar of love would hold it in place. . . . The ideology of a virtuous love that would preserve both the social and the sexual order arose in the ranks of landowning and monied. Through its support of primogeniture and the "free" circulation of wealth, the Hardwicke Act reinforced the dependency of both women and the poor by keeping capital out of their hands. (134)

Throughout the eighteenth century, men firmly maintained the legal upper hand in marriage, although as Lawrence Stone observes, there was a "general movement [during] this period to redress the balance of justice between the sexes, which can be seen in so many aspects of matrimonial law and practice" (*Road* 210). Nevertheless, while men could sue for divorce, no woman attempted to do so between 1700 and 1801 (Stone, *Road* 360). At the time *Otranto* appeared, women had virtually no legal right to exercise control over their children's welfare, and fathers, if they wished, could direct their children's education, employment, and marriage without any consultation with the mother. In the event of separation, unless otherwise arranged by mutual consent, the father, regardless of his own character and behavior, kept the children, and "[a]ccording to the common law courts, visiting rights by the mother, and even her right to communicate by letter, were entirely at the discretion of the father" (Stone, *Road* 170). By the last two decades of the century attitudes began to change, and an increasing recognition of the importance of maternal nurturing led to more frequent private arrangements in which the young children resided with the mother. Yet as late as 1804, "Lord Chief Justice Ellenborough . . . defended the action by a separated husband in forcing his way into his wife's house, wrenching an infant from its mother's breast, and carrying it off with him" (Stone, *Road* 173).

There appears to be a dearth of information on the extent of familial sexual abuse in eighteenth-century England; the only type of incest to which Stone refers in his history of marriage and divorce law is that between consenting adults, which violates the laws of consanguinity. When one considers women's legal powerlessness, however, along with the extent to which eighteenth-century fiction focuses on irresponsible male sexuality, it seems safe to assume that this also may have been a troubling if unspoken issue in social life.[7] Stone cites one relatively late (1832) instance in which a lady with numerous aristocratic connections sued for divorce from her husband, who "had been unfaithful to her on their wedding night, had debauched all the maidservants in the house, had given his wife venereal disease, and was constantly drunk." Her application was defeated after considerable parliamentary debate on the grounds that "divorce by act of Parliament had traditionally been restricted to husbands, except when there were peculiarly aggravating circumstances like incest" (*Road* 360–61).

The topic of rape, and its incestuous overtones in *Otranto,* would not in itself have shocked Walpole's audience, for it occurs often enough in earlier eighteenth-century novels. Richardson's Clarissa pines away, choosing death by passive suicide because Lovelace has "ruined" her, and her family has abandoned her; Fielding's wayward Tom Jones engages in lustful revels with a woman whom for a brief period of time the reader believes is Tom's natural mother. In fact, accidental incest averted in the nick of time or unions revealed as incestuous but later proved not to be so are titillating staples of early eighteenth-century fiction. Yet although the subject would not strike readers as either alarming or unconventional, the same cannot be said of the manner in which Walpole treats it. The "highly inflammable nature of the male," which had long been accepted as a given in earlier novels about chastised, penitent, and reformed rakes (Tompkins 151), becomes in Walpole's Gothic tale a menacing, nearly daemonic force of destruction.

In his presentation of unruly masculine sexuality, Walpole abandons the conventional humorous or moral/sentimental treatments in favor of one that vividly conveys the victim's sense of terror. Walpole's tempestuous, passionate, and "impetuous" Manfred is as obsessed as Richardson's Lovelace but considerably more compulsive in his rapacious and murderously aggressive behavior. Manfred's confidence in his own virility is clear when he makes his proposal to Isabella, after deciding that he must marry her himself in order to produce male offspring to continue the family line: "Lady, you have missed a husband undeserving of your charms: They shall now be better disposed of. Instead of a sickly boy, you shall have a husband in the prime of his age, who will know how to value your beauties, and who may expect a numerous offspring" (23).

In terms of characterization, Manfred is less a person than a force. Walpole does attempt to introduce a slight measure of psychological complexity and moral reasoning into the tale, in the comment that before the "transition of his soul . . . to exquisite villainy" (i.e., after quelling his conscience and his feelings of sympathy for the women's plight), Manfred's temper was "naturally humane; and his virtues were always ready to operate, when his passions did not obscure his reason" (37, 31). But the fact remains that the reader never *does* see any evidence of Manfred's reasoning powers, for he spends most of the story racing about the castle in a "tempest of rage" and desire (18). Manfred never simply enters or leaves a room; he "flings" himself about in a state of constant, unrestrained motion. He epitomizes aggressive, unbridled, and unconscionable phallic energy, untamed by either feudal honor or domesticating feminine influence.

The incest/rape motif is played out in *Otranto* through the dream displacement strategy analyzed by Freud, in which the characters' individual identities become blurred. Isabella becomes a surrogate for Matilda, Manfred's actual daughter, so that the horror of the father's incestuous attacks is sufficiently diluted into acceptable fare for Walpole's readers (and perhaps for Walpole himself). Yet the incestuous nature of Manfred's pursuit of Isabella is underscored when he demands her release from the friar who has given her sanctuary in the church, connected via underground passages to the castle. Manfred's assertion, "I am her parent . . . and demand her" (49), prompts Father Jerome to warn him against his "incestuous designs on [his] contracted daughter" (50).

Isabella's role as a substitute for Matilda is further suggested in the scene where she says to the masochistic Hippolita (who is willing to do anything her lord wishes and tries to persuade Isabella to do the same), "Force should not drag me to Manfred's hated bed. I loathe him, I abhor him: Divine and human laws forbid." Then Isabella, whose own mother died in childbirth, affirms with Matilda that Hippolita is in effect the mother of them both (91).

There is as well a blending of the two young women in their attraction to the same man, the chivalric Theodore who, when he first meets Isabella fleeing from Manfred through the dark underground passages, expresses his willingness to "die in [her] defence" (27). Later in the castle where he meets Matilda, who has taken the bold step of warning him to flee from Manfred's wrath, he makes a similar declaration under the misapprehension that she is the same woman he had met earlier in the obscurity of the underground tunnels. She corrects his error, and at the end of their brief interview they have fallen deeply in love: "the hearts of both had drunk... deeply of a passion, which both now tasted for the first time" (74).

Similarly, at the end of the story, Manfred, "flushed by wine and love," stabs Matilda to death in the church with his dagger, thinking that she is Isabella. The bereaved Theodore finally contents himself with marrying Isabella, "with whom he could forever indulge the melancholy that had taken possession of his soul," presumably because the substitution does not entirely compensate for the loss of his original lover (108, 109, 116).

Contributing to the father-daughter confusion is Isabella's father, Frederic, who develops a violent passion for Matilda's "lovely form" (80) and at one point tacitly agrees with Manfred that each will marry the other's daughter (96). Frederic has escaped from being a prisoner of the infidels in the East and returned to Otranto to rescue Isabella, whose desperate condition has been revealed to him in a dream-vision (80–81). The sexual threat she faces is suggested imagistically when an old hermit directs him to the site of an enormous buried sabre, which bears the inscription,

> *Where e'er a casque that suits this sword is found,*
> *With perils is thy daughter compass'd round.*
> Alfonso's *blood alone can save the maid,*
> *And quiet a long restless Prince's shade.* (82)

Although Frederic's role is a heroic one, his complicity in the drama of family incest is later suggested when the sepulchral ghost of the old hermit warns him against forgetting his mission and succumbing to his desire for Matilda: "Wast thou delivered from bondage... to pursue carnal delights?" (107). Unlike Manfred, Frederic is able to heed the warning and curb his impulses, perhaps in part because he is a genuine noble, whereas Manfred is merely an illegitimate usurper.

The noble Theodore similarly has difficulty controlling his youthful desire to prove his manliness through acts of valor; in defense of Isabella he "impetuously" and almost fatally wounds Frederic, thinking that he is one of Manfred's agents (77). Impetuousness is normally Manfred's exclusive prerogative, and the adverb suggests that even the young hero is not entirely immune to the compulsive, aggressive drive that dictates most of Manfred's behavior. This incident is one of many in which the Oedipal conflict arises; throughout *Otranto* father figures try to behead sons, and sons attack fathers in repeated gestures of mutual emasculation.

The motif of gigantism in *Otranto*, once quite popular in the old romances, provides another representation of overwhelming masculine desire. Although today's reader is more likely to find it amusing, in the case of Walpole's audience the imagery may have been sufficiently subliminal to be genuinely disturbing. The first page of the story introduces the ancient prophecy: "*[T]he Castle and Lordship of Otranto should pass from the present family, whenever the real owner should be grown too large to inhabit it*" (15; Walpole's emphasis). Almost immediately after this statement, the gigantic helmet (which also signifies the "head" of the family), with its "proportionate quantity of black feathers," lands on poor Conrad (17). The suggestion of tumescence is repeated at the end of the story when Manfred speaks of the prophecy made by St. Nicholas in a dream to Ricardo, Manfred's grandfather: "Ricardo's posterity should reign in Otranto, until the rightful owner should be grown too large to inhabit the castle, and as long as issue-male from Ricardo's loins should remain to enjoy it" (114).

Manfred's tyrannical exercise of his sexual impulses and Hippolita's unquestioning subservience to him suggest a critique of patriarchal power in *Otranto* that accords with recent feminist analyses of sexual politics. Walpole apologizes in his preface to the first edition that he can offer no moral more original than the biblical dictum that "*The sins of the fathers are visited on their children to the third and fourth generation*" (5; Walpole's emphasis). Carol Dole, in her examination of Shakespearean prototypes for Manfred, cites an essay of Walpole's in which he argues that the "'unreasonable jealousy of Leontes [in *The Winter's Tale*] and his violent conduct in consequence, form a true portrait of Henry the Eighth, who generally made the law the engine of his boisterous passions'" (32).[8] One finds repeatedly in Walpole's writings evidence of a strong conviction that too much power inevitably corrupts; in *Otranto,* Manfred's claim to exclusive possession of the law is precisely what allows him to behave as if he were above the law.

When Matilda airs her concerns to her maidservant Bianca about Manfred's abusive treatment of Hippolita, the pragmatic Bianca responds, "Oh! Madam, . . . all men use their wives so, when they are weary of them. . . . [Y]our mother . . . knows that a bad husband is better than no husband at all" (39). The saintly Father Jerome, in contrast, "dread[s] Hippolita's unbounded submission to the will of her Lord" (62), and the reader is clearly meant to share his reservations. Hippolita is an eighteenth-century version of Chaucer's patient Griselda. The problem with this ideal type, which Walpole stresses, is her failure to protect her child from the father's abuses. Hippolita's declaration that Manfred is "dearer to me even than my children" (21) becomes a sad comment on maternal failure by the end of the story, when the father murders his own child.

The radical nature of Walpole's challenge to the social ideal of wifely submission becomes even more evident when contrasted with the conservative views expressed by women novelists two decades later. J. M. S. Tompkins has shown that affirmation of the general principle of submission was almost universal in these late-eighteenth-century novels, although there was a somewhat limited range of opinion on the extent to which it should be applied (155–61). Most women writers still sided with Hippolita's assertion that "[i]t is not ours to make election for ourselves: Heaven, our fathers, and our husbands must decide for us" (*Otranto* 91–92). In Walpole's ground-breaking work, however, there is a strong sense that Hippolita's slavish devotion to her husband and to patriarchal law is a gross violation of a more fundamental natural law, one that promotes the health and survival of the young.

Walpole's personal family background also supports the idea of a feminine bias informing *The Castle of Otranto*. As a child, Walpole was much closer to his mother than to his father who, as has been mentioned, had been prime minister of England from 1715 to 1717 and 1721 to 1742 (Horace was born in 1717). Catherine Walpole's death in 1737, when Walpole was twenty, left the father free to marry his long-time and publicly recognized mistress, who had for many years received more of Sir Robert Walpole's personal attentions than his wife had. There is speculation that the wife herself had engaged in her own share of "gallantries," to use the mideighteenth-century euphemism. However that may be, according to Walpole himself his mother treated her youngest son with "extreme fondness," and he explained her strong maternal attachment as arising from her concern about his delicate health (Kallich 9)—although one biographer, R. W. Ketton-Cremer, suggests that Catherine's intense involvement with her son was also a way of compensating for being neglected by her husband (12).[9]

As an adult, Walpole generally kept his distance from both public political activity and private sexual involvement, and his attitude seems to have been a fairly clear case of reaction against a virile and dynamic father who sired six children (although there is some question as to whether Horace was his biological son[10]), kept a mistress, and was the most powerful figure in English public life for over twenty years. Horace Walpole was resolutely celibate, with the possible exception of one brief affair (Ketton-Cremer 30–31), and usually remained detached from the political realm as well. Despite the fact that he held a seat in Parliament from 1742 until 1768, he maintained for the most part an arms-length relationship with the political events of the day, although engaging in a considerable amount of behind-the-scenes manipulation with his influential friends. He was also a greedy voyeur of social and political gossip—many of the raciest anecdotes from Lawrence Stone's study are from Walpole's correspondence.[11]

As his friend Gilly Williams noted, Walpole wrote *The Castle of Otranto* during a period of "political frenzy" (Sabor 66) in which he was uncharacteristically immersing himself in the life his father had represented. Walpole had reached a point of nervous and emotional exhaustion from his efforts to defend his beloved maternal cousin, Henry Seymour Conway, from political misfortunes that he himself had to some extent precipitated in his role as advisor and which were related to larger upheavals in the political world (Ketton-Cremer 200–04). It was during this time that Walpole had a vivid dream about a gigantic hand in armor and almost immediately commenced writing his story. He wrote William Cole in March 1765,

> I was so engrossed with my tale, which I completed in less than two months, that one evening I wrote from the time I had drunk my tea, about six o'clock, till half an hour after one in the morning, when my hand and fingers were so weary, that I could not hold the pen to finish the sentence, but left Matilda and Isabella talking, in the middle of a paragraph. (W. S. Lewis 122)

It is doubtful that Walpole's state of emotional ferment arose solely from the political and diplomatic conflicts in which he had become embroiled; evidently, the episode had also stirred up some powerful and disturbing personal family memories.

Henry Conway appears to have been at this time Walpole's last strong link with the mother he had lost twenty-seven years earlier. Seven years after her death, Walpole wrote to his cousin, offering to share his fortune with him so that Henry might marry the woman he loved, and referring to the maternal connection as the main reason for his generosity: "'If I ever felt much for anything (which I know may be questioned), it was certainly for my mother. I look on you as my nearest relation by her, and I think I can never do enough to show my gratitude and affection to her'" (qtd. in Ketton-Cremer 76).

It is apparent that even though Walpole developed a friendlier and more intimate relationship with his father during the elder Walpole's later years, the son's psychological identification with his mother was much stronger. This sense of identification certainly helps to explain why *The Castle of Otranto* depicts so vividly the nightmare of female subjugation, which makes the novel for all its weaknesses the significant and innovative work it is. The connection between Manfred as the personal father who neglects and abuses his wife, and Sir Robert as the symbolic father of a paternalistic social order, seems inescapable.

John Samson has shown that *Otranto* may be read as a political allegory, with Theodore representing Conway, as the noble but persecuted young man; Manfred representing George Grenville, George III's persecuting and tyrannical (in Walpole's view) minister; and Father Jerome, whose well-meaning but "simple-minded meddling incriminates Theodore," representing Walpole himself (148). Samson makes the astute observation that "what kept Horace Walpole from mental collapse following the Conway incident was his ability to create a saving fiction." Samson's argument is less convincing, however, when he suggests that the frequency of "perverse sexuality" in eighteenth-century Gothic fiction generally, and in *Otranto* particularly, signifies *simply* a "revolt against monarchy" (156, 152). My point is that in *The Castle of Otranto* perverse and destructive sexual relations between husband and wife or parent and child are expressions, and not merely symbols, of inequitable legal and political relations that neither regulate the behavior of the most powerful members of a given society nor protect the most vulnerable.

Walpole's *Otranto* registers, well in advance of Mary Wollstonecraft's *Vindication of the Rights of Woman,* the social ills arising from the cultural effacement of women, and the urgency of the need for change (notwithstanding the fact that Walpole once contemptuously called Wollstonecraft a "hyena in petticoats"; qtd. in Sunstein 306). Although his tale expresses some fear about the loss of old certainties, it also calls for the collapse of the ancient castle.

It should be noted, however, that the Castle of Otranto does not collapse entirely. It is shaken "to its foundations" by a clap of thunder; then the walls behind Manfred are "thrown down with a mighty force," and "the form of Alfonso [the murdered prince, Theodore's grandfather], dilated to an immense magnitude, appear[s] in the center of the ruins" (113). After some more revelations about personal identities, the group retires "to the remaining part of the castle" (115). A case can thus be made for a more conservative reading of *Otranto*'s ending, as a nostalgic call for return to feudal ideals of chivalry and honor; yet even with this interpretation, the novel's protest against the tyrannical subjection of women remains clear.

Thus, however frivolous, "lightweight," and escapist *The Castle of Otranto* may appear to be, it remains a highly important work: both historically, in its novel treatment of family violence; and generically, as the prototypical Gothic novel which conveys its radical social critique via a thrilling, subliminally subversive horror story.

CHAPTER THREE

Sentiment versus Horror:
Generic Ambivalence in Female Gothic
and Ann Radcliffe's A Sicilian Romance

*W*hen in the 1790s women began to produce and read Gothic novels in unprecedented numbers, little had changed since Walpole's day with regard to women's legal position in society. It would not be until 1839 that the Infants' Custody Act would give a mother the right to keep her children under the age of seven with her, in the event of a marital separation. Women had been writing novels all through the eighteenth century,[1] but although their fictions articulated a feminine experience of life, which was generally missing from novels written by men, their work seldom overtly questioned the necessity of women's economic dependence or the notion that they were sexually "purer" than men.

The omnipresence in Gothic horror stories of terrified maidens fleeing from rape and imprisonment in medieval castles and monasteries would seem to indicate that many eighteenth-century women found their condition to be less than satisfactory. Yet the plot resolutions and the narrative commentary in these stories continue to affirm conventional, mainly middle-class domestic values. Alongside the overall conservative tendency, however, there are also distinct signs of a growing conviction that late-eighteenth-century domesticity is not always the protective shrine to feminine purity it is supposed to be. There is also in some of these novels, however obliquely presented, a subtle recognition of feminine sexual desire.

The tension between the ideal and the actual experience (whether social or psychological), or between a civilized sensibility and a disruptive Gothic terror, results in a remarkably ambivalent literary voice.

The women novelists called "Gothic" were actually working in two different modes: the Gothic novel as inaugurated by Walpole, and the novel of sentiment and sensibility that had been popular throughout much of the century ("sentiment" generally tokening the refinement of feeling and emotion into a moral virtue, and "sensibility" an acute susceptibility to external impressions). It is not entirely accurate to say as Leslie Fiedler does that in "Sentimentalism, the Age of Reason dissolves in a debauch of tearfulness" (*Love* xxxiv) for despite its stress on the emotional rather than the intellectual life, the cult maintained the Enlightenment faith in humanity's steady transcendence over its rude and bestial origins. In the words of J. M. S. Tompkins,

> To the eighteenth century [sensibility] was a significant, almost sacred word, for it enshrined the idea of the progress of the human race. Sensibility was a modern quality; it was not found among the ancients, but was the product of modern conditions; the heroic and tremendous virtues might be dying out with the stormy times that evoked them, but modern security, leisure and education had evolved a delicacy of sensation, a refinement of virtue, which the age found even more beautiful. The human sympathies, which a rougher age had repressed, expanded widely, especially towards the weak and unfortunate, and the social conscience began to occupy itself with prisoners, children, animals and slaves. (92–93)

Tompkins quotes a number of striking examples. One letter to *Gentleman's Magazine,* May 1791, gives "an account of an affecting scene of Village Distress, a visit to a young labourer, who has lost his wife and is left with seven children, because 'it might yield to some of your readers a portion of that luxurious pity which I felt'" (103 n. 1; she also includes several highly amusing excerpts about the loyalty of dogs).

A basic tenet of the cult of sensibility was the un-Calvinistic belief that one could rely on one's feelings for moral guidance—particularly one's feelings of social sympathy. The seventeenth-century Cambridge Platonists had argued for faith in inherent human virtue: although we might live in a fallen world, we nevertheless retain something of God's image within ourselves, which we can cultivate and trust. Virtuous action that was inspired only by a fear of the consequences of human or divine law was not true virtue. Moral conduct not only could be guided by the individual conscience but also could be impelled by an innate desire to do right. This idea was sometimes pushed to its extreme, as in the third Earl of Shaftesbury's assertion that "[a] man of thorough good breeding, whatever else he be, is incapable of doing a rude or brutal action."[2]

The cult of sensibility rested on the notion of a morally superior elite, whose members could be identified by their strong susceptibility to external impressions—an elite with whom the middle classes came to identify, against the decadence of the aristocracy and the more rough and tumble world of the lower classes. This elite was further divided into its own gendered moral hierarchy, with women on top. In Edmund Leites's view, this strategy served "to free men from the burden of the demand for moral constancy and the accompanying expectation that good persons will live the whole of their adult lives without significant moral failure" (121). In sexual matters, the burden of repression lay more heavily on the women; but it was not regarded as a burden, for the general consensus was that in this area women had nothing to repress.

The instinctual nurturing of motherhood was often cited as an inspirational example of moral altruism, and most women adhered to the idea that their inherent capacity for social sympathy and sensitivity was superior to men's. As Tompkins comments, women writers of the later popular novels "accepted their function of ennobling men very seriously" (150). Women's sense of their own importance in the moral realm compensated considerably for their exclusion from the public one; their role was to preserve the sanctity of the home life, the private sphere to which their mates could return and be refreshed after venturing out into the contaminating world of commercial competition. Thus a kind of ethical harmony between the sexes could be maintained, which would in turn ensure the security and stability desirable for motherhood.[3]

Such was the ideal, at any rate. Its complications can be seen in the 1740s novels of Samuel Richardson, which on the surface affirm the triumph of female virtue over male appetite—in Pamela's case by her "holding out" successfully for marriage, and in Clarissa's case by her preferring to die with her moral integrity intact rather than marry the man who raped her. In other ways, however, Richardson's novels are testaments to women's social and sexual vulnerability, not only to harassment, imprisonment, and sexual assault but also to their own unadmitted longings.

As Margaret Anne Doody points out, Richardson's work itself grew out of "a minor tradition established by the writers of love stories told in the feminine voice" (*Natural* 24). These stories written by women usually took one of two forms, "the seduction/rape tale and the courtship novel" (*Natural* 18). They also showed a strong interest in psychological analysis (*Natural* 22). Doody states that in the novels of Eliza Heywood, one of the best known of these writers, the heroines "are sexually passionate creatures, naturally responsive to a lover's ardour, oppressed by the force of love within as well as by the lover's ruthless importunity" (*Natural* 18). According to Doody, "moral instruction" is often accompanied in Heywood's stories by "light pornography" (*Natural* 18, 19). A similar mingling of contraries may be seen in Richardson's combination of what Frederick S. Frank calls the "homiletic" moral message and the "horrific" scenes of sexual sadomasochism (59).

Frank goes so far as to argue that Richardson's novels were the direct progenitors of the Gothic novel. He points out that the "ruthless erotic criminal," the "self-gratifying Gothic aesthetic which encourages the reader to take delight in incidents of pain . . . depravity and decay . . . sexual barbarity, social chaos, charnel spectacle, and moral anarchy," the sadistic male sexuality and the masochistic female sexuality, "the Gothic ordeal of the incarcerated maiden," the "live burial," can all be found in later Gothic fiction (49–55). Although it is certainly true that Richardson repeatedly suggests the anarchic and amoral force of the instincts, Frank does not examine Richardson's stronger emphasis on the virtue that triumphs over all this, or the important difference of setting: the first Gothic novels were displaced in time and space, whereas *Pamela* and *Clarissa* are set in contemporary, realistically detailed social worlds.

Additionally, the fact that Eliza Heywood's boldness was a disappearing phenomenon in the literary landscape is perhaps most clearly signaled in the plot resolutions of Richardson's novels; at the end of *Pamela* the heroine remains, as Leites notes, "as innocent of her sexuality . . . as when she began," despite the many indications Richardson has offered about her secret desire (130). The same can be said of Clarissa, who is unconscious (in the literal sense: she has been drugged) when she is deflowered. Moreover, as Erica Harth observes, "Pamela's active campaign for virtue ends in the passive condition of a wife. . . . Whatever social and sexual conflict the novel initiates is ultimately harmonized by love and virtue resolved into 'sentiment,' the dominant affective tone of the eighteenth century" (150, 148).[4]

The desexualizing of women's image in the course of the eighteenth century was partly a consequence of changing socioeconomic conditions.

Public and private spheres were becoming more clearly demarcated as an expanding market economy generated new wealth. And since new wealth meant new property, it became more important to ascertain clearly lines of succession and inheritance, which could be done only when there was general confidence in women's chastity. Mary Poovey quotes Samuel Johnson as saying, "Consider of what importance to society the chastity of women is. Upon that all the property in the world depends. We hang a thief for stealing a sheep; but the unchastity of a woman transfers sheep, and farm and all, from the right owner" (6).[5]

In one sense, the chaste woman was the guardian of the man's property, but in another she *was* the property—or more precisely, the money that sustained property—itself. As more and more young women from the prosperous merchant class furthered their families' interests by marrying the eldest sons of the landed estates, the dowries that women were expected to bring into marriage increased. In effect, "husbands were becoming more expensive, or, to reverse the formula, women were becoming less valuable" (Poovey 12).

Women's relative decline in "market value" throughout the century reflected the more masculine values of Protestantism. Women's enhanced moral status, often referred to in reverent and quasireligious language, appears to have provided a new outlet for religious feeling in a society that no longer worshipped the Holy Mother of God. It also offered some psychological compensation for the fact that women's child-bearing capacity was being devalued into a commodity that could be exchanged not so much for the perpetuation of the ancestral line as for the acquisition of new political and economic power.

The fact that middle-class women were becoming increasingly literate during the course of the century did not seem to alarm their men. Although some concern was expressed about the quality of the reading material preferred by women (especially its unevenness), the activity was generally regarded as a fairly harmless pastime that helped to fill their vacant hours—providing of course that the reading material was appropriate: that is to say, morally and socially instructive. So long as novels adequately reinforced the values promoted in the conduct books, they were usually considered to be acceptable fare for the impressionable minds of the (mostly young) women who read them and who were thought to be deficient in the mental fortitude necessary for pursuing more serious material. As one writer advocated, "A large majority, especially of the fair sex, have not time nor talents for the investigation of abstract principles in moral and social life; wherefore a lighter kind of study is essential" (qtd. in Tompkins 71).[6]

Although the propertied classes recognized that literacy allows a dimension of independent mental experience, which can be dangerous to social stability, this concern was directed mainly toward the lower classes. In the words of Lawrence Stone, the aristocratic elite "followed Hobbes in blaming the horrors of the Civil War on excessive education in the pre-war years. Between 1660 and 1790 most men were convinced that a little learning for the poor is a dangerous thing, since it encourages them to aspire beyond their station" ("Literacy" 85). Stone cites one gentleman who commented in 1792 that Thomas Paine's *Rights of Man* (1791–92) had done "little harm" in Manchester and Birmingham, where "not one in a hundred" of the factory laborers knew their alphabet, but a great deal in Scotland, where "the *bodies*" could all read ("Literacy" 85–86).

Women were deemed less likely to inculcate subversive ideas through their reading, however, since most of them came from the leisured middle and upper classes and generally preferred novels to radical political tracts which might encourage them to "aspire beyond their station." Mary Wollstonecraft's *Vindication of the Rights of Woman* (1792) was one exception to the case, but its impact was limited and also short-lived, thanks to the naive revelations of her husband, William Godwin, about her risque past in his *Memoirs of the author of a Vindication of the Rights of Woman* (1798), published one year after her death (Mellor 2–3).[7]

The Gothic deluge of the 1790s did cause alarm in some quarters, partly because of the somewhat dubious content of these works (the more "improbable" and histrionic ones receiving torrents of abusive scorn from the reviewers), and partly because the huge popularity of Gothic fiction was a public phenomenon that no-one could ignore. As Dorothy Blakey records, the library of William Lane, which circulated his popular Minerva Press publications—novels both written and read largely by women— increased its stock from ten thousand items in 1790 to nearly seventeen thousand in 1802 (114). The huge demand for these novels is further indicated by the fact that the price of a library subscription rose from a guinea a year in 1798 to a guinea and a half by 1802 (Blakey 116).

Lane was a shrewd businessman and was enormously successful in commercial if not in critical terms. Blakey suggests that "it was a definite part of his policy to attract young and timid writers, who would be flattered to part with their manuscripts at any price" (71). Needless to say, the diffident attitude of which Lane took advantage was all too common in the women writers who came to him.

Even the more accomplished and commercially successful writers were careful to include apologetic pleas for critical indulgence in their prefaces. Eliza Parsons apologizes in her introduction to *The Mysterious Warning* (1796) for her deficiencies as a writer, and in her dedication she defends her efforts in a characteristic maternal vein: "The few pretensions I have to merit are merely negative ones: I have never written a line tending to corrupt the heart, sully the imagination, or mislead the judgement of my young Readers" (xviii). These women never laid claim to any intellectual or aesthetic excellence, which not even the "realistic" novel, still regarded as primarily a form of popular entertainment, was yet expected to supply.[8] They emphasized instead their works' morally didactic value, an apparently sincere but nevertheless effective strategy at a time when printed sermons were still very popular with the reading public.

Many women turned to writing because it was one of the few acceptable remunerative endeavors available to them, a fact that helps to explain the allegiance to conservative values in their novels. These women literally could not afford to be too radical. A number of them had personal histories of economic hardship and struggle, several having been left in a state of poverty by their improvident and/or deceased husbands, often with a brood of needy children to clothe, feed, and educate. Isabella Kelly married a "reckless, indigent, and profligate" man who left the family in a state of poverty when he died; she resorted to what she called the "'odious task of writing'" as her only option (Varma's introduction to *Abbey* vi). Charlotte Smith married a "philandering wastrel" who left her in charge of twelve children when he landed in debtor's prison (Ehrenpreis's introduction to *Old* viii). Eliza Parsons married an industrious man, a turpentine distiller, who was devoted to his family but whose spirit was broken by family bereavement and business reversals. When he died of a stroke she was left impoverished, with seven surviving children to support (Varma's introduction to *Mysterious* vii–viii).

For the women writers, the Gothic novel was a vehicle for exploring, via a retreat into an imaginative past (whether through chronological displacement or architecturally induced), their own complex attitudes about their personal desires and their place in the public and social world. There is a great deal in these works that clearly arises from the wish-fulfillment impulse, an aspect of women's Gothic dreams that enters through the delusive gates of ivory rather than the prophetic gates of horn.[9] These female authors were writing out their own fantasies, which offered to many a momentary reprieve from the difficulties and dissatisfactions of daily life. In their escapist dream plots the irresponsible spouse reforms, a sudden inheritance rescues the family from poverty, "low" origins turn out to be "high," and the pursued and terrified young woman narrowly escapes rape. In this respect these works were not greatly different from the sentimental novels that preceded them, although a greater sense of disturbance and instability was also registered in their Gothic aspects.

In Isabella Kelly's *Abbey of St. Asaph* (1795), the Gothic element is enclosed within a romantic drama that portrays the perils of women's dependence on men but provides a resolution suggesting that mutual happiness in such a situation is nevertheless possible. The marriage between a young woman, Elinor, and a gentleman, Clement, becomes invalid after he admits that he lied about his age. He declines to make her an honorable woman despite the fact that they have a child, but by the end of the story, and after the young woman has undergone many harrowing experiences in the social world, the two become reconciled.

Although the plot centers on incidents of betrayal and deception, almost all the characters in this novel exhibit an exquisite sensibility, which shows itself in their susceptibility to states of extreme alarm. Every two or three pages someone collapses from shock or distress. The noble, constant, ideal hero, Lionel Douglas, who "had now reached his eighteenth year, his soul enriched with all the virtues that ever graced humanity" (1: 66, 67), reacts typically after discovering that his beloved Jennet may be in danger: "The brain of Douglas was on fire, while a thousand horrid fears for Jennet's safety, alarmed his bosom.—Reason tottered on her throne, and in a whirl of madness, unknowing how to turn, he descended to the street; Elinor,— Montague, all were forgotten, in the dread of Jennet's fate" (1: 174).

Jennet is a remarkably stalwart heroine whose moral excellence conforms to the "proper woman" stereotype but whose unusually bold and questing spirit does not. She composes herself in difficult circumstances by falling on her knees in "pious meditation" (3: 12), but she is finally overwhelmed when she ventures into the catacombs under the Abbey of St. Asaph. There she is confronted by seemingly inexplicable sights and sounds in "the dwellings of the dead," where the bodies appear in "different stages of decay" (3: 11, 12), and she faints. Her composure is somewhat renewed when she recovers and sees an old man, Sir Eldred, who reassures her that he is not a ghost, explaining that he has been imprisoned there for nineteen years by a usurping brother. When she asks this venerable personage his opinion regarding another legendary ghost, his face breaks into a "smile, the first for nineteen years that had dimpled on his cheek" (3: 21).

The fact that Sir Eldred has suffered few apparent ill effects from his long sojourn underground was not particularly problematic for Kelly's readers, for a character's long-term imprisonment (or "live burial") was a common Gothic plot device in the 1790s. What matters in these fictions, it seems, is the emergence of the long-held secret and not the psychological effects on the individual who has borne it for so long in solitude. Part of the convention also demands that the secret's final exposure is prefaced by ominous, apparently supernatural effects (which more often than not are later explained as arising from natural causes). The readers' lack of interest in particularized psychological exploration suggests their implicit acceptance of the role Gothic characters tend to play as embodiments of social and psychic forces rather than as individual personalities.

One aspect of the ritual of descent in Gothic fiction that undoubtedly appealed to the women readers of the day was its suggestion that the above-ground, or conscious, public version of reality is incomplete; if one dares to venture into the strange and uncanny world below the surface, one finds a different story. In Jennet's case, her underground explorations are preceded by a visit to the old Abbey, in a scene which initiates the movement away from the contemporary social world, with all its obstructions and constrictions: "She entered with reverential awe, and with pleased serenity examined the ancient tombs of long forgotten dead; of men once the terror of invading and domestic foes, and the glory and defence of mighty powers; of women, once the pride of female excellence, and the worshipped wonders of surrounding principalities" (3: 5). After briefly bathing in the ambience of this old Catholic world where women were once "worshipped wonders," she moves from the outmoded sacred to the apparent daemonic as she descends the stairs leading to the catacombs. At one point she sees a human skeleton: "the bare ribs shook,—the ghastly skull rose slow, yet visible, to view; and disconsolately bowing, seemed to implore commiseration. Something glistened within the hollow sockets, which once inclosed the orbs of sight, and a faint shriek issued from the yawning jaws" (3: 13–14). The reader is left with the impression that Jennet may indeed have encountered some unquiet spirit of the dead, until near the end of the novel when reassurance comes in the form of the enlightened Doctor Lewis who, "unconscious of guilt, a stranger to fear, and armed with the righteousness of a quiet mind, resolutely advance[s]" and picks up the skull, to discover a large rat in it (3: 127–28).

The explaining away of the supernatural is accompanied by a resolution of the plot in which all deserving characters end up secure, comfortable, and happy. In addition, Jennet, who has suffered some undue social humiliation because of her lowly background, discovers that she is after all a rich heiress, for the old nobleman she found underground is ultimately revealed as her true father (3: 104–117). She even acquires a new name, her original birth name of Rodolpha. Thus, the heroine's frightening journey has uncovered for her a father figure who will unfailingly honor his traditional patriarchal responsibilities, unlike the callow cad Clement, who is more strongly associated through setting with the modern world of contractual relations dominated by self-interest.

Kelly's novel is typical of Female Gothic from this period, in the way it attempts to resolve the conflict between public values and women's private impulses. Despite its brief foray into Gothic horror, it tends to affirm dominant social values, whatever slight criticism it might suggest about contemporary practices. The belief is maintained that sentiment and moral virtue will serve to correct such social imperfections. The heroine is a sensitive, rational creature who loves devotedly rather than passionately. There is no overt questioning of the validity of the social system that serves women's needs so poorly—which seems understandable, considering how dependent late-eighteenth-century women still were on it. Neither is there any sign of the underground world of sexual desire that one finds in *The Castle of Otranto*. The Gothic nightmare is often suggested in these works, but its full force is almost invariably held in check by the bulwark of sensibility.

Bette B. Roberts, who also examines the emotional conflict at the heart of early Gothic novels by women, states that the "Walpolian blend of romance and novel, the capacity of the genre itself to blur fantasy and reality. . . . lends itself to the ambivalent expression of flight from and reinforcement of an inhibitive patriarchal value system" (225). She argues that while the domestic novel reinforced and idealized the female status quo, "the gothic novel provided an outlet for the literary expression of repressed female wishes and fears resultant from a restrictive milieu" (225–26). Although I agree in the main with Roberts's analysis, my point is that the full Walpolian Gothic horror was one element that most of the late-eighteenth-century women novelists were not prepared to take up. *Sentimental Female Gothic* would seem to be a more appropriate term for such works, rather than the general category of *Female Gothic* currently favored by feminist critics, for it serves to distinguish this group from the main tradition, which includes Mary Shelley's horrific *Frankenstein*.[10]

In the work of the great mistress of Female Gothic, Ann Radcliffe, the values of sensibility are also upheld, but her novels acquire greater force and complexity from the way they allow repressed female sexuality to come dangerously close to the surface of the narrative. In *A Sicilian Romance* (1790) Radcliffe's debt to Walpole is most apparent; thus, it illustrates perhaps better than any other of her tales her unique hybrid of Gothic horror and sentimental ethos.

The main plot of *A Sicilian Romance* concerns the flight of the young and beautiful Julia from an unwanted marriage that her father attempts to impose upon her. At the beginning of the novel, Julia and her sister, Emilia, are living in the Castle Mazzini with their governess, Mme Menon, when their father, the marquis, returns after a long absence with his second wife, Maria (the girls' mother apparently having died when they were children), and the girls' brother, Ferdinand. At this time, the young people are troubled and fascinated by mysterious sights and sounds that emanate from an unused section of the castle. As well, Julia falls in love with one of their guests, Hippolitus (the Count de Vereza), on whom the adulterous Maria also has her eye.

When Julia learns that her tyrannical father is going to compel her to marry the Duke de Luovo, she flees, assisted by Ferdinand and Hippolitus, but in their attempt to leave the castle the two young men are caught; the marquis stabs Hippolitus (not fatally) and confines Ferdinand to a dungeon. Julia, the only one to get away, has a number of hair-raising adventures, and just as she is about to be forced to become a nun, Ferdinand manages to rescue her. When they return to the castle, Julia discovers her long-lost mother in an underground vault beneath the castle's unused section, where the ruthless marquis had imprisoned her many years ago. In the meantime, the marquis discovers his second wife's infidelity, and after a heated argument she poisons him and then commits suicide by stabbing herself. In the end, all the deserving characters are happily reunited: the mother and children; the two old friends, Mme Menon and the marchioness; and the two lovers, Julia and Hippolitus.

Like the first edition of *Otranto, A Sicilian Romance* is purportedly based on an old manuscript that was assembled by the narrator (in Radcliffe's work the device is presented as part of the fiction, whereas Walpole originally pretended there was an actual manuscript). There also are two heroines in Radcliffe's work, but the psychological implications of this duality are not developed as they are in *Otranto*. The two sisters in *A Sicilian Romance* illustrate female loyalty and solidarity, while also serving as points of contrast: Emilia possesses a "mild and sweet temper, united with a clear comprehensive mind," whereas Julia is more volatile: "[She] was of a more lively cast. An extreme sensibility subjected her to frequent uneasiness; her temper was warm, but generous; she was quickly irritated, and quickly appeased; and to a reproof, however gentle, she would often weep, but was never sullen. Her imagination was ardent, and her mind early exhibited symptoms of genius" (1: 7).[11] Julia's "extreme sensibility" is the main quality that identifies her as a fairly conventional sentimental heroine.

At the outset of the story, Radcliffe instructs her readers in the "two classes" of conversation: the sentimental and the familiar. "It is the province of the familiar to diffuse cheerfulness and ease," whereas in sentimental conversation, the type in which the girls' instructress excelled,

> good sense, lively feeling, and natural delicacy of taste, must be united [with] an expansion of mind, and a refinement of thought, which is the result of high cultivation. . . . a knowledge of the world is requisite, and that enchanting ease, that elegance of manner, which is to be acquired only by frequenting the higher circles of polished life. In sentimental conversation subjects . . . are discussed in a kind of sportive way, with animation and refinement, and are never continued longer than politeness allows. (1: 15–16)

This overtly didactic passage, with its insistence on the positive value of cultivated restraint, also serves to distance Radcliffe's work from Walpole's.

Although in both *The Castle of Otranto* and *A Sicilian Romance* the pious and long-suffering mothers are repressed figures, Hippolyta is "buried alive" only in the figurative sense, whereas the marchioness is literally trapped underground. After numerous encounters with the inevitable locked doors, rusty keys, passageways hidden behind tapestries, and dark confusing tunnels and staircases, Julia discovers in a subterranean chamber in the castle's forbidden zone the mother whom she had presumed dead. In the room's "feeble light," Julia sees "the pale and emaciated figure of a woman, seated, with half-closed eyes." The mother's air of "mild dignity" arouses in the daughter "an involuntary veneration" even before her true identity is revealed (2: 158–59).

The mother tells her tale of abuse. Her husband, whose "passions" we are told at the beginning of the story, "were vehement" (1: 6), became enamored of another woman, and when his wife went into a Clarissalike decline (she tells Julia that she "beheld the approach of death with a steady eye, and even welcomed it as the passport to tranquillity"; 2: 164), he had her moved to a hidden underground chamber. He then declared her dead and married his new lover. A servant brought the imprisoned woman food once a week and even allowed her one look at her children from a distance.

On the question of parental responsibility, Radcliffe's presentation differs dramatically from Walpole's, for in *A Sicilian Romance* the failure rests mainly on the shoulders of the father, "whose heart was dead to paternal tenderness" (1: 6; although it could be argued that the mother's desire for death may be another form of abandonment). Although in both cases patriarchal power comes between the mothers and their children, Hippolita's complicity in her own oppression is what keeps her from safeguarding the welfare of her daughter(s), whereas Julia's mother is simply another victim who has been separated from her children by force.

The mother's description of her brief glimpse of her children is clearly meant to be heartbreaking: "I saw you—I saw my children—and was neither permitted to clasp them to my heart, or to speak to them!" (2: 170). She recalls the emotional devastation of the enforced separation from her children: "instead of calming, [seeing my children] agitated my mind with a restless, wild despair, which bore away my strongest powers of resistance. I raved incessantly of my children, and incessantly solicited to see them again" (2: 171). Her "reason" or sanity is never ultimately "subdued," however, for her "firm principles of religious faith . . . imbibed in early youth" sustain her (2: 167–68). She never attempts to escape or to call for rescue because she understands that "the marquis . . . has not only power to imprison, but also the right of life and death in his own domains" (2: 173–174).[12]

While the buried mother motif might strike a modern reader as excessively melodramatic, according to Lawrence Stone recorded examples of "wives imprisoned in their homes or in madhouses" were not infrequent during the eighteenth century, although they diminish after midcentury. He cites one conversation in 1769 between Lady Sarah Bunbury and Lady Mary Coke (to whom Walpole dedicated *Otranto*), in which the younger Sarah Bunbury told her older friend that she would not attempt to leave her husband for her lover, for fear that "'her running away from her husband would give him the right to lock her up for the rest of her life'. Lady Mary disagreed, observing that in fact 'she would not be locked up, tho' I remembered when people were locked up for no fault of their own'" (*Road* 168–69).

The secret that emerges from the forbidden zone of the castle, then, is the social powerlessness of women—or more precisely, the powerlessness of the mother. Radcliffe, in her handling of the revelation, conforms to the Gothic pattern in which the repressed content is initially experienced as something strange and menacing. The cries and moans of Julia's grieving and distracted mother are first interpreted as uncanny events by the other characters, as is the flickering light of the person carrying food to her in the prohibited region of the castle.

The "involuntary veneration" that Julia first feels upon seeing her mother is anticipated in an earlier scene, when her response to overhearing a hymn to the Virgin Mary obliquely connects the Catholic Virgin with her antecedent, the ancient and fruitful Mother Goddess. When Julia, upset by the threat of the unwanted marriage forced upon her by her father, rises from her bed at night, what she sees and hears from her window is described in a lyrical evocation of both eroticism and religiosity.

> The night was still, and not a breath disturbed the surface of the waters. The moon shed a mild radiance over the waves, which in gentle undulations flowed upon the sands. The scene insensibly tranquilized her spirits. A tender and pleasing melancholy diffused itself over her mind; and as she mused, she heard the dashing of distant oars. Presently she perceived upon the light surface of the sea a small boat. The sound of the oars ceased, and a solemn strain of harmony (such as fancy wafts from the abodes of the blessed) stole upon the silence of the night. A chorus of voices now swelled upon the air, and died away at a distance. In the strain Julia recollected the midnight hymn to the virgin, and holy enthusiasm filled her heart. The chorus was repeated, accompanied by a solemn striking of oars. A sigh of exstacy stole from her bosom. Silence returned. The divine melody she had heard calmed the tumult of her mind, and she sunk in sweet repose. (1: 132–133)

The erotic or sensuous aesthetic element in Catholicism clearly had some appeal for Radcliffe, despite her enlightened prejudice against popish superstition. She commented on a journey through the Lake District in 1794, after visiting the ruined monasteries in the area, that "though reason rejoices that they no longer exist, the eye may be allowed to regret" (qtd. in Napier 40).[13]

Because "repose" can be only a temporary pleasure for Radcliffe's protagonists, shortly after this scene Julia decides to flee. After a great deal of difficult, dangerous, and disorienting wandering she returns to her father's castle, arriving first in the dungeon where her mother has been imprisoned. The movement tracks women's spiritual dispossession; it takes Julia from a hymn sung to the holy virgin, to the discovery of a "pale and emaciated figure" who can barely be seen in the "feeble light"—the mother who is finally recovered and restored to her rightful place of honor and her full humanity. Julia declares to her, "Oh! let me lead you to light and life!" (2: 177).

Although the repressed returns in a typical Gothic fashion in this novel, Radcliffe nevertheless handles the horror with velvet gloves. In one characteristic scene, one of the young heroes rescues Julia from a den of thieves. In their flight, they enter a "dark abyss" beneath a secret door: "[I]t is not easy to imagine their horror on discovering they were in a receptacle for the murdered bodies of the unfortunate people who had fallen into the hands of the banditti" (2: 139). Radcliffe then tastefully comments that the "bodies which remained unburied were probably left either from hurry or negligence, and exhibited a spectacle too shocking for humanity" (2: 140).

At the same time, however, there is a great deal of sexual suggestiveness in this episode. Julia's lover encounters the apparently dead body of a young woman, her face concealed by her robe: "[T]he long auburn tresses which fell in beautiful luxuriance over her bosom, served to veil a part of the glowing beauty which the disorder of her dress would have revealed. / Pity, surprize, and admiration struggled in the breast of Hippolitus" (2: 132). The young woman turns out, of course, to be Julia. In the context of this dark and uncivilized world, there is a subtle yet vivid recognition of the indiscriminate, amoral aspect of carnal desire, while events in other parts of the novel affirm the importance of prudence and discrimination in human relationships.

A similar confusion occurs at the outset of the story when Julia watches from a window as her stepmother the marchioness arrives with her entourage at the castle after many years' absence, along with Julia's and Emilia's brother Ferdinand, whom they have not seen since childhood. Julia points out "the graceful figure of a young man" in the group whom she hopes is their brother, but he later turns out to be Hippolitus, who soon becomes her suitor (1: 34–35, 39).

The suggestion of a natural and instinctual sexual desire is also conveyed in Radcliffe's prose rhythm, which enacts and affirms a specifically feminine erotic response. One gentleman praised Radcliffe's work because "she has forborne to raise one questionable throb, or call forth a momentary blush" (qtd. in Tompkins 250),[14] but he evidently was not reading very carefully. Tompkins astutely points out the "voluptuous colouring" that accompanies the "chaste propriety" of Radcliffe's prose (250) and comments that her "books are full of the half-revealed, of objects that are betrayed sufficiently to excite curiosity but not sufficiently to allay it, of hints and traces that lead the mind into a region of vague sublimity" (257). The teasing, exciting effect of Radcliffe's technique, which "fine-tunes" the art of timely interruption employed by Walpole, is suggested in Tompkins's description: "If there is suspense in *Otranto,* in *Udolpho* everything is suspended. Perils threaten and withdraw; lovers part and meet and part again; mysteries are suspected and explained, but the explanation is misleading; false trails are laid; confessions are interrupted—if only by the dinner-bell; sudden knocking alarms us—even if it is only the servant" (261). Tompkins never explicitly states that what we have here is the enactment of female eroticism in elaborate and extended foreplay, but perhaps she does not need to.

Radcliffe's imagery also is sexually charged, as many modern critics have noted. It is questionable, however, whether the eighteenth-century reader was as aware as the twentieth-century critic is about the way Radcliffe's descriptions "invite the reader to *think about* sex," as Ann Ronald argues (179, 182; my emphasis). Certainly there is no indication from contemporary reviews that there was anything offensive to feminine modesty in Radcliffe's lush prose. It seems more likely that the exaltation inspired by undulating landscapes, cascading waterfalls, and impressive mountain peaks; the thrill and trepidation of encountering forbidding castle gates, uncovering secret passageways hidden behind tapestries, of unlocking previously locked doors; and the discovery of passion, terror, and sometimes love in dark subterranean realms was registered emotionally rather than mentally by Radcliffe's readers.

In Radcliffe's Gothic fiction, the repressed element of feminine sexual desire does return, but not completely enough to be explicitly articulated. Whatever challenge is made to existing mores is made indirectly rather than overtly—another sign of the woman writer's conflict between public values and private impulses. Most critics agree about the presence of unresolved contradictions in Female Gothic. Cynthia Griffin Wolff says that the heroine's encounter with the Gothic edifice as symbol of the female body often occurs "when she is undergoing the seige of conflict over sexual stimulation or arousal" (210). Ronald speaks of the "mixed messages" that have characterized women's Gothic novels from the eighteenth century to today (185), and Nina da Vinci Nichols argues that in *The Mysteries of Udolpho* Radcliffe "never quite resolves minor contradictions in Emily's roles as aetherialized maiden, as brave young detective, and as symbolic quester of identity. In part, ambivalence is the result of dividing Emily's goals between the novel's narrative and symbolic levels" (192).

As well, Raymond W. Mise has pointed out that the association of forced marriage with sexual assault in the early women's Gothic novels seems to indicate an anxiety that many young women may have felt about marriage, stemming in part from their "lack of confidence in [their] own sexuality" (228). In the light of this idea, Radcliffe's novels can be seen as serving to familiarize her young readers with the pleasures of eros.

Preoccupation with issues of sexual identity can be seen as well in the wicked stepmother motif, which appears in three of Radcliffe's major novels (*A Sicilian Romance, The Mysteries of Udolpho,* and *The Italian*). The stepmother corresponds symbolically with the murderous or rapacious male, in her role as a destructive character who opposes the desires of the young female protagonist. The stepmother Maria in *A Sicilian Romance* is a narcissistic older woman for whom the gratification of personal sexual pleasure is more important than the exercise of maternal love. In fact she seems to have no maternal feeling whatsoever.

Radcliffe's comments on Maria's attempts to defy the law of biological gravity are censorious and sarcastic, as when Maria, unbeknownst to her husband, "allow[s] herself a free indulgence in the most licentious pleasures" (1: 23). When the false marchioness gives up her attempt to seduce Julia's suitor and begins a new liaison, the reader is told that she "now bestowed her smiles upon a young Italian cavalier . . . who possessed too much of the spirit of gallantry to permit a lady to languish in vain" (2: 235). Her name suggests that she is a debased version of the Virgin Mother, and when she is found dead of a self-inflicted knife wound after a hysterical argument with her accusing husband about her infidelity, her body is found appropriately prone on her couch and "bathed in blood" (2: 197).

If one reads this novel as a form of dreamscape in which the various characters represent different aspects of the dreamer's self, the "splitting off" of the maternal and sexual impulses that was endorsed by the laws and customs of eighteenth-century society becomes more apparent. The need to kill off or bury sexual desire as a paradoxical but necessary sacrifice to maternity was to a large extent a consequence of the mother's legal position in Radcliffe's day. According to Lawrence Stone, "by committing adultery a woman lost all moral and legal rights as a mother, and was by definition unfit to have custody of her children. A wife convicted, or merely accused, of adultery could be virtually certain that she would never be permitted to set eyes on her children" (*Road* 171). Although these severe rules were not always followed in practice, they were nevertheless the final authority in cases of dispute.

Radcliffe herself was childless, but she appears to have had a clear sense of social priorities. In *A Sicilian Romance* her didactic impulses seem to connect her most strongly with the character of Mme Menon, the wise, dispassionate, and widowed instructor of the two young sisters, whose role of educating the girls to become mature and responsible adults mirrors one aspect of Radcliffe's own apparent aims as a writer. Nevertheless, the wayward and turbulent power of sex keeps disrupting the placid surface of her protagonists' lives, and Radcliffe gives it remarkably loose rein.

The three adult females in this story clearly represent different aspects of the feminine: Mme Menon as guide, protector, and teacher; the natural mother, first seen in a feeble light, pale and emaciated yet dignified and venerable, as the dishonored source of life; and the stepmother as erotic desire. While the nurturing aspects are allowed fictional reconciliation—Mme Menon and the girls' mother are old friends—the self-pleasuring aspect is vividly done away with, ending ambiguously "bathed" in blood. Yet Maria's death makes it possible for the young protagonist, who has been propelled through many trials and horrendous discoveries, to fulfill her own desires in fruitful marriage to the man she loves.

Radcliffe concludes her tale on a lofty note, forsaking her Gothic subversiveness and giving moral sentiment the last word: "We learn, also, that those who do only THAT WHICH IS RIGHT, endure nothing in misfortune but a trial of their virtue, and from trials well endured, derive the surest claim to the protection of heaven." Yet the paragraph that precedes this pronouncement is perhaps more revealing about what Radcliffe's work actually offered her many women readers: the true marchioness survives to see "*her* race renewed in the children of Hippolitus and Julia," who is now safely ensconced in marriage and motherhood. The contented grandmother, "surrounded by her children and friends, and engaged in forming the minds of the infant generation . . . *seemed to forget that she had ever been otherwise than happy*" (2: 216; my emphasis). In its combination of moral didacticism and its compensatory erotic suggestiveness, Radcliffe's Female Gothic did not demand the collapse of the old castle—but it did, perhaps, help its female audience to make the best of a bad bargain.[15]

CHAPTER FOUR

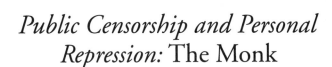

Public Censorship and Personal Repression: The Monk

*T*he Monk, by Matthew Lewis, raised a storm of moral indignation when it appeared in 1796, although not until the second edition revealed that its author was a member of Parliament. At this time literary censorship had become one of the government's main tools for suppressing radical political dissent, and it was perhaps for this reason that the critics who derided Lewis's impropriety also failed to grasp *The Monk*'s pervading argument, which concerns the dangers of excessive repression in both the individual and the social spheres.

The protagonist of Lewis's novel is a monk named Ambrosio, who knowingly commits rape and murder and then later learns that he has unknowingly committed incest and matricide. At the outset of the tale, Ambrosio is reverenced throughout Madrid as a paragon of excellence and purity, but he falls prey to the seductions of Matilda, a demonic emissary of the devil, who first appears in the guise of a young novice named Rosario. The narrow education Ambrosio received in the monastery has left him ignorant about the power of sex, and his proud belief that he is superior to the impulses of carnal desire makes him all the more susceptible to the charms of Matilda, who draws him into the moral depravity that culminates in his murdering his mother, Elvira, and raping and murdering his sister, Antonia.

The Monk includes a long subplot concerning the adventures of Agnes, the sister of Antonia's youthful suitor Lorenzo, and Raymond,

Agnes's lover. Their attempt to elope is foiled by the appearance of the first overtly supernatural being in the story, the Bleeding Nun, who keeps Raymond in her power until he exorcises her unquiet spirit with the aid of the Wandering Jew. By this time, Agnes has entered a convent that adjoins Ambrosio's monastery, but when Raymond eventually finds her they meet secretly, and she becomes pregnant. When her condition is discovered by Ambrosio and the cruel Mother Domina, the latter has Agnes locked away in the underground vaults of the convent, where she gives birth prematurely, and her baby dies. Agnes is finally rescued, and at the same time Ambrosio kills Antonia and is captured by his pursuers in a nearby tunnel. Agnes survives and marries Raymond; Lorenzo marries another beautiful young virgin, Virginia, who eventually becomes "sole Mistress" of his heart (420).

Like Walpole, Lewis had discreetly concealed his authorship in the first edition of his novel, which appeared in March 1796.[1] After the book sold well enough to warrant a second edition by the following September, however, and no critics had raised concerns about its immorality, Lewis (who had been elected to Parliament in July) added "By M. G. Lewis, Esq. M.P." to the title page (Parreaux 43, 87–88). He no doubt understood that revealing his authorship would offend some people. The gesture seems to have been prompted partly by the spirit of youthful impudence (he turned twenty-one that summer), and perhaps by a more serious desire to assert his distance from the dominant conservative mood in Parliament, with which his own libertarian leanings were at odds—it would have been evident to most readers that no M.P. who supported the current legislative agenda could have penned this sensational Gothic novel.

Because of the parts of *The Monk* that critics subsequently found objectionable, Lewis came very near to being charged with and convicted of blasphemy (or blasphemous libel), an offence punishable in common law by fine and imprisonment or corporal punishment (Parreaux 94). Although a number of reviewers objected to the sexual violence in *The Monk,* as well as to its passages of lush, erotic prose, the section that roused the greatest ire, and whose irony clearly was lost on the critics, was one in which the narrator describes in an apparently approving tone how Elvira expurgated the Bible so that it would be suitable reading material for Antonia.

Coleridge was the first reviewer to raise the issue. In *The Critical Review,* February 1797, he praised the author's skill and his "rich, powerful, and fervid" imagination (*Miscellaneous* 371) and then passed some judgements on the aesthetic weaknesses and psychological improbability of *The Monk*. He then turned to his main concern—its moral perniciousness:

> [I]f a parent saw [*The Monk*] in the hands of a son or daughter, he might reasonably turn pale. . . . The temptations of Ambrosio are described with a libidinous minuteness. . . . [T]he shameless harlotry of Matilda, and the trembling innocence of Antonia, are seized with equal avidity, as vehicles of the most voluptuous images. . . . [Lewis's] great acquirements and splendid genius [have been] employed to furnish a *mormo* for children, a poison for youth, and a provocative for the debauchee. (*Miscellaneous* 374)

Coleridge's next target was the passage in which the narrator explains Elvira's reasons for censoring the Bible. He quoted and emphasized with italics the lines, "'the *annals of a brothel would scarcely furnish a greater choice of indecent expressions*'" and "'[The Bible] but too *frequently inculcates the first rudiments of vice.*'" He was outraged at the "impiety of this falsehood" and thundered, "We believe it not absolutely impossible that a mind may be so deeply depraved by the habit of reading lewd and voluptuous tales, as to use even the Bible in conjuring up the spirit of uncleanness" (375).

The climax of Coleridge's argument comes when he declares, "Nor must it be forgotten that the author is a man of rank and fortune.—Yes! the author of the Monk signs himself a *LEGISLATOR!*—We stare and tremble" (376). What bothered Coleridge was not just the incongruity between the author's sordid imagination and Lewis's public role as member of a law-making body concerned with safeguarding the status quo; it was equally important that Lewis was "a man of rank and fortune." At this time, the middle classes were applying considerable pressure on the gentry and aristocracy to reform and to conform to their own bourgeois moral code; thus any sign of aristocratic decadence provided fresh fuel for public indignation.[2]

The second major attack came in July 1797, from Thomas James Mathias in *The Pursuits of Literature,* a long satirical poem that first appeared in 1794 and had passed through three previous revised editions, accumulating "strata of garrulous footnotes in which the author passed judgement on current publications" (Peck 26). Mathias was treasurer to the queen and in the opinion of André Parreaux may have had his own political reasons for singling out Lewis: "[O]ne wonders whether what was really desired was not, perhaps, the end of Lewis's *political* career" (134). Mathias declared it inconceivable that a legislator in our parliament, a member of the House of commons of Great Britain, an elected guardian and defender of the laws, the religion, and the good manners of the country, has neither scrupled nor blushed to depict, and to publish to the world, the arts of lewd and systematick seduction, and to thrust upon the nation the most unqualified blasphemy against the very code and volume of our religion. (qtd. in Parreaux 107)

Whereas Coleridge had simply accused Lewis of impiety, Mathias urged prosecution: "I believe this 7th Chap of Vol. 2 is *actionable* at Common Law" (qtd. in Parreaux 109). He went on to provide a list of legal precedents justifying his position.

Mathias had earlier made a somewhat bombastic but canny observation about the power of the written word, in which he managed to combine a hallelujah for freedom of the press with an assertion about the necessity for censorship: "Wherever the freedom of the press exists, (and WITH US may that freedom be perpetual!) I must assert *that*, LITERATURE, *well or ill conducted, IS THE GREAT ENGINE by which, I am fully persuaded, all civilized states must ultimately be supported or overthrown*" (qtd. in Parreaux 105). His view was representative of the contemporary extremist position in which the power of literature to affect prevalent attitudes became an either/or proposition. It could either "support or overthrow" the state, and any literature that did not further the official purposes of the state—with which religion was still closely tied—deserved to be suppressed.

A number of critics did attempt to rise to Lewis's defense. A gentleman named Soame penned a poem titled *The Epistle in Rhyme, to M. G. Lewis, Esq. M.P.*, published in 1798, in which he praised *The Monk* for possessing "Dante's force, and beauties all her own!" But one of Soame's footnotes also acknowledges the tenor of the times: "Mr. L. should have recollected that we live in an age which is extremely nice in the choice of words at least." Soame recommended, apparently in all seriousness, that the author substitute for straightforward words such as *lust* the type of diction found in the circulating library: "amiable weakness, exquisite sensibility, &c." This compromise "would have ensured his book an avowed reception with readers of the most scrupulous delicacy, and an ostensible station even in the *boudoir* of devotees" (qtd. in Parreaux 128).

By this time, Lewis was already busy doing just that. Anxious to avoid prosecution, in February 1798 he produced a fourth edition now titled *Ambrosio, or The Monk* (a third unexpurgated edition had already been printed in April 1797; if anything the demand for *The Monk* had only been stimulated by the controversy). Not only was all the indecent diction either removed or substituted, but almost all the references to physical love or desire were cancelled, and a large portion of the story was eliminated, including the scene where Ambrosio rapes Antonia (Parreaux 120–21). The strategy worked; no charges were laid. In the meantime, however, three extant editions of the original text were in circulation, some were still available for purchase (by 1801 they sold at a guinea apiece; Peck 35), and a thriving business in pirated editions soon followed. For the forces of the moral vanguard, it was a limited success.

Although *The Monk* is set in a fictional past and makes frequent overt criticism of the despotism of the Catholic Church, it is not difficult to discern the novel's implicit criticism of the unusually repressive political conditions that prevailed in England in the 1790s. Public enthusiasm about the overthrow of the French monarchy in 1789 had shifted to dismay over the bloody Reign of Terror and fear about a similar eruption of revolutionary chaos at home; the scene of mob violence in *The Monk,* where an enraged populace beats and tramples to death the Mother Domina, enacts English fear of—and fascination with—the atavistic behavior that became rampant in France after the traditional controls of its inflexible, moribund aristocratic regime were overthrown. In addition, France's imperialist ambitions had become clear by 1792, in military invasions that violated some long-standing international treaties. England had become involved in the conflict, but in 1796 domestic confidence in its own military powers was not very strong (A. Briggs 137–40).

Although a number of the reform societies formed in England in the early 1790s continued to function, in general there was a strong movement toward conservatism. In Birmingham in July 1791, a group attempting to celebrate "the ideas of 1789" ignited a two-day riot by an opposing mob rallying round the cry of church and king (A. Briggs 133–34). In 1792 a Royal Proclamation condemned "divers wicked and seditious writings," and the prime minister, William Pitt, initiated isolated persecutions of reformers. In May of 1794, fourteen members of the two leading London reform societies were arrested and tried for treason, but all were acquitted. This was the last victory for English civil liberties for many years; one year later *Habeas Corpus* was suspended. Two acts were also passed that increased the government's powers of censorship, one forbidding large public gatherings without special permit, and another criminalizing spoken and written treason (A. Briggs 129–37). One year before *The Monk*'s first publication, the attorney-general, Sir John Scott (later Lord Eldon), had boasted that in the preceding two years "there had been more prosecutions for libels than in any twenty years before" (qtd. in Parreaux 119).

The epigraph to *The Monk,* from Shakespeare's *Measure for Measure,* provides an initial indication of the novel's concern with the relation between public censorship and personal repression. The quotation refers to Angelo, whose self-deceptive pride is a model for Ambrosio's; Angelo "Scarce confesses / That his blood flows, or that his appetite / Is more to bread than stone" (1.3.50–53). At first sight, this assessment seems to refer merely to the suppression of instinctual impulses whose recognition would disrupt one's sense of personal identity. As Lewis seemed to have recognized, however, the plot of *Measure for Measure* presents the problem in both its individual and social dimensions.

Both *Measure for Measure* and *The Monk* are concerned with tyranny, whether it be the tyranny of the instincts, the tyranny of self-censoring pride, or the tyranny of social injustice, which can arise from either extreme. In *Measure for Measure,* the duke appoints Angelo as his ruling deputy during the duke's feigned absence from Vienna, which because of the duke's permissiveness has degenerated over the years into a state of anarchic license and social chaos. The duke explains:

> We have strict statutes and most biting laws,
> The needful bits and curbs to headstrong weeds,
> Which for this fourteen years we have let slip;
> . . . so our decrees,
> Dead to infliction, to themselves are dead;
> And liberty plucks justice by the nose. (1.3.19–29)

Conditions in Ambrosio's society, under the yoke of the Spanish Inquisition, are at the opposite extreme from the current situation in the duke's Vienna. The Monk lives in a totalitarian state ruled by fear and persecution to an even greater extent than Lewis's England was.

Both Angelo and Ambrosio mercilessly impose long-unused penalties for illegitimate pregnancy. In *Measure for Measure* Angelo sentences a man (Claudio) to death for impregnating his lover prior to marriage. In *The Monk,* Ambrosio discovers evidence of Agnes's pregnancy and planned

escape from the convent to marry her lover, whereupon he hands her over
to the Mother Domina and the convent's "severe and cruel" punishment,
despite the young woman's passionate pleas for mercy (47). Both men subsequently discover the stirrings of physical passion within themselves for a
virtuous young woman, and both experience the urge to fulfill their desire
as a form of transgression. Both seem to react to the young women as pro-
jections of their own ideally virtuous personas, which they unconsciously
feel impelled to destroy. After meeting Claudio's sister, Isabella, who is
about to become a nun (but like Agnes later realizes that her true calling is
to marriage and motherhood), Angelo reflects:

> Can it be
> That modesty may more betray our sense
> Than woman's lightness? Having waste ground enough,
> Shall we desire to raze the sanctuary
> And pitch our evils there? O fie, fie, fie!
> What dost thou, or what art thou, Angelo?
> Dost thou desire her foully for those things
> That make her good? O, let her brother live;
> . . . Ever till now,
> When men were fond, I smil'd and wond'red how. (1.3.179–187)

Ambrosio becomes entranced by the purity of Antonia for similar reasons:
"Grown used to her modesty, it no longer commanded the same respect
and awe: He still admired it, but it only made him more anxious to deprive
her of that quality, which formed her principal charm" (256).

In both cases, succumbing to the frailty of personal desire humanizes
the men somewhat, and they briefly consider softening their judgements
before giving in to their habitual need for dominance. Angelo's capitula-
tion takes the form of demanding Isabella's body in exchange for Claudio's
life. Ambrosio begins to feel some compunction about his harsh treatment
of Agnes after giving in to the seductive spell of Matilda. He considers
pleading for her cause with the Mother Domina, but Matilda dissuades
him, mainly on the grounds that his intervention might raise suspicions
about himself (230–31).

Angelo's and Ambrosio's psychological dependence on a self-image of
moral superiority is precisely what leads them into moral culpability. As the
duke's speech indicates, the balance between "liberty"—freedom of speech
or action—and "justice"—balance between extremes—is a delicate one, in
both the social and the psychological realms. And as the plots of both

Measure for Measure and *The Monk* suggest, maintaining this balance requires an adequate knowledge of both oneself and others.

The section of *The Monk* dealing with Elvira's well-meaning but fatally misguided efforts to safeguard her daughter's virtue, which so angered Coleridge and Mathias, illustrates Lewis's argument about the dangers of "cloistered virtue." The phrase was used one hundred and fifty years earlier by Milton in his anticensorship tract, *Areopagitica* (1644), a work provoked by similarly repressive governmental policies. It is probable that Lewis was familiar with Milton's tract and also possible that it may have influenced his own critique of censorship in *The Monk*.

Areopagitica was Milton's response to a recent parliamentary ordinance imposing severe penalties for unlicensed printing. Beginning with the historical argument that censorship has always been the recourse of degenerate cultures, Milton goes on to develop the idea of the fortunate fall implicit in *Paradise Lost*. His analysis of "cloistered virtue" deserves to be quoted at length because of its close correspondence with the moral and psychological premises of *The Monk*:

> And perhaps this is that doom which Adam fell into of knowing good and evil, that is to say of knowing good by evil.
>
> As therefore the state of man now is, what wisdom can there be to choose, what continence to forbear, without the knowledge of evil? He that can apprehend and consider vice with all her baits and seeming pleasures, and yet abstain, and yet distinguish, and yet prefer that which is truly better, he is the true wayfaring Christian. I cannot praise *a fugitive and cloistered virtue,* unexercised and unbreathed, that never sallies out and sees her adversary, but slinks out of the race where that immortal garland is to be run for, not without dust and heat. Assuredly we bring not innocence into the world, we bring impurity much rather; that which purifies us is trial, and trial is by what is contrary. That virtue therefore which is but *a youngling in the contemplation of evil,* and knows not the utmost that vice promises to her followers, and rejects it, is but a blank virtue, not a pure; her whiteness is but an excremental [external] whiteness. (665–66; my emphasis)

As Wendy Jones has observed, the danger of "untested virtue" is a problem that pertains to both Antonia and Ambrosio (146). Jones traces the connections made in *The Monk* between the suppression of individual expression, especially the ability to tell one's own story, and the suppression of erotic desire.

Initially, both Antonia and Ambrosio are presented as naive "younglings in the contemplation of evil," which consequently overpowers them. The narrator repeatedly reminds the reader of the two characters' inexperience and their resulting inability to discern the darker motives of both others and themselves, often referring to their awareness or unawareness of inner desires or feelings in terms of "consciousness" and "unconsciousness."

Lewis's usage of such terms was not completely unprecedented or original. According to the OED, the first recorded use of 'conscious' in the sense of "having internal perception or consciousness . . . of one's sensations, feelings, thoughts, etc." is in John Locke's 1690 *Essay on Human Understanding*, and the first recorded use of 'unconscious,' in the sense of "not realized or known as existing in oneself" comes from Coleridge's *Biographia Literaria* of 1817. However, both words appeared occasionally in the Gothic novels of the 1790s, usually to indicate whether or not a character recognized his or her feelings of attraction to the opposite sex. In *The Abbey of St. Asaph*, for example, Kelly writes, "Douglas had long unconsciously adored [Jennet], but neither knew the nature nor extent of his feelings, until he fancied her wondrous beauty had attracted the admiration of Henry Montague" (I, 72). The frequency with which Lewis employs the terms is, however, unusual, as are the variety of situations to which he applies them, and their emphasis serves to draw attention to the novel's psychological concerns.

A first indication that *The Monk* is concerned with exploring dimensions of consciousness is the fact that the last word of Lewis's "Advertisement" is *unconscious:* an adjective that ostensibly refers to Lewis himself. Admitting that he unwittingly may have incorporated more "plagiarisms" into the tale than the ones he acknowledges (a story from *The Guardian*, a folk-tale, a Danish ballad, and a collection of old Spanish poetry), Lewis explains: "[B]ut I doubt not, many more may be found, of which I am at present totally unconscious" (6). Here the conventional meaning of simple unawareness applies, with the added suggestion of knowledge that may have once been conscious, has since been forgotten, but may yet be retrieved.

In Ambrosio's case, the terms *conscious* and *unconscious* usually signify his awareness or unawareness of either his lustful desires or his moral condition. Before he succumbs to the sirenlike Matilda, "[t]hough still unconscious how extensive is its influence, He dread[s] the melodious seduction of her voice" (68). For some time after meeting Antonia, Ambrosio remains "wilfully blind to the danger of exposing himself to [her] charms," but when he recognizes his desire, "his aim be[comes] more decided, and his attentions [assume] a warmer colour" (256). He is "not unconscious, that his attempts [to corrupt her moral understanding are] highly criminal," and he suffers some discomfort from his "consciousness of his faults" to the abandoned Matilda (257).

Shortly after these observations, the narrator uses the word *unconscious* to describe Antonia's reaction to a question Ambrosio puts to her. When he asks whether she has ever seen the man she would desire for a husband, she vehemently denies it; the narrator comments that this "was an untruth, but She was unconscious of its falsehood: She knew not the nature of her sentiments for Lorenzo" (260).

Ambrosio shares Antonia's naivete about human nature. The reader is informed that even after the Monk's sexual initiation with Matilda, he is still so "little acquainted with the depravity of the world" that he does not suspect how "few of his [female] Penitents would have rejected his addresses" if he were to attempt to seduce them. Even if Ambrosio were aware of their inclinations, however, his concern for his reputation, which is "infinitely dear" to him, would prohibit such transgressions (240). In Freudian terms, his superego—the aspect of self that identifies with societal ideals—serves to suppress libidinal desire. In Jungian terms, his reliance on his persona—his public mask—restrains him.

Throughout the story, the narrator provides a great deal of instructive commentary on unconscious motivation, most of it concerning Ambrosio. Matilda's earlier initial ambush in the garden, when she confesses to Ambrosio that she is not a young man but a woman who adores him, reveals Ambrosio's ignorance of his own feelings and his consequent conflict between conscious aims and unconscious impulses: "While She spoke, a thousand opposing sentiments combated in Ambrosio's bosom." The narrator elaborates that

> there were others also which did not obtain his notice. He perceived not, that his vanity was flattered by the praises bestowed upon his eloquence and virtue; that He felt a secret pleasure in reflecting that a young and seemingly lovely Woman had for his sake abandoned the world, and sacrificed every other passion to that which he had inspired: Still less did He perceive that his heart throbbed with desire, while his hand was pressed gently by Matilda's ivory fingers. (62)

In other words, Ambrosio fails to recognize his own deepest needs: his need to feel more accomplished and virtuous than other men; his longing to occupy a pre-eminent position in one woman's heart; and his natural physical desire. His unawareness of all these things only compounds his vulnerability to Matilda's charms (in both the romantic and necromantic senses of the word).

Matilda's temptation of Ambrosio proceeds in stages, carefully designed to undermine what little resistance he has and to capitalize on his deluded notions about himself. At first she claims that she loves him purely, without any physical desire, but she manages during the confrontation to expose one of her breasts. The sight arouses another conflict in Ambrosio between conscious and unconscious responses. He experiences both "anxiety and delight," and his sensations are vividly described in very physical terms as a welling up of energies seeking release, suggestive of male ejaculation: the anxiety and delight *fill* his heart, "A raging fire [*shoots*] through every limb; The blood [*boils*] in his veins," and once again he is thrown into confusion, "a thousand wild wishes [bewildering] his imagination" (65; my emphasis).

During sleep, however, the conscious mind is at rest, and the unconscious has free play in dreams. That night Ambrosio has a series of disturbing erotic dreams in which Matilda's naked breast is a prominent feature, and which alert him to the dangers of the situation. The images and the intense sensory quality of the dreams force him into a partial recognition of the weaknesses in his character. He decides that he has been "a slave to flattery, to avarice, and self-love" and resolves again to banish her from the monastery (68). But because his self-awareness is still so limited, he is unable to follow through on his resolution.

Shortly before Ambrosio finally yields to Matilda, the narrator again emphasizes how much the Monk's arrogance fuels his self-delusion. Once again "Ambrosio's bosom [becomes] the Theatre of a thousand contending passions," but his "attachment to the feigned Rosario, aided by the natural warmth of his temperament" leads him to allow her to remain in the monastery. The narrator adds,

> The success was assured, when that presumption which formed the groundwork of his character, came to Matilda's assistance. The Monk reflected, that to vanquish temptation was an infinitely greater merit than to avoid: he thought, that He ought rather to rejoice in the opportunity given him of proving the firmness of his virtue. St. Anthony had withstood all seductions to lust; Then why should not He? Besides, St. Anthony was tempted by the Devil, who put every art into practice to excite his passions; Whereas, Ambrosio's danger proceeded from a mere mortal Woman, fearful and modest, whose apprehensions of his yielding were not less violent than his own. . . .
>
> Ambrosio was yet to learn, that to an heart unacquainted with her, Vice is ever most dangerous when lurking behind the Mask of Virtue. (83–84)

This passage, like many others in *The Monk,* yields itself to retrospective irony in light of the final revelation that Matilda never was merely a mortal woman and that the fear of discovery that Ambrosio assumes she shares with him never was one of her concerns. The statement about Vice hiding behind the mask of Virtue applies both to Matilda's feigned modesty and to Ambrosio's own mask or persona of superior virtue, which he initially assumes reflects his actual nature.

By extension, such retrospective irony also serves Lewis's concern with bringing repressed cultural and psychological material to the conscious attention of his audience, for the reader shares Ambrosio's shock upon discovering Matilda's true identity and suddenly recognizes his or her own selective rejection of information that had been increasingly suggestive of Matilda's demonic role. As Peter Grudin comments, discussing the medieval sensibility that informs *The Monk,* and showing Matilda's connection with the medieval incubus/succubus, the novel's "Gothic atmosphere. . . . is theologically . . . archaic" (144). By postponing the revelation that the forces of evil embodied in Matilda are real and powerful, the novel exposes the limitations of the reader's resistant post-Enlightenment bias.

In another passage of extended narrative commentary on Ambrosio's moral and psychological condition, Lewis examines the role of education in the formation of personality. The reader is informed that Ambrosio's natural temperament was too vital and energetic for monastic life; "He had a Warrior's heart"; "He was naturally enterprizing, firm, and fearless. . . . There was no want of generosity in his nature. . . . His abilities were quick and shining, and his judgment vast, solid, and decisive" (236). The monks, however, take advantage of the young child's ambition to belong to their order (and the commentary subtly indicates that Ambrosio's youthful desire to belong somewhere, anywhere, is a consequence of having lost his family at a young age). They "carefully [repress] those virtues, whose grandeur and disinterestedness were ill-suited to the Cloister":

> While the Monks were busied in rooting out his virtues, and narrowing his sentiments, they allowed every vice which had fallen to his share, to arrive at full perfection. He was suffered to be proud, vain, ambitious, and disdainful; he was jealous of his Equals, and despised all merit but his own; he was implacable when offended, and cruel in his revenge. Still in spite of the pains taken to pervert them, his natural good qualities would occasionally

break through the gloom cast over them so carefully: At such time the contest for superiority between his real and acquired character was striking and
unaccountable. (237)

The commentary ironically inverts conventional ideas about what is
"good" and what is "perverted"; Ambrosio's natural warmth and exuber-
ance of feeling are exchanged for conformity and a false but socially acceptable humility.

In addition to perverting his natural propensities, the monks "[ter-
rify] his young mind [with] all the horrors which Superstition could furnish them." Impressed by their detailed depictions of the torments of
eternal perdition, the imaginative young man becomes inwardly "timid and
apprehensive," and his powers of independent judgement are weakened.
His enforced separation from ordinary life and its "common dangers" only
compounds the damage.

The monks' efforts to reshape the young Ambrosio in their own image are criticized in terms very similar to Rousseau's critique of education
in *Emile*.[3] Lewis's description of how Ambrosio's "acquired" character becomes a perversion of his "real" one seems to corroborate Rousseau's opening premise in *Emile* that "[e]verything is good as it leaves the hands of the
Author of things; everything degenerates in the hands of man. He forces
one soil to nourish the products of another, one tree to bear the fruit of another" (37).

A main thrust of Rousseau's criticism was aimed at the excessive arti-
ficiality of existing social institutions, especially France's, and his comments
on the conflict between "inclinations" and "duties," or what Freud would
later term the "id" and the "superego," seem to provide a fit description of
Ambrosio:

> He who in the civil order wants to preserve the primacy of the sentiments
> of nature does not know what he wants. Always in contradiction with him-
> self, always floating between his inclinations and his duties, he will never be
> either man or citizen. He will be good neither for himself nor for others. He
> will be one of these men of our days: a Frenchman, an Englishman, a bour-
> geois. He will be nothing. (*Emile* 40)

In the light of Rousseau's complaint, Ambrosio's training can be interpreted
as more than simply another instance of outmoded Catholic despotism, for
it may also reflect Lewis's own critique of England's Protestant upper-class
education system (Lewis attended Marlebone Seminary, Westminster
School, and Christ Church, Oxford).

Yet although the narrator seems to agree with Rousseau's contention that one thwarts human potential "[w]hen, instead of raising a man for himself, one wants to raise him for others," the novel as a whole does not support the dichotomy Rousseau proposes between a hypothetical "natural man" and that debased product of human interference, "civil man." Rousseau declares that "[n]atural man is entirely for himself. He is numerical unity, the absolute whole which is relative only to itself or its kind. Civil man is only a fractional unity dependent on the denominator; his value is determined by his relation to the whole, which is the social body" (39–40). Rousseau's argument is itself very self-contradictory,[4] and although he postulates at certain points a possible harmonious reconciliation between natural man and the social order, the anarchic implications of some of his statements are inescapable, and led many to regard him as a harbinger of the French Revolution.

Whereas Rousseau argues that we should endeavor to free ourselves entirely from the constraints of the collective social body, *The Monk* suggests that the conflict between the demands of individual desire and those of the social order is a universal, inescapable part of the human condition, and that because we derive our emotional sustenance and our sense of identity from the imperfect web of relationships in which we find ourselves, we need to acknowledge those conflicting demands in order to establish a viable balance between them.

However, there is one observation made by Rousseau that receives a strong endorsement in *The Monk*: "Women have stopped being mothers; they will no longer be; they no longer want to be. If they should want to be, they hardly could be" (*Emile* 46). Here Rousseau is talking specifically about breast-feeding, and advocating a return to what we now call "natural bonding." In fact, his ideas on this point did anticipate a return to the practice on the part of many middle- and upper-class Englishwomen in the cult of domesticity that took hold at the end of the eighteenth century (Stone 170). Yet motherhood was still a very problematic issue in Lewis's time, and it is perhaps an indication of how truly "unspeakable" the issue was that so few reviewers articulated their response to what is unarguably one of the most horrific aspects of the novel: its repeated and graphic violations of the feminine, and particularly the maternal, realm.

When at the end of the novel Ambrosio has irrevocably consigned his soul to the Devil, the triumphant Lucifer reveals that Ambrosio has murdered his own mother and raped and murdered his sister. The demon then sums up Ambrosio's fatal weaknesses: "I saw that you were virtuous from vanity, not principle, and . . . . I observed your blind idolatry of the Madonna's picture" (440). On the most superficial level, the latter observation plays up to popular prejudice against popish superstition, but on a deeper level it points to the true source of Ambrosio's violent response to the women he encounters: his unconscious longing to recover the maternal bond that was lost to him when his mother abandoned him at the age of two. As Antonia's Aunt Leonella relates, Elvira, the daughter of a shoemaker, had secretly married a young nobleman, and when his father discovered the union three years later the couple fled from his wrath to the Indies, leaving their two-year-old son behind them "in the abruptness of [their] flight" (13). The angry marquis took the child from Elvira's family and (as is later revealed) gave him up to the Church.

The fact that Ambrosio is repeatedly and intensely aroused by the sight of the female breast (gazing at the bosom of the Virgin whose picture hangs in his room, and later seeing Matilda's and then Antonia's exposed breasts) provides one indication of his overruling desire for his mother. As Wendy Jones comments, his fascination with the female breast, the "universal synecdoche of the mother," shows that it is the desire for the mother that really "haunts" Ambrosio. Jones also makes the astute observation that Antonia is the "metaphorical substitute for the mother and that Ambrosio unconsciously recognizes his mother in her" (134).

Another sign of his craving for maternal love is the way he envisions sexual union as a kind of return to infantile bliss. When he gazes upon the Virgin's picture, he addresses it as if it really were the unfailing maternal presence he has missed since the age of two, in terms that reveal the lack of separation between his adult sexual drive and his desire to recover the original mother-child intimacy. He wonders if he, "the sole uncorrupted Pillar of the Church" (an undoubtedly intentional phallic joke on Lewis's part) will be able to withstand the temptations with which he will be faced: "Should I meet in that world which I am constrained to enter some lovely Female, lovely . . . as you Madonna!" (40). He goes on to muse, "What sweetness, yet what majesty in her divine eyes! . . . Oh! if such a Creature existed, and existed but for me! Were I permitted to twine round my fingers those golden ringlets, and press with my lips the treasures of that snowy bosom!" (40–41).

Jones argues that Ambrosio's sexual compulsiveness is a "displacement" of his longing for his mother, but my view is somewhat different. The narrator repeatedly reminds us that Ambrosio is "in the full prime and heat of manhood," which suggests that the monk is propelled as much by the strength and force of his own libido as by the desire to recover his mother. Because Ambrosio lacked maternal nurturing at an early age, he failed to develop a healthy separation between desire for the mother's comfort, care, and safety, and the desire for sexual satisfaction. In other words, it is the conflation of the two, rather than the displacement of one by the other, that prevents him from ever finding emotional fulfillment through sexual activity.

The image of the Madonna stimulates Ambrosio's imagination to the point that he almost admits the depth and urgency of his desire, before he interrupts his flow of fantasy with the harsh truth: "Fool that I am! . . . Away, impure ideas! Let me remember, that woman is for ever lost to me" (41). Because his own "first woman," his mother, was irretrievably lost to Ambrosio, so for him are all women. He consoles himself by indulging in delusions of moral grandeur, assuring himself that his uncommon virtue would protect him from temptation, and reasserting the division between matter and spirit that characterizes the sublimation of the pagan Mother Goddess in the Christian concept of the Virgin Mary: "What charms me, when ideal and considered as a superior Being, would disgust me, become Woman and tainted with all the failings of Mortality" (41).

As Syndy M. Conger has commented, however, the "rhythmic return of idea to matter, and of desire to death, is as inexorable [in *The Monk*] as it is frequent" ("Sensibility" 123), and nowhere is this pattern more noticeable than in Lewis's treatment of the various mother figures. Whether this return takes the form of coarse humor, grotesque physical corruption, or savage desecration and violation, it reasserts the material dimension of the maternal. As well, the motif of corruption and bloodshed emphasizes not only the violence that has been committed against the feminine world in the history of the Judaeo-Christian tradition, but also the destructive aspect of the Great Mother herself.

From the enormously pregnant Venus of Willendorf to the devouring Kali of Indian tradition, images of the mother have been fashioned by the primitive imagination in recognition of her immense power, as individual mother and as representative of the *mater* from which all life springs.[5] In the patriarchal Western world, however, the *mysterium tremendum*[6] of the feminine principle has been either rigidly suppressed or given only partial expression via the Mother of God reverenced in the Catholic tradition. Lewis's Protestant society had done away with even that vestige of a sacred feminine principle and on the social level continued to infantilize women and to enforce their prohibition from the public sphere.

Within this cultural context, *The Monk* can be read as both a veiled portrayal of the violence done against women in Lewis's own world and an attempt, violent in itself, to recover contact with the ancient Magna Mater.

The crude humor of the first chapter provides a disarming introduction to *The Monk*'s emphasis on physiological realities, when the garrulous Leonella tells her listeners that the monks have propagated the story that Ambrosio is "a present to them from the Virgin" and that he "knows not in what consists the difference of man and Woman. The common People therefore esteem him to be a Saint." At this, the innocent Antonia asks, "Does that make a Saint? . . . Bless me! Then am I one?" Viewed retrospectively, the conversation points to the perils inherent in both Ambrosio's and Antonia's "cloistered virtues," but initially the passage suffices as a humorous deflation of the spiritual and moral pretence underlying Ambrosio's public performance as preacher. Leonella is on the point of explaining that "a Man has no breasts, and no hips, and no . . ." when Ambrosio's timely entrance prevents her from mentioning the unmentionable biological truth (17–18).

The first moment of conflict in the plot, when Ambrosio discovers Agnes's note, concerns the issue of illegitimate pregnancy. Its significance is underscored by a noticeable shift to a more intense, dramatic tone and by the fact that it marks the point at which the narrative begins to break off into two parallel plots, which signify the difference between desire that is morally and psychologically "legitimate" and that which is "illegitimate." Although by conventional social standards Agnes's pregnancy and her desire to be reunited with her lover may be deemed illegitimate, the story allows her desires an implicit sanction that Ambrosio's do not receive. Jones similarly notes the distinction drawn in *The Monk* between "permissible" desire for "sexually appropriate" objects and "repressed desire, which can never know its true object and is therefore incapable of satisfaction" (133).

Not only the emotional power of Agnes's desperate and passionate pleading but also the validity of some of her arguments render her case far more persuasive than Ambrosio's rigid reliance on convent rules. She tells him that she loves the father of her unborn child "with the purest, the most irreproachable passion," that she was about to marry him when a "horrible adventure, and the treachery of a Relation" separated them, and that she joined the convent under the misapprehension that he was "for ever lost" to her. Her final appeal is the most unanswerable: "take compassion on the innocent Being, whose existence is attached to mine. If you discover my imprudence to the Domina, both of us are lost" (47). Her emotional and physical intensity—she holds him by his garment while begging and weeping at his feet—appears to upset Ambrosio and only seems to provoke his harshness. Ambrosio seems to act more like a rigid, intolerant Puritan than a Catholic monk; he orders her to release him and calls anxiously for the nuns (46, 48).

In keeping with the novel's pattern of withheld information, the parallels between Ambrosio's and Agnes's situations, and the terrible consequences of his lack of charity, are not made clear until near the end of story. The devil reveals that Ambrosio himself was the son whom Leonella had told her listeners about in the first chapter, who was left behind when his parents fled from a similarly "horrible" situation which involved the "treachery of a relation." Ambrosio learns too late that he was after all "legitimate" and discovers that the woman he murdered was the very one to whom his own existence was once "attached."

Agnes's tale, told after her rescue and therefore in a situation that seems to reassure the reader of a return to normality, is actually even more horrific than Ambrosio's rape and murder of Antonia. Both episodes occur in the murky obscurity of the abbey's underground vaults, the "lower zone" of the Bahktinian grotesque, and the symbolic locus of the subconscious. However, Antonia's rape has received considerably more critical attention than has Agnes's depiction of her baby's birth and death and the subsequent putrefaction of its body. The reason may be that the scene is, in Peter Brooks's words, "almost unbearable" (258).

Agnes recounts that she was left alone in the dungeon with a heavy chain wound around her waist and fastened to the wall and that the witch-like prioress, before leaving her, prayed for the death of the infant, "on whom though unborn [Agnes] already doated" (410). Agnes's "mental anguish . . . advanced the period of [her] labour" and the baby was born prematurely:

> But I knew not how to treat it, or by what means to preserve its existence. I
> could only bathe it with tears, warm it in my bosom, and offer up prayers for
> its safety. I was soon deprived of this mournful employment: The want of
> proper attendance, my ignorance how to nurse it, the bitter cold of the dun-
> geon, and the unwholesome air which inflated its lungs, terminated my sweet
> Babe's short and painful existence. It expired in a few hours after its birth,
> and I witnessed its death with agonies which beggar all description. (412)

Her statement that she did not even know how to nurse the baby might seem questionable, until one considers that the infant's prematurity likely necessitated special care, which she lacked the experience and knowledge to provide. Also, the comment serves to emphasize the importance of the fact that she was completely isolated and lacked any guidance or support from other women, something that the taunts of the prioress stress as well: "No aid shall be given you in your labour; Bring your Offspring into the world yourself, Feed it yourself, Nurse it yourself, Bury it yourself" (410). Thus the episode suggests that even in the birth of a child, the "natural," instinctual, and individual experience cannot be clearly differentiated from the social.

Agnes's sanity finally collapses upon the death of her baby, and her refusal to part from the corpse is depicted in grisly detail as the ultimate physical degradation, the conjunction of birth with the inexorable dissolution of the material body in death. The passage is somewhat unstable tonally; some of Agnes's statements seem to verge on grotesque humor, as if even for Lewis perhaps the scene is too much to bear:

> [The corpse] soon became a mass of putridity, and to every eye was a loathsome and disgusting Object; To every eye, but a Mother's. In vain did human feelings bid me recoil from this emblem of mortality with repugnance: I with-stood, and vanquished that repugnance. . . . Hour after hour have I passed upon my sorry couch, contemplating what had once been my Child: I endeavoured to retrace its features through the livid corruption, with which they were over-spread. During my confinement this sad occupation was my only delight . . .
>
> My slumbers were constantly interrupted by some obnoxious Insect crawling over me. Sometimes I felt the bloated Toad, hideous and pampered with poisonous vapours of the dungeon, dragging his loathsome length along my bosom: Sometimes the quick cold Lizard rouzed me leaving his slimy track upon my face, and entangling itself in the tresses of my wild and matted hair: Often have I at waking found my fingers ringed with the long worms, which bred in the corrupted flesh of my Infant. At such times I shrieked with terror and disgust, and while I shook off the reptile, trembled with all a Woman's weakness. (413, 415)

The conjunction here of clichéd phrases and grotesque situation—in this mass of putridity that only a Mother could love, her "delight" in tracing its former features through its livid corruption, and her "Woman's weakness" in succumbing to terror at the touch of worms and reptiles—would seem to present a rather gruesome parody of sentimental literary treatments of maternity. At the same time, the situation is truly horrifying and would drive anyone insane regardless of sex.

As well, as Rictor Norton has discussed, the passage gives evidence of Lewis's considerable poetic skill:

> the rhetorical phrasing, rhythm, rime, alliteration, assonance . . . . the aug-
> mentation or lengthening (felt-bloated), the acrostic scrambling (bloated
> toad; reptile-trembled), the chiasmus (lizard roused; fingers ringed), the rime
> (pampered-vapours), and numerous alliterations (shrieked-shook; woman's
> weakness; dungeon-dragging; loathsome length along my bosom). (38)

Lewis's skillful manipulation of sound and rhythm contributes enormously to the passage's emotional impact.

Although Agnes emerges from her descent into this moist and ooz-ing metamorphic tomb/womb to tell her tale, it is not before she herself has degenerated to an animalistic condition, signified by her "half-naked" body and her "over-grown and matted hair which hung over her face and bosom in disorder" (369, 396). Like most of the other women characters in the novel, Agnes enacts the "rhythmic return of idea to matter, of desire to death," a pattern that repeatedly invokes the female body as the myste-rious center of the birth/death cycle.

The pattern begins with the first inset narrative, the "History of don Raymond," which as Peter Brooks has shown makes the breakthrough "from a world which has . . . been largely natural and social" into a world where the supernatural and the daemonic exert tangible and undeniable force (256). The movement into supernatural horror begins with natural horror, in the vivid image of "blood on the sheets," which because it is initially unex-plained evokes a range of associations with birth, defloration, and death.

Raymond has been told to look at the sheets by the woman, Mar-guerite, of the inn at which he is staying, and he soon understands her mes-sage after overhearing a conversation revealing that her husband heads a gang of bloodthirsty thieves (107–08). When Raymond realizes that Mar-guerite remains in unwilling bondage to her husband, Baptiste, out of fear for herself and her children, he sees her with new eyes: "How different did She now appear to me! What before seemed gloom and sullenness, I now found to be disgust at her Associates, and compassion for my danger" (111). During their sabotage of the criminals, Raymond succeeds in wrestling Baptiste to the ground and holding him while Marguerite grabs Baptiste's dagger and "plunge[s] it repeatedly in his heart till he expire[s]" (118).

Marguerite's situation as wife-in-bondage is so convincingly por-trayed that the reader cannot help but applaud, if not wholly approve of, her act of bloody vengeance. The violence of the act is also mitigated some-what by the fact that while Marguerite and Raymond are escaping, Baptiste's remaining cohorts are slaughtering the domestic servants in the barn (118). As well, almost immediately after this scene, we see Marguerite displaying warm and effusive maternal affection toward two of her children (119, 121). Her stabbing of her husband prefigures Ambrosio's stabbing of Antonia, yet the different motivations for the two acts and the fact that the Ambrosio's victim is an innocent woman seem to invite a softer judgement of Marguerite's crime on the part of the reader.

Marguerite's narration of her own history also prefigures certain elements in Agnes's relationship with Raymond. Marguerite came from a respectable family and fell in love with a man (of inferior character to Raymond) who became "Master of [her] affections" (122). Although she admits that "my passions over-powered my virtue," she maintains like Agnes that she loved the man in faith and fidelity. Her lover fell in with Baptiste's gang, and after he died Marguerite "became the property of the infamous Baptiste" (123). In decorous, euphemistic language, she recounts that he raped her: "He obtained those favours by violence, which I persisted to refuse him" (124). Marguerite insists that because her "nature was licentious and warm, but not cruel," she hated the barbaric life into which she was forced as an unwilling witness. Like Agnes, her "conduct had been imprudent, but [her] heart was not unprincipled" (124).

Throughout *The Monk* there is an implicit stress on the legitimacy of female desire, especially in the case of the young women characters. Although Lewis is not as explicit as Shakespeare was in *Measure for Measure* that his characters' premarital relations were "mutual" crimes (2.3), he does suggest, not only with Marguerite but also with Agnes, that the woman was not just a passive victim of her lover's unbridled passion. Raymond gallantly uses the passive voice in describing the occasion to Lorenzo: "[I]n an unguarded moment the honour of Agnes was sacrificed to my passion"; but then he goes on to add, "Scarcely was the first burst of passion past, when Agnes recovering herself started from my arms with horror" (186, 187). The possibility that the burst of passion was mutual in spite of Agnes's swift repentance is further suggested by Agnes's own description of what happened, in which she uses the active voice—"in an unguarded moment I violated my vows of chastity. I shall soon become a Mother" (47)—as well as by Raymond's later comment about "*our* momentary lapse from virtue" (190; my emphasis).

As in the case of Marguerite, Agnes's capacity for maternal love seems to be inextricably connected to the strength of her original passion, in the letter she writes to Raymond: "A Being for whom I already feel a Mother's tenderness, solicits me to pardon my Seducer" (189). Feminine desire is also affirmed by the fact that the first fruit of Marguerite's illicit union is the noble and artistic young Theodore, whose name means "gift from God."

In the next phase of Raymond's journey, when he meets and falls in love with Agnes, he first encounters the destructive aspect of the feminine embodied in Agnes's aunt, Donna Rodolpha. Like Leonella, Donna Rodolpha plays that stock character in 1790s Gothic fiction, an aging woman whose sexual (or romantic) desires are unabated. But whereas Leonella is a comical figure, Donna Rodolpha is vengeful and destructive. When she realizes belatedly that Raymond's confession of love refers not to herself but to Agnes, she reacts like a Fury, vowing revenge against both Raymond and his paramour: "As She uttered these last words her fury mounted to such a pitch as to stop her powers of respiration. She panted, groaned, and at length fainted away" (137).

Raymond meets up with Donna Rodolpha's supernatural counterpart, the legendary Bleeding Nun, when he unsuccessfully attempts to help Agnes flee from the Castle of Lindenberg and Donna Rodolpha's wrath. It is important that Raymond first sees the Bleeding Nun as an image in the form of a drawing made by Agnes, for the sketch captures the nun's iconographic function as an emblem of female transgression, and of the fall from desire to death. Surrounded in the sketch by a group of terrified people, the figure was "of more than human stature, clothed in the habit of some religious order. Her face was veiled; On her arm hung a chaplet of beads; her dress was in several places stained with the blood which trickled from a wound upon her bosom. In one hand She held a Lamp, in the other a large Knife, and She seemed advancing towards the iron gates of the Hall" (138). The literal cause of her "wound" is explained somewhat later in the story, but the image also suggests the universal female "wound" from which menstrual blood flows, the vagina as sign of women's biological vulnerability and power. As well, the wound is located on the breast, another sign of female fertility (the breasts developing with the onset of menstruation). The nun's costume is "stained" with its mark, both in the sense of bearing its ineffaceable imprint, and in the sense of carrying the moral stain or fault that the Judaeo-Christian tradition has associated with the female body.

The nun is a daemonic descendant of the ancient goddesses of life and death; she is larger than life, and she carries in each hand a symbol of her powers: the light-giving lamp and the death-wielding knife. Iconographically, the Bleeding Nun is also connected with the "Sorrowful Mother" of Catholic mythology, who grieves for the death of the child to whom she gave birth (whereas Matilda's Madonna picture represents the beginning of the relation, in the "Mother and Child"). Having been culturally repressed, she re-emerges in her most archaic and daemonic guise for Lewis's Protestant audience. The nun transgresses the boundary between life and death, and she moves toward the gates of the hall as if she were approaching the gates of Hell.

According to Agnes, the Bleeding Nun was rumored to be a ghost who had haunted the castle for about a century, "shrieking, howling, groaning [and] swearing" during her nocturnal rambles (140). Agnes recounts the legend to Raymond in a tone of skeptical humor, declaring that she herself has "too much reason to lament superstition's influence to be its Victim" (141). Agnes's rational skepticism is thrown into doubt, however; for although there is an element of grotesque parody in her sketch of the figures who are staring at the nun, the portrait of the nun herself is vivid and powerful. The reader's concurrence in Agnes's skepticism is finally completely undermined when Raymond discovers that the being with whom he absconded was not Agnes disguised as the nun, but the Bleeding Nun herself.

One could argue in turn that Agnes unwittingly may have performed a necromantic act in sketching the nun, and that her action is the ironic vehicle for the release of psychically archaic material into a modern social world. It could further be argued that the image's "coming to life" and subsequent interference with the lovers' aims has been facilitated by Agnes's skepticism itself, by her failure to acknowledge the validity and energy of the daemonic.

In Agnes's picture the nun is presented as "advancing towards the iron gates of the Hall," and this motion is completed when the nun violently throws open the door of the room where Raymond has been trying unsuccessfully to sleep. She then slowly removes her veil to reveal the death's head underneath it. Raymond is transfixed by her "Rattle-snake's" eyes. He becomes "inanimate as a Statue" and can neither move, speak, nor withdraw his eyes. She then sunders the final division between the quick and the dead by touching him in a macabre embrace of death, grasping his hand with her "icy fingers" and "pressing her cold lips" to his (160–61).

The repeated visits of this Medusalike creature cast a spell that keeps Raymond immobilized for several months at the inn where he has been staying, long after the physical injuries occasioned by his carriage's overturning have been healed. Symbolically, the carriage signifies the harnessing and directing of libidinal energy toward a chosen aim, for purposive activity in the social realm. In Raymond's case, its overturning represents the thwarting of his desire for legitimate marriage; before he can fulfill that desire, he must confront and come to terms with the destructive aspect of the archetypal feminine.

The exorcism of the nun's ghost is effected by the appearance of "*the wandering Jew*" (177), a Faustian figure who had bargained for eternal life on earth and whose lament to Raymond provides a warning against attempting to evade the inevitable cycle of life and death: "Fain would I lay down my miserable life, for I envy those who enjoy the quiet of the Grave: But Death eludes me, and flies from my embrace" (169). The nun has three demands, which only Raymond can fulfill because in her earthly life she was the great aunt of Raymond's grandfather, her original name being Beatrice de las Cisternas (an infernal version of Dante's paradisal Beatrice). To fulfill the demands of his ancestral heritage, Raymond must retrieve her bones from "Lindenberg Hole," give them proper burial in the family vault, and let thirty masses be said for the repose of her soul.

It is also significant that in order for the nun's spirit to be exorcised, and for her destructive power to be allayed, her story must first be told. Again, there is an implicit parallel here with the Gothic writer's storytelling, which serves to discharge instinctual and primitive psychic energies whose force otherwise would be intensified through their repression, and which otherwise would remain, as Jung states, "in an untrained, undeveloped, infantile, archaic condition" (*Structure* 124).

The story behind the Bleeding Nun, as related to Raymond by the wandering Jew, provides yet another instance of excessive repression followed by excessive indulgence of the passions. Like Ambrosio, Beatrice entered the Church at an early age, and like both Ambrosio and Agnes, she did not do so by her own choice. When she became older, her "warm and voluptuous character" began to reveal itself, and she soon ran off with Baron Lindenberg to his castle in Germany, where she led a debauched and licentious life (173). She became involved with the baron's brother, who persuaded her to murder the baron while he slept in their bed; the brother then stabbed her to death in Lindenberg Hole after she had accomplished the deed: "He plunged [the dagger] still reeking with his Brother's blood in her bosom, and put an end to her existence by repeated blows" (175).

The tale of the double murders comprises a midpoint in Lewis's incremental repetition of sexual betrayal and family violence, between Marguerite's stabbing of the man who raped her and Ambrosio's stabbing of Antonia after raping her. This sequential patterning is one of the methods by which *The Monk*, like the Bleeding Nun, gradually unveils its full horror. This technique also has its analogy in the disturbing dream that keeps returning in various shapes and forms, until the dreamer "gets" the message.

Between this episode and Antonia's murder, the horror of death, that this "sensible warm motion [should] become / A kneaded clod," (*Measure for Measure* 3.1.120–21), is enacted in two more scenes, both involving mother figures: Ambrosio's murder of Elvira, and the mob's murder of the Mother Domina. When Elvira discovers Ambrosio on the verge of raping Antonia and threatens to expose him, he grabs her by the throat, dashes her upon the ground, and drags her toward the bed, where he smothers her with a pillow while "pressing his knee upon her stomach with all his strength" (303). The fact that Elvira and Antonia live on the Strada di San Iago points to another Shakespearean connection, Desdemona's death in *Othello;* but in addition to smothering Elvira as Othello smothers Desdemona, Ambrosio also does violence to the very womb in which his own life took form. After her struggle ends and she finally dies, "Ambrosio [beholds] before him that once noble and majestic form, now become a Corse[*sic*], cold, senseless and disgusting" (304).

Antonia's reaction upon finding her mother's body the next morning is not dissimilar to Ambrosio's, for the young woman betrays an automatic and natural enough repugnance to death: "She clasped the inanimate form to her bosom, felt that it was dead-cold, and with a movement of disgust, *of which She was not the Mistress,* let it fall again from her arms" (307; my emphasis).

The death of the negative mother figure, the Mother Domina (who functions as a witch-Hecate figure in her power to bless or curse childbirth), is even more repulsive than that of Elvira. When the Domina is publicly accused of murder, the surrounding crowd "proceed[s] to take upon her a most summary and cruel vengeance. . . . heed[ing] nothing but the gratification of their barbarous vengeance." They fling mud, filth, and verbal abuse at her, pass her from one "Tormentor" to another, stifle her "cries for mercy" with "howls and execrations," "spurning her, trampling her, and treating her with every species of cruelty which hate or vindictive fury could invent." After she is felled by a well-aimed flint and dies, the "Rioters still [exercise] their impotent rage upon her lifeless body," beating it and kicking it until it becomes "no more than a mass of flesh, unsightly, shapeless, and disgusting" (356).

Ambrosio is the only male character in the story to suffer such a violent sundering of the body, to be hurled into the lower zone of self-annihilation and returned to the original "slime from the depths." In the book's final episode, the devil drops him from a great height onto the rocks beneath. Ambrosio's "broken and dislocated limbs" are useless, and although he hears "the river's murmur as it roll[s] beside him," he cannot reach it to quench his thirst. His dissolution, an inversion of the biblical creation, takes seven days, and finally a "violent storm" comes, the "winds in fury" tear up rocks and forests, and the river he longed to reach, swollen by the rains, carries his body away (442). The natural forces being described here are another version of the "female nature" from which Ambrosio was alienated, and to which he had been so antagonistic.

In this concluding scene, nature exhibits the soothing and nurturing as well as the destructive manifestations of the feminine that have been portrayed so vividly throughout the rest of the novel. In its fury at man's perversion and violation of the natural, nature cleanses by destroying him and returning him to the watery world that preceded his individual existence.

Ambrosio's ultimate fall was ensured much earlier in the story, in an episode whose mythical context illuminates the theme of desecration of the feminine body. In order to persuade the still-hesitant Ambrosio to fall in league with the devil, Matilda reveals through her magic mirror Antonia undressing and about to take her bath. The narrator compares Antonia to the Venus de Medicis (for the second time; also see p. 9), and the atmosphere of a natural outdoor scene is evoked by the erotic description of "a tame Linnet [which flies] toward her, nestle[s] its head between her breasts, and nibble[s] them in wanton play." Antonia, who has up to this point, though "unconscious of being observed," modestly "veil[ed] her charms," reveals them when she playfully drives away the Linnet. At this sight, Ambrosio, whose "desires [are] worked up to a phrenzy," cries, "I yield!" and his fate is decided (271).

Although the narrator thinks of Venus when he (too) gazes on Antonia's "lovely form," Diana is actually the pagan goddess who is invoked in this scene—the virgin huntress whom Actaeon spied on while she was bathing in the woods with her nymphs. Actaeon was punished for invading the goddess's secret domain by being turned into a stag (Ovid 78–79). Ambrosio is similarly punished for his violation, for after seeing Antonia he becomes possessed by a rapacious and bestial sexual appetite.

Peter Brooks has argued that *The Monk* marks the historical moment at which "the Sacred has reasserted its claim to attention, but in the most primitive possible manifestations, as taboo and interdiction" (249). Brooks suggests that the Gothic writers of the late eighteenth century all recognize that a "resacralization" of their secularized world is no longer a possibility. He associates this resacralization with an ethical imperative with which, he says, God can no longer be associated. God thus becomes a force that inspires fear rather than worship (250–51). My interpretation is that *The Monk* initiates a return to a phase of religious experience preceding religion's later association with morality, one in which the world is perceived as being infused with the sacred. Gothic fictions belong to the destructive phase of re-creation. To use Mircea Eliade's comments on primitive ritual, they "put an end to existing forms (worn away by the fact of their own existence) in order to make room for the birth of a new form" (69). Another point on which I differ with Brooks, and which is central to this study, is that although Gothic novels may not communicate direct and explicit moral messages, these works can be intensely moral in their implications.

Certainly, one of the strongest primitive manifestations in *The Monk* is the appearance of the ancient Mother Goddess in both her "daemonic" and "divine," destructive and creative aspects. The only redemptive scene in this generally bleak novel occurs when Antonia, after being stabbed "twice in the bosom" by Ambrosio and found by her would-be-rescuers as "a Female bleeding upon the ground," finally succumbs to death. In contrast to the Bleeding Nun, Antonia's "eyes [sparkle] with celestial brightness: Her frame seem[s] to have received new strength and animation," and she cries, "Mother, I come!" (392–93). In Lorenzo's dream at the beginning of the story, "harmonious voices pealed along the Vaults; and the glory into which Antonia was received, was composed of rays of such dazzling brightness, that [he] was unable to sustain the gaze" (28). Later, Elvira's ghost visits Antonia, raising "the Linen which covered her face" and saying, "Yet three days, and we meet again!" (318). Although these earlier episodes seem to assure the reader that Antonia ascends, Christlike, into heaven, at the actual point of death she becomes a Persephone figure, who rejoins her mother rather than her father.

The Monk consistently undermines the Protestant world view by evoking the awe and dread with which the Mother Goddess was once regarded. The novel's apparent critique of Catholicism veils its actual critique of the Protestant spirit, and the social and moral consequences of women's devaluation in the modern world. Ambrosio's problem is not his Catholicism per se, but his conformity to a puritanical ideal of what Catholic priests should be like. The Protestant reformers' objection to Catholic celibacy lay less in the ideal itself than in the frequency with which that ideal was relaxed behind convent walls. Certainly, the Catholic religion accepted human fallibility and sexuality to an extent that the Protestant religions did not. As Edmund Leites states, "[t]he Puritans developed techniques to increase the capacity for moral self-regulation and rejected the relief given by the medieval cycle of sin, guilt, and repentance, where failure was expected and therefore given a sort of cultural sanction" (139).

The Monk also examines, through the divergent histories of the brother and sister, Ambrosio and Antonia, the importance of a strong and loving maternal presence in individual moral development. Although both siblings are destroyed by the evil forces for which their cloistered virtues failed to prepare them, Antonia remains spiritually and morally intact, whereas Ambrosio succumbs to all Matilda's sophistical arguments, to her "dramatic conspiracy of the verbal, the musical, and the visual" (Grudin 139), and loses his soul. As the narrator explains, there are several reasons why Ambrosio is unsuccessful in "infusing corruption into Antonia's bosom" while he pretends to be her friend and advisor:

> [T]he excellent morals which She owed to Elvira's care, the solidity and correctness of her understanding, and a strong sense of what was right implanted in her heart by Nature, made her feel that his precepts must be faulty. By a few simple words She frequently overthrew the whole bulk of his sophistical arguments, and made him conscious how weak they were when opposed to Virtue and Truth. (257)

Not only does Antonia possess a basic sense of what might be called "natural law" (a fact that implicitly repudiates Locke's notion of the *tabula rasa*), but she also has had the advantage of Elvira's unceasing "care," the emotional nourishment that is a prerequisite to any child's moral development and that Ambrosio has lacked.

At the age of two, Ambrosio was transferred from his mother's care into a community of men, and the ultimate consequences of his loss of feminine guidance were devastating. If, as has already been suggested, Ambrosio's monkish education can be seen as a reflection of practices still current in Lewis's day, it may also be possible to understand the Monk's maternal loss as an extreme yet representative depiction of the plight of children in late-eighteenth-century England, where women were so severely disempowered.

As in the case of Horace Walpole, it appears that Lewis's personal experience may have sensitized him to this larger social problem. According to Louis Peck, Lewis's biographer, his mother ran off with a music master when Lewis was six years old, leaving Matthew and his three younger siblings behind. Frances Lewis did not see her children for a long time after this, moving from place to place and hiding her addresses so that her husband could not find her. A year later, she gave birth to a girl, apparently "the 'Miss Lacey' mentioned frequently in Matthew's and his mother's [later] letters, whom Mrs. Lewis was so solicitous to establish in life and to whom in her will she left everything she owned" (Peck 7). As Peck explains it, Frances Lewis was "*obliged* to withdraw from society" (7; my emphasis) as well as from her own children because of her transgression. Peck also recounts that "[t]his family affair placed Matthew for years in the awkward position, which he assumed with great tact and common sense, of intermediary between his parents, both of whom he loved" (7). Peck is not specific, however, about the age at which young Matthew assumed this task, nor does he examine the likelihood that in the first years of his mother's absence the boy could have felt anything but grief, anger, and powerlessness.

As his writing skills developed, Lewis used them to retrieve his mother via a long-distance literary relationship, and although his letters reveal "sincere if sometimes effusively expressed affection" for his mother (Peck 8), they also betray a lingering sadness and resentment:

> I cannot help recollecting the pain and anxiety you have occasioned to my dear my worthy Father, and that it is owing to your conduct that my Sisters are deprived of maternal care and attention, and, of receiving the benefits of those little instructions and observations, so necessary to make young Women accomplished, and which are in the power of a Mother alone to point out to them with success. (Qtd. in Peck 8)

This may have been as close as Lewis could come to expressing his own feelings of pain, anxiety, and deprivation. He also explained to his mother, in response to her question as to whether she should refer to him as her nephew, that to save himself social embarrassment when questioned about her, "I do not say that I have a Mother living" (qtd. in Peck 8).

Lewis's father, a senior civil servant, apparently had a more inflexible, less expressive and demonstrative personality than Frances Lewis, and although Matthew Lewis regarded his father with respect and affection, the son was temperamentally more in sympathy with his mother. It would be very easy to interpret the murder of the mother in *The Monk* reductively, as Lewis's acting out of his own repressed rage, but the novel's cultural critique also indicates a clear comprehension of the dilemmas facing women such as his mother in Lewis's time. From a very young age, he succeeded in maintaining relationships with both estranged parents in what seems to have been a remarkable effort of will and understanding. Given the close attention to the question of individual freedom and the affirmation of female desire that we find in *The Monk,* it seems likely that Lewis's own criticism of his mother's weakness may have been less severe than his criticism of the social censorship of women, which "obliged" her to abandon her children in her pursuit of sexual and emotional satisfaction.

In the violent destruction of its central male protagonist by supernatural agency, *The Monk* presents a characteristically Gothic warning about the dangers of censorship, whether social or psychological. The topical issue addressed in the novel—the government's current program of inhibiting free speech—is only one aspect of the larger problem with which Lewis is concerned: that is, the inflexibility and imbalance that arise whenever the feminine dimension of life is suppressed.

CHAPTER FIVE

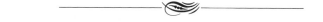

The Industrial Demon: Frankenstein

*W*hen Mary Shelley's *Frankenstein* was published (anonymously) in 1818, it did not create quite the stir that *The Monk* did, nor did it sell well enough to warrant a second edition.[1] Five years later, however, Richard Brinsley Peake staged a dramatization titled *Presumption; or, The Fate of Frankenstein* (1823) that stimulated enough public interest in Shelley's novel to call for a reprinting. Within the next three years, *Presumption* inspired fourteen other dramatizations (Forry 3).[2] Since that time dramatic and cinematic productions have helped to disseminate internationally the story that Brian Aldiss has called "the first great myth of the Industrial age" (23).

The basic features of Shelley's novel are generally well known, despite the great variety in its subsequent permutations.[3] A young "mad scientist" named Victor Frankenstein becomes obsessed with creating human life, to the point of neglecting almost everything else, including his family and friends. He abandons in horror the being he creates, immediately after electrically charging it with the "spark of life." The neglected creature, or "monster," thence becomes a destructive force who murders almost all of Frankenstein's family and friends. Frankenstein finally dies after frantically pursuing the creature through the icy Arctic wastes; the creature is last seen (by the man to whom Frankenstein has told his story) traveling away on a raft until he is "lost in darkness and distance" (223),[4] after having declared his intention to commit suicide by burning himself on a funeral pyre.

Working within the Gothic tradition, Shelley made the first major innovation in the genre, taking up the scenario of unadmitted guilt and unconscious possession that her father William Godwin had used in *Caleb Williams* (1794)[5] and expanding it to address some of the social and moral problems arising from current developments in science and technology. Numerous critics have shown how her idea for the creation of a humanoid can be traced both to ancient myth and folklore and to contemporary scientific developments, but few have examined its relevance to related developments in industrial technology and production.[6]

Radu Florescu has suggested that Shelley's depiction of the monster as an extension of its creator's guilt may have been influenced in part by the Jewish legend of the Golem, a creature made from clay and animated by magic. In some stories about the Golem, the creature carries out errands for which its creator does not want to be held responsible, and ends up rebelling against its master (222–25)—a dynamic which is very similar to the one Shelley develops between Frankenstein and his monster. However, the process by which Frankenstein's monster is made differs significantly from that of the legendary Golem, in that he is constructed from an assortment of parts, rather than shaped from a single material. In this respect, Shelley may have been partly inspired by a more modern phenomenon: the mechanical men for which the area around Neuchâtel, Switzerland, was famous, and which Shelley might have seen when she stayed there with her new husband and her stepsister Claire Clairmont during the summer of 1814 (Florescu 55). These androids (the term by which they were commonly referred to; Florescu 233) were constructed on the same mechanical principles as the clock and were widely regarded as marvels of human technological ingenuity.

Florescu also notes the probable influence of the scientific theories of Erasmus Darwin (whom Shelley mentions in her 1831 introduction to *Frankenstein;* 8–9) and Sir Humphry Davy, in Shelley's depiction of the monster's creation (215–20).[7] More recently, David Ketterer has argued that Shelley was reading Davy's work at the same time that she was developing the section on Frankenstein's conversion from alchemical studies to modern science ("Frankenstein's 'Conversion'" 57–61). Samuel Holmes Vasbinder and Anne K. Mellor have further shown that Shelley's portrayal of Frankenstein's project was informed by an extensive knowledge of current trends in scientific research. In Mellor's view, Shelley draws a distinction in *Frankenstein* between "good" observational science and "bad" invasive, manipulative science, represented by the work of Darwin and Davy respectively (*Mary*

89–102). Both Vasbinder and Mellor demonstrate that Shelley undoubtedly knew about the numerous experiments in galvanism that had been conducted in England and on the Continent over the preceding two decades: in particular, Professor Luigi Aldini's electrical stimulation of the corpse of a recently executed convict, in London in 1803 (Vasbinder 79–80; Mellor, *Mary* 105–106).[8] Mellor argues that *Frankenstein* presents a prophetic critique of the dangers of moral irresponsibility in scientific enquiry (*Mary* 114).

Shelley's critique extends as well to include the new industrial modes of production which were developing alongside recent advancements in science and technology. In this respect, it is especially significant that Frankenstein's monster is not born but *manufactured,* assembled from inanimate materials (specifically, dead body parts). In Martin Tropp's words, the attic where the monster "is constructed like a machine" is really a "one man factory" (31, 30). Warren Montag has argued that by excluding from *Frankenstein* any overt presentation of life in urban-industrial England— the land of "Blake's 'dark satanic mills'"—Shelley highlights the unnaturalness of Frankenstein's project: "[T]he product of [Frankenstein's] labor, the monster . . . is the sole embodiment of the industrial in an otherwise rural world, and this is the source of his monstrousness" (309, 310).

Thus, Frankenstein's monster can also be understood as a nightmarish portent of the assembly line construction of the Industrial Age, and the division of labor that Adam Smith celebrated in *The Wealth of Nations* (1776) as leading to "a proportionable increase of the productive powers of labour" (6), but that also created great devastation in the lives of England's working poor during Mary Shelley's time. The breakdown of Frankenstein's personality signifies more than the inevitable consequences of scientific monomania; it also presents a warning about collective psychic and social fragmentation in the industrial/scientific era.

In his disregard for the spiritual ramifications of his project, Shelley's Frankenstein epitomizes the dangers attending the scientific world view. His actions and their consequences constitute the typical warning encoded in Gothic fiction, that rejection of the spiritual can lead to an eruption of the daemonic.

The first important articulation of the separation between scientific and spiritual matters had occurred in Baconian science. Invoking the Protestant prohibition against "Idols of the human mind," Bacon had argued in his *Novum Organum* (1620) against the confusion of science with "superstition and theology," and "the absurd mixture of matters divine and human" (16, 37, 38). He asserted that "[i]t is therefore most wise soberly to render unto faith the things that are faith's" (16, 38).

As Michael McKeon points out (and as *Frankenstein* suggests), one symptom of this historical development is that the "felt immanence of spirit in matter loses its conviction" (66). The new approach assumed a greater self-sufficiency, which demanded skepticism rather than reverence, whereas in the medieval view, any effort to manipulate the material world was believed to require a ritual that would connect the seeker with the immaterial world, whose powers were understood to be far greater than those of any individual.[9]

Frankenstein's fascination with and subsequent rejection of alchemical studies calls attention to the rupture between the medieval and modern worlds, a break that is signaled by the scorn Bacon expressed for medieval magic and alchemy and their lack of attention to empirical reality:

> But if any one should condescend to consider such sciences as are deemed rather curious than sound, and take a full view of the operations of the alchemists or magi, he will perhaps hesitate whether he ought rather to laugh or to weep. For the alchemist cherishes eternal hope, and when his labors succeed not, accuses his own mistakes, deeming, in his self-accusation, that he has not properly understood the words of art or of his authors. . . . [W]e may well apply to [the discoveries of alchemists] the fable of the old man, who bequeathed to his sons some gold buried in his garden, pretending not to know the exact spot, whereupon they worked diligently in digging the vineyard, and though they found no gold, the vintage was rendered more abundant by their labor. (64–65)

Frankenstein confesses much the same thing in recounting his early infatuation with the works of Cornelius Agrippa, Albertus Magnus, and Paracelsus: "The raising of ghosts or devils was a promise liberally accorded by my favourite authors, the fulfilment of which I most eagerly sought, and if my incantations were always unsuccessful, I attributed the failure rather to my own inexperience and mistake, than to a want of skill or fidelity in my instructors" (40). Although Bacon chastised modern natural philosophers for making exaggerated claims about their powers—those "silly and fantastical fellows who . . . have loaded mankind with promises, announcing and boasting of the prolongation of life, the retarding of old age . . . the bringing into our power the management of celestial influences," and so forth (66)—he himself was not immune to the Promethean impulse. Bacon argued that an unprejudiced, dispassionate and methodical inquiry into the nature of material reality would

> remove despair and excite hope, by bidding farewell to the errors of past ages, or by their correction. . . . [I]f many useful discoveries have occurred to mankind by chance or opportunity, without investigation or attention on their part . . . much more may be brought to light by investigation and attention, if it be regular and orderly. . . . We may, therefore, hope for further, better, and more frequent results from man's reason, industry, method, and application, than from chance and mere animal instinct, and the like, which have hitherto been the sources of invention. (84)

Thus in its promise of ameliorating, consoling, and offering hope for the human condition, science would take upon itself the office of religion—but it would do so in a material and tangible, rather than spiritual and intangible, fashion.

The self-inflation that seems incipient in Bacon's optimism is equally demonstrated by Victor Frankenstein, whose hopes, as Laura Crouch has shown, "were only slightly more . . . presumptuous than those of other chemists of his day," including Davy, who prophesied that scientific knowledge would eventually lead to a more enlightened and egalitarian world (Crouch 36, 40). Frankenstein, the prototypical mad scientist, declares, "I will pioneer a new way, explore unknown powers, and unfold to the world the deepest mysteries of creation"; "A new species would bless me as its creator and source: many happy and excellent natures would owe their being to me" (48, 54). There is no safeguard against such hubris in the modern science that Frankenstein pursues, for it does not require the ritual of spiritual self-purification demanded by the older alchemical tradition.

Frankenstein admits that the grandeur of the old studies was what fascinated him and that works of modern natural philosophy only left him "discontented and unsatisfied. Sir Isaac Newton is said to have avowed that he felt like a child picking up shells beside the great and unexplored ocean of truth. Those of his successors in each branch of natural philosophy with whom I was acquainted, appeared even to my boy's apprehensions, as tyros engaged in the same pursuit" (39).[10] In his creation of a humanoid, Frankenstein demonstrates the Promethean tendency inherent in the newly secularized science to aspire to the divine power from which it claims to have released itself. His electrical "animation" of a lifeless being has the paradoxical aim of infusing spirit into base matter via material means. His "arts" are "unhallowed" (9) not because they are affiliated with occult magic, as some readers have assumed, but because they are part of the un-sanctified modern science of Shelley's time.

The proponents of the new science, in their advocacy of systematic investigation and experiment, had no small influence on subsequent developments in production and manufacture. Many of the early leaders of the Industrial Revolution combined practical technological skill with considerable scientific expertise, just as Frankenstein himself made some technical "improvements of some chemical instruments" while engaged in theoretical study (51). Thomas Telford, for example, who investigated such practical subjects as the strength of iron chains and rods for bridge-building, and the movement of canal boats through water, was elected a member of the Royal Society of Edinburgh in 1827. A letter about his pursuits written to a friend in 1796 reveals an absorption in his task and an optimism about its results remarkably similar to Victor Frankenstein's attitude:

> *Knowledge is my most ardent pursuit . . .* [and] I am now deep in Chemistry—the manner of making Mortar led me to inquire into the nature of Lime and in pursuit of this, having look'd into some books on Chemistry *I perceived the field was boundless*—and that to assign reasons for many Mechanical processes it required a general knowledge of that Science. I have therefore had the loan of a MSS Copy of Dr Black's Lectures. I have bought his Experiments on Magnesia and Quick Lime and likewise Fourcroy's Lectures translated from the French by a Mr Elliott. And *I am determined to study with unwearied attention until I attain some general knowledge of Chemistry as it is of Universal use in the [practical] Arts as in Medicine.* (Qtd. in Musson 102; my emphasis)

Although Telford's ambitions are clearly less grandiose than Frankenstein's, the similarity between his and Frankenstein's attitudes does suggest Shelley's acute sensitivity to the temper of the times.

One industrialist elected to be a Fellow of the Royal Society was Josiah Wedgwood, the famous potter, who promoted new developments in clays, glazes, coloring, and temperature control at his factory in Etruria, where a number of "[s]cientific men were engaged, at liberal salaries," in various forms of research and experimentation (Musson 106).

The Wedgwood family also demonstrated the moral and social irresponsibility—or perhaps obliviousness would be a better word—that often accompanied enthusiasm for industrial development. Wedgwood's son, Josiah ("the Second"), most of whose employees worked eleven-hour days exclusive of mealtimes, appeared before Peel's committee on child labor in 1816. While Wedgwood agreed that child labor should be curtailed, he objected to any governmental legislation on the issue, affirming the prevalent laissez-faire philosophy that "from all I know at present of manufactories in general, and certainly from all I know of my own, we had better be left alone." At that time, Wedgwood employed 387 people, of whom thirteen were under ten years of age, and 103 between ten and eighteen (Pike 106, 105).

Vasbinder has suggested that Shelley "to some extent shares the optimism of the scientists of her day that science will show man the way to knowledge and truth and make him master of the universe" (71), but the plot of *Frankenstein* hardly seems to support such a conclusion. While I am not trying to argue that Shelley advocates a return to the good old preindustrial days, it does seem clear that she is very critical of the prevailing ethos of the industrial era, and that, as Fred Botting comments, *Frankenstein* interrogates "the ideology which frames and constructs scientific projects . . . the assumptions it operates with and the interests it serves" (176).

Growing up in London, Shelley probably had little if any direct experience with the new mode of production that was making its appearance in other parts of England. Yet it is certain that in her politically informed household she would have been made keenly aware of the social problems and questions of governmental responsibility that attended its development. As a young teenager, she would compose weekly lectures to be delivered by her younger brother William on subjects such as "The Influence of the Government on the Character of the People" (Mellor, *Mary* 11). Sections of her father's novel *Fleetwood* (1805) were based on his earlier visits to some of England's mills and factories: Josiah Wedgwood's potteries at Etruria, the industrial parts of the Midlands, and Robert Bage's paper works at Elford in 1797; the factory of his old friend Frederick Norman in Stowmarket in 1803; and a silk mill in Spitalfields in 1804 (P. Marshall 264).

A lengthy subplot in *Fleetwood* "denounces child labour in no uncertain terms" (P. Marshall 264); the protagonist Ruffigny describes how children as young as four years of age sit in front of the spinning wheels in the silk factories of Lyons for twelve hours a day, with a "stupid and hopeless vacancy in every face" (*Fleetwood* 1: 244). Ruffigny declares, "Every boy learns more in his hours of play, than in his hours of labour. . . . Put him into a mill, and his understanding will improve no more than that of the horse which turns it" (1: 247–48). The children at the silk mills "were all sallow; their muscles flaccid, and their form emaciated" (1: 244). They "were made sacrifices, while still tender. . . . This is the case in no state of society, but in manufacturing towns" (1: 250).[11]

Mary Shelley knew this novel well, as she did almost everything her father wrote. When Percy Shelley had first asked for Godwin's approval of Shelley's plan to end his marriage with his estranged wife Harriet and live with Godwin's daughter, Mary and Percy proposed to leave England and settle in Uri, Switzerland, the locale of Godwin's fictional Ruffigny. The choice was apparently an unsuccessful attempt to compliment and placate Godwin, whose opposition to the union was nevertheless firm (St. Clair 355–56).

Mary was also greatly influenced by the intellectual legacy of her deceased mother, Mary Wollstonecraft Godwin. In *A Historical and Moral View of the French Revolution* (1794), which Shelley read about a year and a half before she began writing *Frankenstein* (*Journals* 55–56), Wollstonecraft decried the dehumanizing effects of the specialization of labor in a manufacturing economy:

> Commerce also, overstocking a country with people, obliges the majority to become manufacturers rather than husbandmen; and then the division of labour, solely to enrich the proprietor, renders the mind entirely inactive. The time which, a celebrated writer says, is sauntered away, in going from one part of an employment to another is the very time that preserves the man from degenerating into a brute; for everyone must have observed how much more intelligent are the blacksmiths, carpenters and masons in the country, than the journeymen in great towns; and respecting morals, there is no making a comparison. The very gait of a man, who is his own master, is so much more steady than the slouching step of a servant of a servant. (386)

The "celebrated writer" to whom Wollstonecraft refers is Adam Smith. One of the social evils that Smith thought the industrial division of labor would cure was the "slothfulness" of laborers:

> A country weaver, who cultivates a small farm, must lose a great deal of time in passing from his loom to the field, and from the field to his loom. . . . The habit of sauntering and of indolent, careless application, which is naturally . . . acquired by every country workman who is obliged to change his work and his tools every half hour and to apply his hand in twenty different ways almost every day of his life, renders him almost always slothful and lazy, and incapable of any vigorous application. (8)

Smith argues that in contrast, productivity invariably increases when labor is divided according to different mechanical operations and "every man's business" is reduced "to some one simple operation" that becomes "the sole employment of his life" (7).[12]

Shelley's awareness of the moral issues being raised by the new modes of production was also undoubtedly enhanced by her contact with the progressive socialist Robert Owen, who had become friends with Godwin in 1813 and was a frequent visitor to the Godwin household during the spring of 1814, when the sixteen-and-a-half-year-old Mary was residing at home (Sunstein 62–63). Mary apparently discussed Owen's ideas with her half-sister Fanny, who admired the man but was skeptical about his optimism: "[H]ow he can expect to make the rich give up their possessions, and live in a state of equality is too romantic to be believed" (qtd. in Sunstein 63).

Owen owned the New Lanark textile mills in Scotland, a model of humane management based on cooperative principles that featured educational and recreational opportunities for adults and children. In 1815 he began to agitate for legislation prohibiting the employment of children under the age of ten and limiting the hours of work for children in factories to ten hours a day. With the assistance of Robert Peel, he achieved some limited success. By 1819 an act was finally passed prohibiting "the employment, in cotton mills only, of children under the age of nine, and limit[ing] the hours of work of children between nine and sixteen to twelve in the day, exclusive of meal-times" (Pike 100–01). At this time it was still the norm for very young children to put in fourteen-hour workdays in the mills and factories, exclusive of mealtimes.

The social misery and havoc created by the new system of production was evident to anyone who kept an open eye and ear to public affairs. In 1811, the year that Mary Shelley turned fourteen and spent eight months away from her family in a boarding school on the west coast, workers' riots broke out in several parts of England. In the Nottingham area in the early months of that year, dissatisfaction with workers' conditions in the textile industry led to systematic sabotage against the frames of unpopular hosiers (those who treated their employers fairly being left alone). Small groups of framework knitters broke into the workshops and removed the jack-wires (not to destroy them but to keep them for ransom), which were indispensable to the machines' operation.

On March 11 a crowd of several hundred gathered to protest low wages and unhealthy working conditions; the general mood became so heated that the military were called in and the crowd forcefully dispersed. That night there was an outbreak of frame breaking in near-by Arnold, which the general populace cheered on and aided by obstructing the authorities. The disturbances were renewed in November, when outbreaks of "Luddite" frame breaking occurred nightly throughout most of the month. The military was called in again, but the authorities were stymied by the systematic nature of the attacks and by popular support for the saboteurs (Darvall 64–70). Percy Shelley was familiar with the Nottingham area, and "the desperate conditions he saw there in 1811 in part inspired his 1812 poem *Queen Mab*" which he gave to Mary in 1814 (J. Smith 14).

In February 1812 frame breaking was made a capital offense. Byron, who later became an intimate friend of the Shelleys and was said to have proposed the ghost-story contest that led to the writing of *Frankenstein,* was one of the few members of the House of Lords to strenuously oppose the bill. He accused the government of ignoring the "unparalelled [*sic*] distress" and destitution of the workers and argued that the government's inaction was to blame for the desperate measures that workers had finally taken: "[H]ad proper meetings been held in the earlier stages of these riots, had the grievances of these men and their masters . . . been fairly weighed & justly examined, I do think that means might have been devised to restore these workmen to their avocations & tranquillity to the Country" (22, 25). His opposition to the death penalty for frame breaking had already earned him the young Mary Shelley's admiration even before they met (Sunstein 51).

Despite her later apparent conservatism, Shelley maintained, in the words of Johanna Smith, "a lifelong sympathy for the poor" (13), and it is clear that at the time of writing the 1818 *Frankenstein* she shared her husband's passionate indignation about the indifference of the ruling classes to the desperate condition of the laboring poor (see J. Smith 13–16). Percy Shelley's concern with the problem of child labor is expressed in his *Philosophical View of Reform* (1819–20), where he argues that the greed-inspired system of industrial manufacture turns "children into lifeless and bloodless machines at an age when otherwise they would be at play before the cottage doors of their parents. . . . Children . . . are put in requisition, and the vigorous promise of the coming generation blighted by premature exertion" (237).

Leigh Hunt, who became friends with the Shelleys while Mary was composing *Frankenstein,* also published an essay on the subject just a month before Mary's book was completed. His description of how child laborers become subhuman creatures traces a process of cause and effect similar to that of the monster's moral degeneration in *Frankenstein:*

By the present system, children are snatched from the healthy air and their recreations to be imprisoned all day long in a kind of hell upon earth; their natural cheerfulness is checked, or turned into callous impudence; their bodies are blighted with unnatural warmth and inaction, their minds with equally unnatural thought or sullenness . . . instead of ruddy and sparkling faces, they have pale and careful ones. . . . It is first a sense of premature sorrow . . . and then a sense of the gross and selfish injustice exercised towards them by others, that renders these schools of industry the certain schools of . . . despair, and the *probable* schools of . . . theft, of riot, of *Luddism,* and when the excess of provocation is complete, or rather the long-suffering patience exhausted, of bloody revolution. (251, 252)

It is clear that from her friends, her family, and her reading, Shelley had received ample exposure to the argument that Frankenstein's creature forcefully makes, that misery can make one a fiend (145).

Parts of Mary Shelley's journals and letters, particularly her bad-tempered comments about the peasants she encountered when she eloped to the Continent with Percy in company with her stepsister Jane (later renamed Claire), have led more than one critic to believe that Shelley actually felt a "deep aversion to the lower classes" (Mellor, *Mary* 25). What needs to be taken into account, however, is the personal context of the letters and the journal entries that reveal her revulsion to the filth and squalor she witnessed at this time. The impecunious group traveled in considerable physical discomfort; Mary had been seasick on the trip over; she had just become pregnant;[13] she had just turned seventeen; and she had likely realized fairly quickly that she would have to compete with Jane for Percy's attentions.[14] Mary's attitude is more generous in one of her later letters, written during their second trip to Switzerland, when their arrangements were better planned and more comfortable; she also had a healthy baby boy, and Jane had transferred her interest from Percy to Byron. Only a few weeks before commencing her composition of *Frankenstein,* Mary wrote:

There is more equality of classes here than in England. This occasions a greater freedom and refinement of manners among the lower orders than we meet with in our own country. I fancy the haughty English ladies are disgusted with this consequence of republican institutions, for the Genevese servants complain very much of their *scolding,* an exercise of the tongue, I believe, perfectly unknown here. (*Letters* 1: 21).[15]

Thus, however conflicted Shelley may have been between her democratic ideals and her personal desire for security and stability (and perhaps prestige), it is apparent that at the time of writing *Frankenstein* she had not lost her youthful consciousness of "The Influence of the Government on the Character of the People" (Mellor, *Mary* 11). England had turned its back on its own poor in much the same way that Victor Frankenstein turns his back on his own creature, who argues persuasively that his monstrous behavior is not innate but simply a logical consequence of paternal abandonment.

Frankenstein's actions—and inaction—can thus be seen as representing a collective failure of responsibility during this period of rapid industrial development. However, the creature's symbolism is more complex, for he represents not only the weak and vulnerable victims of industrialization, and the potential of victims to become victimizers, but as an agent of destruction he also embodies the unregulated, unchecked force of industrialization itself. Here it is important to look at his psychological role as Victor Frankenstein's double, for the personal dynamics form an essential component of *Frankenstein*'s psychopolitical critique.

Although the presence of the double or doppelgänger theme in *Frankenstein* has been noted frequently, to understand this theme fully requires some reference to modern psychological theory pertaining to dissociation and the double, as in the work of C. G. Jung or Otto Rank. Jung has pointed out that "the split-off personality [of the double] is not just a random one, but stands in a complementary or compensatory relationship to the ego-personality" (*Archetypes* 261). Associated with the ancient trickster figure and thus with "counter-tendencies in the unconscious," the double can in some cases take the form of "a sort of second personality, of a puerile and inferior character," which Jung designates "the shadow" (*Archetypes* 262).

Rank has employed similar ideas in his survey of double figures in literature, where, he says, the main character is almost invariably a man with a very narcissistic, emotionally undeveloped personality who is incapable of forming a loving, reciprocal relationship with a woman. Embodying this incapacity, the double figure acts to impede the main character's friendships and love relationships. Rank points out that in most stories about the double the main character begins by underestimating the power of his shadow, whose powers are then enhanced because he is not taken seriously enough at first. The protagonist thinks that the double is still dependent on him and his conscious control, when in fact it has become quite independent and "works in secret" against the protagonist.

In her 1831 preface, Shelley gives special emphasis to the moment at which Victor Frankenstein's double is released into an independent life, when she describes having envisioned the scene in the waking dream that inspired her writing of the novel (9–10). Her account underscores the centrality of this scene to the overall story. Frankenstein's own retrospective account of the event similarly involves a terrifying nightmare, but in his case it is one that conflates his fiancée and his dead mother. This nightmare, along with Frankenstein's earlier description of the events leading up to the monster's creation, provides an important clue as to the motives underlying his obsessive quest to create life.

After he animates the creature, and the defects of his own workmanship become horrifyingly clear to him—the creature's "yellow skin [which] scarcely covered the work of muscles and arteries beneath . . . his watery eyes, that seemed almost of the same colour as the dun white sockets in which they were set, his shrivelled complexion and straight black lips" (57)—Frankenstein rushes out of the room, collapses onto his bed, and falls asleep. He dreams that he sees Elizabeth, the woman he is supposed to marry, in "the bloom of health," but when he kisses her lips they become like the monster's, "livid with the hue of death." As he holds the corpse in his arms, it becomes transformed into his dead mother: "[A] shroud enveloped her form, and I saw the grave-worms crawling in the folds of the flannel" (58).

Frankenstein's unconscious merging of the monster, his mother, and Elizabeth is understandable in the light of the information he gives earlier, that when he was seventeen years old his mother died prematurely from tending her "favourite" foster child, Elizabeth, who was sick with scarlet fever (42). As David Ketterer, one of the few critics to examine the doppelgänger theme in any detail, suggests, "Frankenstein must blame Elizabeth for causing his mother's death" (64).

Ketterer traces a number of ironic reversals that indicate that the monster can be seen in part as a "psychological projection" (59). Chris Baldick similarly notes that in "taking flight from the monster . . . Victor can be seen to be shunning the recognition of his own desire; his failure to acknowledge either as his own will make him their slave" (48). Jeffrey Berman states more precisely that Frankenstein's "horrified retreat from the Creature may lie in the psychic mechanism of projective identification, the projection of virulent aggression onto another figure, who is then seen as a deadly persecutory double" (62). Berman demonstrates that Frankenstein presents a classic case of pathological narcissistic rage, with all the accompanying "typical defense mechanisms" of "splitting, denial, defensive idealization, omnipotence, and devaluation" (62). William Veeder also examines self-division and projection in *Frankenstein* and suggests that "Victor's riven psyche attempts to heal itself through the creation of the monster" (*Mary* 81). My view, in contrast, is that the release of the monster marks the moment at which Frankenstein's psychic fragmentation, or "bifurcation" as Veeder refers to it, becomes irremediable.

What needs further consideration here is the complex range of emotions that Victor Frankenstein projects onto the monster, as well as the way Frankenstein "aids and abets" the monster's crimes, thereby enabling the monster to develop greater autonomy. The brevity of Frankenstein's account of his mother's death suggests his difficulty in dealing with his own grief and anger. He speaks of his despair and "the void that presents itself to the soul" upon the death of a loved one, but shortly thereafter he speaks of his recovery, and then about the resumption of his plans to go to Ingolstadt to study (43). In Ingolstadt, obeying the dictates of the "resistless, and almost frantic, impulse" driving him to discover the secret of "bestowing animation upon lifeless matter" (54, 52), he becomes physically emaciated and detached from normal life, neglecting to visit or correspond with his family for a period of almost two years.

In his self-destructiveness, Frankenstein attempts unconsciously to rejoin his mother in death, and through his project he seeks the means of bringing her back to life: "[I]f I could bestow animation upon lifeless matter, I might in process of time (although I now found it impossible) renew life where death had apparently devoted the body to corruption" (54). As many critics have noted, he uses an unwitting but revealing pun when he describes the creature, once it has been brought to life, as a hideous "mummy . . . endued with animation" (58).

The murderous monster unleashed by him activates everything that the rational, skeptical, and emotionally impoverished scientist has rejected and forgotten: the relational impulses that remain in a primitive and undeveloped condition because they have been excluded "from conscious training and adaptation" (Jung, *Structure* 124). The monster states that in murdering Victor's young brother, William, he was moved by rage at being excluded from human intimacy and companionship, but in his subsequent scapegoating of Justine, his motivation becomes more specific: he is furious at being deprived of both a mother and a mate.

The monster's longing for a woman's love is evident in his emotional reaction to the picture of Frankenstein's mother that he finds on William's body. In spite of his "malignity, it soften[s] and attract[s] him. . . . [He] gaze[s] with delight on her dark eyes, fringed by deep lashes, and her lovely lips." But his "rage" soon returns, for like Lewis's Ambrosio he remembers that he is "forever deprived of the delights that such beautiful creatures could bestow" (143).

His anger at these "beautiful creatures" is revealed when he encounters the sleeping Justine. He thinks, "Here . . . is one of those whose joy-imparting smiles are bestowed on all but me," and decides that "the murder I have committed because I am for ever robbed of all that she could give me, she shall atone. The crime had its source in her: be hers the punishment!" (143–44). Whereas at other points in his story the monster takes on the rhetoric of Milton's vengeful Satan, exiled from his Father, at this point he sounds like Milton's Adam, unheroically trying to scapegoat Eve (as does Lewis's Ambrosio). In transferring responsibility for his own actions onto the woman, he not only tries to evade his guilt, but he also gives vent to the rage he feels at his own maternal deprivation. At the same time, he acts out Frankenstein's anger at the mother who long ago transferred her affections to another child and whose death left him also motherless.

In the case of Elizabeth's death, the monster's actions are linked more strongly with his frustrated sexual drive; her murder is almost explicitly presented as a form of rape. As Baldick has suggested, "Victor's fear of sexuality and Elizabeth's murder are parts of a single 'complex' . . . [T]he creation of the monster is an attempt to create life without encountering female sexuality" (49). The monster, in destroying what he cannot have, destroys the physical separation between himself and the woman (or Woman) he desires. Accepting the force of sexual desire that Frankenstein tries to reject by repeatedly postponing marriage with Elizabeth,[16] the monster first insists that his creator must make him a mate who can assuage the "burning passion" that "consume[s]" him (144). Frankenstein agrees to the monster's demand but, typically, postpones the fulfilment of his promise, although he imagines that the monster's persecutions will cease once a mate has been created for him.

Frankenstein delusively envisions the "one consolation for [his] unparalleled sufferings [as] the prospect of that day when, enfranchised from [his] miserable slavery, [he] might claim Elizabeth, and *forget the past* in [his] union with her" (153; my emphasis). But the past that Frankenstein wishes to forget has a longer history than he imagines, for it includes the first appearance of Elizabeth in his life as the child who displaced his mother's affections, and her later illness, which occasioned his mother's death. Furthermore, as Berman discusses, a close reading of the entire family history according to Frankenstein reveals that it is in fact a highly romanticized, "massive falsification of reality" and that Frankenstein's narcissism and anger can be traced quite logically to deficient parenting on the part of both mother and father (65–69).

Frankenstein is unconsciously in league with his enemy, whom he begins to call a "daemon" after William's murder (76),[17] and there are many indications that he will be aiding his creature by "setting up" the murders of Elizabeth and his closest friend Henry Clerval. Frankenstein's reasoning about his decision to leave his family again and travel to England with Clerval strongly suggests this unconscious collaboration with the monster. Frankenstein speaks of his concern that during his absence he would be leaving his friends "unconscious of the existence of their enemy, and unprotected from his attacks"; but he states that because the creature "promised" to follow him wherever he went, he felt fairly sure that the monster would keep his word: "through the whole period during which I was the slave of my creature, I allowed myself to be governed by the impulses of the moment; and my present sensations strongly intimated that the fiend would follow me, and exempt my family from the danger of his machinations" (153). He claims that he remained in a state of intense anxiety about his family's welfare while he postponed the fulfilment of his promise to the monster for "some time" (161). This period actually adds up to about one year—a delay that could only intensify the monster's frustration and anger.

Frankenstein also declares that he was concerned during this time that the life of his friend, Henry Clerval, might be in jeopardy: "Sometimes I thought that the fiend followed me, and might expedite my remissness by murdering my companion. When these thoughts possessed me, I would not quit Henry for a moment, but followed him as his shadow, to protect him from the fancied rage of his destroyer" (162). Then, with no apparent recognition of the contradiction in his account, he states that he decided to go off alone to make a mate for the monster, leaving his friend unprotected with friends in Perth.

At this point, however, Frankenstein comes very close to acknowledging his complicity with the monster: "I felt as if I had committed some great crime, the consciousness of which haunted me. I was guiltless, but I had indeed drawn down a horrible curse upon my head, as mortal as that of crime" (162). Here he demonstrates the "powerful consciousness of guilt" that Rank has shown to be one of the most typical features of the double motif in literature. Rank argues that it is the uncomfortable awareness of guilt "which forces the hero no longer to accept the responsibility for certain actions of his ego, but to place it upon another ego, a double." The guilt may arise from various sources, but generally it "measures on the one hand the distance between the ego-ideal and the attained reality, [while] on the other, it . . . creates strong tendencies toward self-punishment, which also imply suicide" (76).

Frankenstein has another sudden but brief recognition of identity with his persecutor, after he has destroyed the nearly finished mate (while the enraged monster looks on) and been confronted with the corpse of his friend. He exclaims, "Have my murderous machinations deprived you also, my dearest Henry, of life? Two I have already destroyed; other victims await their destiny" (176). He suffers an emotional collapse, prolonged by his conviction that "*I had unchained an enemy* among [my fellow beings], whose joy it was to shed their blood, and to revel in their groans" (185; my emphasis). He declares to his father that William, Justine, and Henry all died "by [his] hands" and by his "machinations" (185, 186). His repeated use of the word *machinations* to describe both the monster's and his own activities provides yet another indicator of the secret alliance between himself and his creation.

The fact that such moments of truth "burst uncontrollably" (185) from Frankenstein indicates the great energy of the unconscious movement toward a conscious recognition of the truth, despite the resistance put up by the ego. But at this point the ego's resistance hardens; when his father dismisses his statements as symptoms of temporary mental derangement, Frankenstein does little to dispel that idea. Ironically, the excuse he offers for not telling the truth is that people would think him insane.

The division between his conscious and unconscious awareness becomes strengthened again after he agrees to marry Elizabeth, in a final effort to achieve some semblance of normality in his life. This self-division only aggravates his unease. At this point, rather than speaking outright about his guilt, he is plagued by a feeling of anxiety and "prophetic" doom (191), as if he dimly understands that his life has already become one of "sterility and failure" (Keily 169) and that he has lost all hope of creating new life, even in the conventional way of having children and raising a family with Elizabeth.

As Frankenstein's account reveals, his double now actively assists him in maintaining his self-deception: "[A]s if possessed of magic powers, the monster had blinded me to his real intentions; and when I thought that I had prepared only my own death, I hastened that of a far dearer victim" (191). On his wedding night he once again leaves the victim unprotected, sending Elizabeth to the bedroom alone while he wanders through the hallways with his ineffectual phallic pistol in hand and leaving his monstrous double free to do the "dirty work."

There is unmistakable irony in Frankenstein's statement that when he heard Elizabeth scream, "the whole truth rushed into [his] mind" (195)—for he never does discover the whole truth, either about his actual relation with the monster or about his own neurotic fears and wishes. Only after he finds Elizabeth dead, "thrown across the bed," and then recovers from his fainting spell can he "[rush] towards her, and [embrace] her with ardour" (196), having been spared from the "dreadful" (194) experience of sexual consummation. As well, as Mellor has suggested, the sight of the dead Elizabeth arouses in Frankenstein his deepest desire, "to possess the dead female, the lost mother" ("Possessing" 225).[18]

The idea that the psychodynamics traced so carefully in *Frankenstein* point to a larger concern with social injustice has been argued by Baldick, who demonstrates the "strict . . . causal logic" of the situation. He says that "the monster's condition [is] an exact mirror image of Victor's divorce from social bonds," with the difference that "Victor's solitude is voluntary and the monster's is enforced" (52):

> Victor's case of deferred gratification in his abstinent withdrawal from Elizabeth into his researches reflects clearly that general exchange of sexual for artistic or scientific fulfilments which Freud saw as the necessary price of cultural achievement. *Frankenstein* seems to formulate a law of psychic economy (essentially that of the return of the repressed) according to which the cost of sublimation has to be paid in an equal and opposite brutalization. It is of this cost, perhaps, that the monster's outrages are designed to remind us. (50)

One could say that just as Frankenstein is guilty of "monstrous empathic failure" (Berman 56), so was Mary Shelley's society, and that more generally, periods of rapid technological and commercial expansion may be times when such narcissistic personalities flourish,

> personalities . . . presenting excessive self-absorption usually coinciding with a superficially smooth and effective social adaptation, but with serious distortions in their internal relationships with other people. They present various combinations of intense ambitiousness, grandiose fantasies . . . and overdependence on external admiration and acclaim. Along with . . . continuous search for gratification of strivings for brilliance, wealth, power and beauty, there are serious deficiencies in their capacity to love and to be concerned about others. (Kernberg 264)[19]

Mary Shelley may have been thinking of *Frankenstein* a year before the revised edition appeared, when in an 1830 letter to Robert Owen she drew a comparison between national and individual characters, with reference to the then-popular system of phrenology: "I wonder if Nations have *bumps* [*sic*] well as individuals" (*Letters* 2: 122).

The reason Frankenstein gives for making his creature so monstrous (in the sense of larger than average) is that he does not want to waste valuable time dealing with the "minuteness of the parts" (53–54). His frantic haste and its terrible consequences can be correlated to England's headlong rush into industrial manufacture. The first steam engines were of enormous size for similar reasons; for fifty years before Jeremy Watt developed a smaller version, "modern technology meant huge, clumsy mechanical monsters dotting the landscape" (Tropp 34).

Similarly, Frankenstein's evasion of familial responsibility, undervaluing of family life, and avoidance of the domestic sphere associated with women can be correlated to the attitude of the ruling paternalistic elite, whose policies eschewed any recognition of a human community transcending class, and favored the demands of the emerging market economy over the familial needs of the lower classes.

Public debate over the enfranchisement of the propertyless working class had been a heated, even an incendiary, issue both when Shelley was first writing *Frankenstein* and when she was revising it for the 1831 edition. At the later time, despite her trepidation about social disorder, she still referred to the elite as "Aristocrats" and "Autocrats" who should "have the good sense to make the necessary sacrifices to a starving people" (*Letters* 2: 124, 120). A number of the revisions she made in the later edition serve to strengthen the social criticism in *Frankenstein*. The commercial attitude, for example, is more sharply attacked in the later version's reference to Henry Clerval's father as a "narrow-minded trader" (44), whereas in the early version he was simply a man who thought that "learning was superfluous in the commerce of ordinary life" (1818 version 22).[20]

Particularly, Shelley's revisions with regard to her characterization of Robert Walton, the frame narrator, serve to strengthen the impression that Frankenstein's madness is not an isolated phenomenon. Whereas in the 1818 version Walton seems to be a somewhat more balanced and humane individual than Frankenstein, in the later version he more directly replicates Frankenstein's weaknesses. It is only in the later version that Frankenstein cries, "Do you share my madness?" (28). As the man who listens to and then writes down Frankenstein's story, Walton plays the part of the echo in more than one way, for he also echoes or duplicates Frankenstein's narcissistic preoccupation with his personal ambitions. The changes serve to clarify Frankenstein's symbolic role as a symptom rather than an aberration of particular cultural conditions.

The novel's epistolary format dramatizes the two men's condition of being "away from home," both physically and psychologically. Walton's letters to his married sister back in England are, for all their affectionate effusiveness, nevertheless a long-distance form of communication, lacking immediacy in space and time. Aboard ship, Walton lives in an exclusively masculine world, and we never actually see any of his sister's letters to him. Her function seems merely to be the recipient of male news and ideas.

Walton has had little feminine influence in his life aside from that of his sister, having lost both his parents at an early age and been raised by an uncle (16). In the 1831 version only, Walton pays tribute to his sister for her important feminine tutelage: A "youth passed in solitude, my best years spent under your gentle and feminine fosterage, has so refined the groundwork of my character, that I cannot overcome an intense distaste to the usual brutality exercised on board ship" (20). Yet like Frankenstein he develops a burning desire to "accomplish some great purpose," which compels him to distance himself physically from the source of his original nurturing and from human companionship (1818 version 10; 1831 version 17).

In both versions Walton sees himself, like Frankenstein, as a scientific discoverer who will uncover nature's secrets for the benefit of humanity. He imagines that in his voyage to the Arctic he "may there discover the wondrous power which attracts the needle; and may regulate a thousand celestial observations, that require only this voyage to render their seeming eccentricities consistent for ever," thereby conferring "inestimable benefit . . . on all mankind to the last generation" (1818 version 7; 1831 version 16). The later version, however, adds a statement of faith in the power of his individual will that more forcefully establishes the themes of self-inflation and desire for mastery over nature: "But success *shall* crown my endeavours. Wherefore not? Thus far I have gone, tracing a secure way over the pathless seas: the very stars themselves being witnesses and testimonies of my triumph. Why not still proceed over the untamed yet obedient element? What can stop the determined heart and resolved will of man?" (23). His blind optimism can be taken as a reflection of the attitude commonly expressed by England's captains of industry during this time, on a "ship of state" sailing blithely toward dangerous waters.

The later version also intensifies the impression that Walton's quest has an obsessional quality similar to Frankenstein's. In the earlier version, when writing of his conversations with Frankenstein, Walton recounts only how he admitted to the stranger his great desire for a friend who would "complete" him, thus articulating the principle that Frankenstein forgets, that no man is an island. In the later version, however, Walton confides with "fervour" to Frankenstein how much his project means to him, revealing "the burning ardour of [his] soul": "[H]ow gladly I would sacrifice my fortune, my existence, my every hope, to the furtherance of my enterprise" (28).

The 1831 version also highlights Walton's self-contradiction in a way that the 1818 version does not: a contradiction revealing that, like Frankenstein, he is unaware of how driven he actually is by an inner compulsion. He twice assures his sister that he will be prudent: "I shall do nothing rashly: you know me sufficiently to confide in my prudence and considerateness, whenever the safety of others is committed to my care"; "I will be cool, persevering, and prudent" (1818 version 10, 11; 1831 version 21, 23). Yet in the later version he also writes about telling Frankenstein that "[o]ne man's life or death were but a small price to pay for the acquirement of the knowledge which I sought; for the dominion I should acquire and transmit over the elemental foes of our race" (28).

Above all, Walton appears to be as oblivious as Frankenstein is to the many contradictions in the latter's history that indicate, as Richard J. Dunn has commented, that it is in fact one of "consumptive egoism" (412–13). Walton believes that despite the "wildness" and "madness" he discerns in Frankenstein's eyes, he also detects a "beam of [extraordinary] benevolence and sweetness" and comes to regard the man as "the brother of [his] heart" (1818 version 13, 14; 1831 version 25, 27). What is simply admiration in the early version, however, becomes infatuation in the later one, with the addition of the following comment:

> Sometimes I have endeavoured to discover what quality it is which he possesses, that elevates him so immeasurably above any other person I ever knew. I believe it to be an intuitive discernment; a quick but never-failing power of judgement; a penetration into the causes of things, unequalled for clearness and precision; add to this a facility of expression, and a voice whose varied intonations are soul-subduing music. (29)

His blind adulation of Frankenstein is due partly to his sense of identification with the man and partly to his own desperate need for human companionship. Having exiled himself from society, Walton expresses regret for the lack of it: "I have one want which I have never yet been able to satisfy. . . . I have no friend" (1818 version 19; 1831 version 19).

Dunn has also pointed out that as narrators both Walton and Frankenstein reveal a distinct lack of "reflective powers" (413) and that overall the concentric narrative structure of *Frankenstein* demonstrates a failure in communication and understanding, as part of a larger "failure of human community" (408). One could add to this observation that the "community" fails mainly because it does not include women and children.

The ending of the novel repudiates both Frankenstein's and Walton's asocial ambitions. The crew remains uninfluenced by Frankenstein's efforts to inspire them to continue journeying north into the barren wastes of the Arctic, and under threat of mutiny compels Walton to return his ship of discovery back "home" to England. There is no final, definitive narrative disclosure that reveals all; the reader must be content, as Frankenstein never is, to accept some mystery. There is no sure basis for either optimism or pessimism. After witnessing Frankenstein's death and the creature being "born away by the waves, and lost in the darkness and distance" (223), Walton continues to "[waft] toward England," and toward his sister (215). Whether he will ever learn what Frankenstein has failed to understand is a question that remains open.

Relatively few critics have examined *Frankenstein*'s relevance to historically specific political and socioeconomic concerns[21] or what bearing its psychological themes might have on these issues; yet Shelley's own record of her reading before and during her writing of *Frankenstein* gives ample indication of the multilayered perception informing the novel. Following her father, Shelley was in the habit of reading several books at the same time (Mellor, *Mary* 11), and her journals show that she often read a combination of different types of works: political, scientific, classical, poetic, and fictional (including a great deal of Gothic fiction), as well as works on educational theory.

Baldick has called attention to Shelley's political concerns, showing that the monster can be traced to "that venerable cliché of political discourse, the 'body politic'. When political discord and rebellion appear, this 'body' is said to be not just diseased, but misshapen, abortive, monstrous" (14); "[t]he fragmented society, the patchwork or clockwork individual—these become the themes of Romantic social analysis from Schiller through

Carlyle and beyond" (35). He points out that the monster's ugliness, apparent not just to Frankenstein, but to everyone, dramatizes the political question of "the relation of parts to wholes" (33–34).

The part of English society most severely afflicted by industrialism was the disenfranchised poor, whose plight is signified in the monster's first acts of violence: the destruction of a family dwelling and the killing of a child. The former involves his destruction of "every vestige of cultivation" in the garden around the De Lacey cottage (138).

It is not surprising that in subsequent stage adaptations of *Frankenstein*, however widely the production diverged from the original source, the burning of the cottage was almost always retained (Nitchie 392), for the monster's action symbolizes the situation of the working class during this period, when enclosure of common land was accelerating. According to Frank Darvall, "3,110,000 acres [were] converted from common field tillage between 1800 and 1820 as against a total of only 3,400,000 in the preceding 40 years from 1760 to 1800" (15–16); industry was beginning "to draw its workers into factories and to the town, destroy[ing] the old partnership between industry and agriculture whereby the village craftsman was also a small cultivator in the village fields, with a cow and pigs on the common pasture, and the village labourer also, in the winter or in his wife's spare time, a spinner of wool or a knitter of lace and stockings" (17). As Darvall notes, the situation "created a great ferment of opinion in the country, a range of new and often unrecognized problems" (17), not the least of which was widespread hunger. Compounding the problem were the crop failures that occurred from 1809 to 1812; rising prices and falling exports due to the war and the closing off of the American market; the financial panic of 1810, when banks failed and there were a large number of commercial and industrial bankruptcies; and the reduction of wages and the demand for labor in certain industries because of earlier overexpansion. According to one report, in 1812 one-fifth of the population of Lancashire required charitable relief (Darvall 20).

The dilemma of the struggling laborers whose wages were less and less sufficient to support them was exacerbated by the fact that they had less opportunity to maintain the small gardens around their cottages or to keep the pigs or cows that formerly would have given them a subsidiary income. Along with this loss, "industry, with its declining earnings, was making year by year greater demands upon its workmen" (Darvall 32).

It was also making greater demands upon England's children, as some citizens were realizing and as Mary Shelley's circle was keenly aware. One practice that was beginning to arouse some limited criticism at the beginning of the century was that of indenturing young children who were orphaned or whose families were too poor to support them. Local parish officers would "put the children out" to serve as apprentices for a specified number of years, very often in factories located so far away that it was impossible for those who still had parents to maintain any physical contact with them. According to the 1814 through 1815 "Parish Apprentices Report,"

> There are, without doubt, instances of Masters, who in some degree compensate to Children for the estrangement which frequently takes place at a very early age from their parents, and from the nurses and women in the Workhouses of London, and who pay due and proper attention to the health, education, and moral and religious conduct of their Apprentices; but these exceptions to the general rule by no means shake the Opinion of Your Committee as to the general impolicy of such a system. (Qtd. in Pike 98)

The recommendation of the committee was that a fixed limit be established as to the distance from home the children might be "put out."

The majority of children working in the "manufactories," and particularly those who had no parents nearby to defend them, were subject to the vagaries of their masters, some of whom treated them humanely, but many of whom subjected the children to harassment, flogging, and other forms of physical abuse. As one adult survivor put it, "The beautiful and romantic valleys of Derbyshire, Nottinghamshire, and Lancashire, secluded from the public eye, became the dismal solitudes of torture, and of many a murder" (Pike 78; citing John Fielden, *The Curse of the Factory System*, 1836). As well, many children suffered physical injury and mutilation by being caught in the machines, which happened more frequently at the end of their long workday, when some of the exhausted ones would fall asleep on their feet.

Against this social background, the monster's second act of destruction—the killing of little William—and the exchange between him and the child which precedes it, comes into high relief. When the monster first approaches William and claims that he means no harm, the child replies:

> "Let me go," he cried; "monster! ugly wretch! you wish to eat me, and tear me to pieces—You are an ogre—Let me go, or I will tell my papa."
>
> "'Boy, you will never see your father again: you must come with me."

"'Hideous monster! let me go. My papa is a Syndic—he is M. Frankenstein—he will punish you. You dare not keep me.'

"'Frankenstein! you belong then to my enemy—to him towards whom I have sworn eternal revenge; you shall be my first victim.'" (142)

The scene reveals not only the absolute directness and even cruelty of which young children are capable, but also—and what is more important—the truth of what the monster really "means," in the sense of both what he symbolically represents at this point and what he will actually do.[22]

William's confidence that his social privilege will protect him from the monster's destruction proves to be unfounded. In a state of rage and despair, the monster strangles the boy to death. The emphasis given to William's superior social position in this scene seems to suggest an implicit criticism of England's aristocratic elite, who throughout most of the eighteenth and early nineteenth centuries believed that a large body of "industrious poor" was necessary for the maintenance of the nation's health and stability (Harth 138) and who failed to recognize that the social inequity they favored was itself a source of instability.

Evidence of Shelly's own feelings about the mistreatment and abandonment of children can be found in an essay she wrote on Rousseau. A seemingly disproportionate amount of the essay is devoted to the fact that Rousseau had forced his common-law wife to give up at birth the five children she bore him and leave them at a local foundling hospital where, Shelley noted, "few survive; and those who do go through life are brutified by their situation, or depressed by the burden, ever weighing at the heart, that they have not inherited the commonest right of humanity, a parent's care." Shelley went on to compare Rousseau's "kindly-seeming society [to] a Moloch, whom to pacify, little children were ruthlessly sacrificed," and she added that "the whole system takes a revolting and criminal aspect from which we turn with loathing" (qtd. in O'Rourke 545–46, 547).[23]

The monster's declaration that his murder of little William was only the beginning of the revenge he would wreak also indirectly prophesies the far-reaching destructive effects of industrialization. He recounts that his heart swelled "with exultation and hellish triumph" as he gazed on his dead victim, and he cried, "I, too, can create desolation: my enemy is not invulnerable; this death will carry despair to him, and a thousand other miseries shall torment and destroy him" (143).

As mentioned previously, however, the monster's symbolism is multivalent; he plays the role of both victimizer and victim. He is the

destructive force of industrialization; he is a monstrous nation; he is an enraged citizen; he is Victor's shadow; and he is a needy, abandoned child. He
not only inflicts pain and devastation on the innocent and vulnerable, but
he also demonstrates the moral and spiritual degradation that follows upon
the frustration of basic human and developmental needs. Rejected from
human community, unable to exercise the benevolent impulses inculcated
in him by his observation of the De Laceys and with which he initially approached others, barred from creating or constructing anything of his own
making, he exercises power in the only manner left to him: "I, too, can
create / desolation."

A similar condition of frustration leading to moral degeneration prevailed in many of the mills and factories in early industrial England, which
were infamous for the violent and dissolute behavior of their workers. A
government report that came out fifteen years after the first publication of
Frankenstein stated that in one mill the "appearance and language of the
workers, after the bacchanalian orgies of the previous evening . . . proved
the state of demoralization which exists here"—a situation that extended
to the lives of the younger employees who shared accommodation in the
mill with the older ones: "[I]t was painful to find in the bothy, the eating
and sleeping room of such a nest of profligates, two or three young females
without a parent or relation there or in the neighbourhood to look after
their conduct, or to make any attempt to rescue them" (Report of the Central Board: Factories Commission, P.P. 1833; Pike 64). The reporter described the place as resembling more "a receptacle of demons than the
workhouse of industrious human beings."

Working conditions were just as abysmal in the mines of industrial
England, and the extensiveness of mining activity in this period provides
another example of the profound attitudinal shift that had taken place since
the time of the Reformation. According to Carolyn Merchant, before the
modern (post-Renaissance) age, mining had long been regarded as "an
abuse of [the] mother, the earth," even in the relatively pragmatic Roman
civilization. This view "served as a cultural constraint. . . . One does not
readily slay a mother, dig into her entrails for gold or mutilate her body":

> For most traditional cultures, minerals and metals ripened in the uterus of
> the Earth Mother, mines were compared to her vagina, and metallurgy was
> the human hastening of the birth of the living metal in the artificial womb

of the furnace. . . . Miners offered propitiation to the deities of the soil and subterranean world, performed ceremonial sacrifices, and fasting before violating the sacredness of the living earth by sinking a mine. (3, 4)

Merchant cites Pliny (A.D. 23–79) as saying that earthquakes are "expressions of the indignation felt by our sacred parent" at being violated by men's excavation of her ores (30). But with the advent of new technologies related to the growth of commercialism and industrialization, this view, along with its ethical restrictions, lost its authority (2).[24]

When staying with friends in Scotland in 1813, Mary Shelley was taken into the lower depths of a coal mine as a practical joke by one of her father's colleagues (Sunstein 60). It seems unlikely that the impressionable young teenager would have forgotten the sight, which may in turn have influenced her portrayal of Frankenstein's labors.

Frankenstein states that during the time of his efforts to manufacture a living creature, he "appeared rather like one doomed by slavery to toil in the mines, or any other unwholesome trade, than an artist occupied by his favourite employment" (56). His analogy again brings to mind the situation of England's laborers, whose physical and emotional health was being sacrificed in "unwholesome trades" in the name of national prosperity, while England was rapidly becoming the world's industrial leader.

The word *labour(ed)* appears four times in chapter 4, where Frankenstein describes his efforts to manufacture a living creature. According to the *OED,* the use of the word *labour* to denote childbirth was current in the Renaissance, and in the Middle Ages it was used to denote physical exertion. Not until Adam Smith's *Wealth of Nations* was it used to denote the physical work of laborers and artisans as a kind of commodity that provided the material wants of the community. In Shelley's depiction of the monster's creation, all three meanings seem to apply.

Frankenstein describes his project in terms of invasion and penetration, which suggest a masculine assault on an implicitly feminine natural world: "I pursued nature to her hiding-places. Who shall conceive the horrors of my secret toil, as I dabbled among the unhallowed damps of the grave. . . . I . . . disturbed, with profane fingers, the tremendous secrets of the human frame" (54–55). The passage is dense with feminine imagery: the word "conceive" connoting birth and conception; female nature's "hiding-places" and "damps of the grave" suggesting the age-old womb/tomb association with the earth as Mother.

Frankenstein's language also reveals his desire to usurp the feminine power of biological creation, to eliminate its duality and bypass the womb:

"The moon gaze[s] on [his] midnight labours" as he strives to emulate, in his "workshop of filthy creation," a woman in labor, giving birth (54). He later uses the term *labour* to describe his effort to construct a female mate for the monster, in a manner that again accentuates the contrast between the woman's "natural" and his own "unnatural" creation: "as I proceeded in my labour, it became every day more horrible and irksome to me. . . . It was, indeed, a filthy process in which I was engaged" (164). At the point where his "labour [is] considerably advanced" (164), he decides to destroy his work.

The moon—symbol of cyclically recurring feminine biology—is repeatedly referred to in these scenes as a kind of witness to Frankenstein's perversion of the natural. After gazing on Frankenstein's midnight labors, the moon then "force[s] its way through the window shutters" of his bedroom so that Frankenstein can see by its "dim and yellow light" the creature to whom he has given life, attempting to communicate with him (58). Later, when he destroys the nearly completed female, he sees "by the light of the moon, [his] daemon at the casement" (166).

The Greek moon goddess Artemis was the patroness of childbirth and had the power to bless or curse the outcome of a woman's labor; her beneficence usually depended on whether she had been sufficiently honored and appropriately propitiated. But Frankenstein is an irreligious skeptic in whose "education [his] father had taken the greatest precautions that [his] mind should be impressed with no supernatural horrors." He claims that he had never "trembled at a tale of superstition, or . . . feared the apparition of a spirit" and that "[d]arkness had no effect upon [his] fancy" (51). Thus, Frankenstein's assault on feminine nature is also presented as a "profane" desecration of *hallowed* ground. Shelley's personal sense of the sacred feminine is suggested in a journal entry made a few weeks after the death of her first baby: "Day of our Lady—the virgin Mary Mother of God" (72).

Mellor has commented that in his effort to eliminate women's "primary biological function," Frankenstein is actually trying to create "a society for men only" ("Possessing" 220). It is also a society without the young children who belong to the female sphere, and therefore it is a society with no future. However, the "men only" world that Frankenstein desires is not just a neurotic fantasy, for it was already being created in Shelley's England, where women were still disallowed any legal control over their own or their children's lives. In the case of lower-class women especially, their one refuge, the family, was being eroded by the demands of an industrial economy ruled by men.

But as Mellor also observes, in the case of Victor Frankenstein's violations, female Nature wreaks her revenge "with the very electricity he has stolen:

lightning, thunder, and rain rage around him" ("Possessing" 227). Nature also inflicts on him madness, physical collapse, and, finally, an early death.

Frankenstein's critique of women's place in society has attracted the attention of numerous feminist critics, many of whom have emphasized the important role Shelley's parents played in shaping her egalitarian values. Shelley acknowledges her debt to William Godwin's *Political Justice,* which she mentions along with *Caleb Williams* in her dedication of *Frankenstein* to Godwin. Throughout her life Shelley also identified with her absent mother, both imaginatively and intellectually. Wollstonecraft's *Historical and Moral View of the French Revolution,* discussed previously, as well as her *Vindication of the Rights of Woman* (1794) both strongly influenced Shelley's thought. Lee Sterrenburg points out, for example, that Wollstonecraft's perception in the *French Revolution* of how "[o]ppression breeds parricidal monsters" is also a concern in *Frankenstein* (163).

Yet Shelley also independently re-evaluated many of her parents' ideas and reworked them as she developed her own more mythic response to the problems of her day. She also incorporated into *Frankenstein* ideas from other contemporary political works. As James O'Rourke comments, there is currently a "growing body of [critical] literature that is demonstrating the mastery with which Mary Shelley negotiated the dominant intellectual currents of her time" (566).[25]

A particularly informative case in point is Volney's *Ruins of Empires,* to which Shelley draws attention when she makes this the first book from which the monster learns when listening to Felix De Lacey teach Safie the English language. In turn, *Frankenstein*'s immediate social relevance becomes clearer when one considers the numerous similarities between Volney's and Shelley's depictions of social injustice.

The *Ruins* was first published in 1791; its author, Count Constantin François Volney (1757–1820), was a moderate French revolutionary who was later jailed (for ten months) for his opposition to the excesses of the Reign of Terror. The bulk of the *Ruins* takes the form of a disquisition on history and moral philosophy addressed by a ghostly phantom, or "Genius," to the narrator, who has traveled to foreign lands to view the remnants of ancient civilizations. The primary argument of the *Ruins* is that social justice is derived from basic "physical laws of the human heart" and that whenever those laws are persistently violated, social and cultural decline inevitably follow (53).

Given that the *Ruins* was "a best seller which was to be reprinted many times for a generation," and more specifically that Shelley's husband Percy "adored" the work while William Godwin objected to its style, it seems reasonable to assume that Mary Shelley was familiar with it (St. Clair 37, 340, 529 n. 6). The impassioned rhetoric of both Frankenstein and his monster and some of the phrasing they use bear such a strong resemblance to Volney's bombastic style that their speeches sometimes seem to constitute an indirect allusion to Volney's ideas. Upon viewing the ancient ruins at Palmyra, for instance, Volney's speaker laments, "Ah! what are become of those ages of abundance and of life? . . . *Great God! whence proceed such fatal revolutions?* . . . Ah! hapless man, said I, in my grief, *a blind fatality sports with thy destiny! A fatal necessity* rules with the hand of chance the lot of mortals!" (24, 26; my emphasis). "Fatal necessity" is a phrase that Frankenstein is also fond of using. According to Volney, "Fatality is the universal and rooted prejudice of the East: It was written, is there the answer to everything: hence result an unconcern and apathy the most powerful impediments to instruction and civilization" (26 n.). Challenging this view, the spectral Genius of History criticizes the notion that "a blind fatality dispenses good and evil on the earth" and that prudence and wisdom cannot guard against it (29). Although Shelley might agree with the idea that Fortune can be blind and indiscriminate, it seems that in Frankenstein's case, his "fatality" is primarily the consequence of his own blindness.

The Genius then provides a somewhat Hobbesian view of primitive existence that strongly resembles the monster's account of his own personal history: his growth in awareness from a confused, disordered flux of sensory impressions to a consciousness of the world, and of himself as a distinct entity in it (102–115).[26] Volney's account also stresses ideas that are central to *Frankenstein:* the importance of the external environment in influencing mental growth, and the need for human community. The Genius states that at first, "formed naked both in body and mind, man found himself thrown, as it were by chance, on a confused and savage land; an orphan, *abandoned by the unknown power that produced him,* he saw no supernatural beings at hand to warn him of those wants which arise only from his sense, or to instruct him in those duties which spring only from his wants" (37; my emphasis). Similarly, the monster finds himself "desolate" in the forest near Ingolstadt after leaving the apartment already abandoned by Frankenstein—"a poor, helpless, miserable wretch" exposed to the elements from which he has not yet learned to protect himself (103).

Volney's Genius goes on to say that like other animals,

without experience of the past, *without foresight* of the future, [man] wandered in the depth of the forest, guided only and governed by the affections of his nature; by the pain of hunger he was led to seek food, and provide for his subsistence; by the inclemency of the air he was urged to cover his body, and he made him clothes. (37; my emphasis)

The monster too wanders in the depth of the forest, and as he recounts, "No distinct ideas occupied my mind; all was confused. I felt light, and hunger, and thirst, and darkness." He also feels the cold, until he finds a cloak with which to cover himself (103).

In the Genius's account, human intelligence was first stimulated by physical necessity: "the impressions which [man] received from every object, awakening his faculties, developed, by degrees, his understanding, and began to instruct his profound ignorance; his wants excited industry, dangers formed his courage; he learned to distinguish useful from noxious plants, to combat the elements . . . to defend his life; and he thus alleviated its miseries" (37). The monster also learns to distinguish "the insect from the herb, and, by degrees, one herb from another." As well, one day he discovers a fire left behind by some wanderers, and eventually learns by trial and error how to make one himself (104).

The next stage of development, according to the Genius, was to discover the advantages of community: "Wandering in woods . . . the first men, beset with dangers, assailed by enemies, tormented by hunger . . . felt their own individual weakness; and impelled by a common need of safety . . . they united their resources and their strength . . . thus men associated to secure their existence, to augment their powers, to protect their enjoyments."(38) The monster similarly discovers first a hut, where he finds the earliest human-made food and drink (bread, cheese, milk, and wine) and then a village whose attractiveness and productivity appeal to him, until the villagers chase him away (106). After this incident, he discovers the De Lacey family and has the opportunity to observe surreptitiously, through a hole in the wall of the cottage, their frequent demonstrations of mutual sympathy, concern, and pleasure.

Volney's Genius applauds the creative impulse through which humanity has transcended the limitations of its original state: "Yes, creative man, receive my homage! thou hast measured the expanse of the heavens, calculated the volume of the stars, arrested the lightning in its clouds, subdued seas and storms, subjected all the elements. Ah! how are so many sublime energies allied to so many errors!" (37–38). Upon hearing Felix read Volney's work, the monster repeats this last question in his own words: "Was man, indeed, at once so powerful, so virtuous, and magnificent, yet so vicious and base? He appeared at one time a mere scion of the evil principle, and at another, as all that can be conceived of noble and godlike" (119).

The Genius offers an explanation of the rise and fall of civilizations, with a description of the flourishing phase which could be applied to conditions in Mary Shelley's England, with its rapidly increasing productivity and growing dominance in international trade:

> Productions increasing beyond consumption, the necessity of commerce was felt, and exchanges took place between people and people, which augmented their activity and reciprocal advantages. . . . [c]ertain countries . . . became emporiums of flourishing commerce, and seats of powerful domination. . . . The people, growing rich, applied their superfluity to works of common and public use. (45)

The Genius's depiction of the declining phase, invariably ushered in when the "spirit of egotism and usurpation" becomes ascendant, can also be related to the negative aspects of England's industrial and economic revolution.[27]

Volney's analysis of the conditions that trigger cultural decline closely correspond to the state of affairs in England, where the visible growth in national "prosperity" was obscuring an actual decline in social equity. The Genius declares that whether in the form of aristocracy, theocracy, or monarchy (48), the few have exploited the many on the selfish premise that "they shall labor for us, and we will enjoy without labor" (40). Thus "millions of hands were employed in sterile labors" (50) and "[t]he art of governing became the art of subjecting the many to the few" (52). The Genius also criticizes the abuses of colonialism in a section that elicits tears of empathy from Frankenstein's "primitive" monster when he hears it (*Ruins* 175; *Frankenstein* 119).

While avoiding the spirit of self-congratulation that infected much eighteenth-century moral and political philosophy, the Genius nevertheless cautions against the opposite extreme of nostalgic primitivism: "Guard against the illusion and the paradoxes of the misanthrope: man, dissatisfied with the present, ascribes to the past a perfection which never existed" (66). Applauding human developments in science and technology, especially that of "the holy art of Printing" (68), he moves into prophetic mode, employing the utilitarian argument that "[man] will grow wise and good because it is [in his] interest to be so" (68): "Individuals will feel that private happiness is allied to public good. . . . And *when nations, free and enlightened, shall become like great individuals* . . . civilization will become universal" (69; my emphasis). If the fate of Shelley's Frankenstein is any indication, it would seem that she had little confidence in England's ability to sustain the economic affluence and international prestige that it was enjoying at the beginning of the nineteenth century.

The Genius states that in order for the day to come when citizens of nations will no longer be divided against one another, "man" must study the natural laws that govern him: "those laws, *the common source of good and evil,* . . . are at all times, and in all places, present to man; they act upon his senses, they warn his understanding, and dispense to every action its reward or punishment. Let man, then, study these laws! *let him comprehend his own nature*" (35; my emphasis). In her perceptive portrayal of Frankenstein's psychological imbalance, Shelley takes up Volney's argument that an understanding of the "natural laws" governing the human psyche is a prerequisite for any significant social improvement. However, her insight into those laws is far more penetrating than Volney's, partly because her work is more imaginative and less heavily optimistic and didactic. Rather than having a transcendent Genius imparting wisdom as Volney does, Shelley uses a misbegotten monster to show how far from the ideals expressed in works such as Volney's was the actual condition of life in England.

Another reason that Shelley's psychosocial analysis is so much more complex and astute than Volney's is her acute understanding of the importance of maternal nurturing in childhood development. She herself had grown up feeling like a motherless child; although her father remarried a few years after her mother, Mary Wollstonecraft, died, Mary did not have a filial bond with her stepmother, a forceful but tactless and not especially intelligent woman, and the two never got along smoothly. As a child, whenever Shelley was feeling depressed or discouraged, she would go visit her mother's grave. The understanding that her mother had died giving birth to her was reinforced by the annual family visit to Wollstonecraft's grave on September 10, just after Mary's birthday on August 30 (Sunstein 36, 34). It may be that some of her insight into Frankenstein's longing to rejoin his dead mother derived from her own personal experience.

In addition to the perception that her own maternal deprivation had taught her, Shelley had become acquainted with the trials and demands of motherhood herself by the time she started writing her novel. *Frankenstein* was strongly influenced by Shelley's personal experiences of motherhood in the preceding two years.[28] Her baby girl was born prematurely and died a few days later when Shelley was seventeen. Shelley wrote in her journal,

"Dream that my little baby came to life again—that it had only been cold
& that we rubbed it before the fire & it lived—I awake & find no baby—
I think about the little thing all day—not in good spirits" (70). When Shelley started writing her novel, she had a six-month-old baby (William) to
care for and was still legally unmarried; and for the last five months that
she was completing her book, she was pregnant again. But instead of seeing her situation as unique, Shelley "was able to expand her own personal
responses . . . into a compassionate study of an overly masculine society and
its offspring" (P. Scott 189).

In *Frankenstein,* the scene in which the monster kills little William is
one of the most disturbing and strongly prophetic moments in the novel.
The family breakdown and human suffering arising from the new industrial system, which in England did not begin to be addressed until after the
passing of the 1832 Reform Bill (one year after the revised edition appeared), has since been played out repeatedly in virtually all developing
industrial nations throughout the world.[29] Although the most technologically advanced nations today have achieved for the moment some balance
between social concerns and economic development, the "desolation" and
"despair" that Shelley's monster predicted (143) still characterize the life of
workers in many "developing" countries that have become manufacturing
centers for multinational corporations. Despite all the apparent advantages
of modern technology, the social horror that Shelley identified has not gone
away; it has simply shifted its locale.

CHAPTER SIX

The Descent of Man and the Anxiety of Upward Mobility: The Strange Case of Dr Jekyll and Mr Hyde

D r Jekyll and Mr Hyde, a Gothic horror story about a Victorian gentleman who lives a secret life of vice, appeared at a time when the problem of female prostitution had become the subject of much heated public controversy in England. Shortly before the autumn of 1885, when Stevenson dreamed of the "fine bogey tale" that inspired his novella, the *Pall Mall Gazette* (6–8, 10 July 1885) had published a sensational and widely read series of articles by W. T. Stead on child prostitution, the first three of which had been mailed to Stevenson by a friend (Walkowitz 283 n.39) and which claimed that the demand for child prostitutes, and especially for young virgins, was being stimulated by the sadistic tastes of a corrupt and callous class of well-to-do Victorian gentlemen. With its stress on upper-class depravity and hypocrisy, the piece may have paved the way for the strong public response to Stevenson's tale, first printed in an inexpensive "shilling shocker" edition in January 1886. Although Stevenson already had achieved some recognition for his earlier *Treasure Island* (published serially in 1881), *Dr Jekyll and Mr Hyde* was his first major popular success: "Within six months almost forty thousand copies were sold in England" (Wood 102).

The main events of the story occur within the closed circle of a group of upper-middle-class gentlemen and are related by a narrator who appears to share the men's urbanity and sophistication. The tale opens with a description of Mr. Utterson, a lawyer, and is presented largely from his perspective. Utterson becomes intrigued by a connection between his upright friend Dr. Henry Jekyll and a repulsive and disreputable character, Mr. Hyde. Mr. Richard Enfield, Utterson's "distant kinsman, the well-known man about town" (29), had late one night seen Hyde trample down a young girl; financial reparation to the girl's parents took the form of Hyde's going to Jekyll's home and emerging with a check signed in Jekyll's name.

The truth of the relationship between the two is that Hyde is Jekyll's double, a concretized shadow released by Jekyll when he found the hypocrisy of his life as public benefactor and private sinner to be increasingly uncomfortable. Through chemical experimentation, Jekyll discovered a potion that could transform him into a brute, governed wholly by his grosser appetites and untrammeled by the moral scruples that previously had troubled him. Over the course of time, however, Jekyll discovers that he can no longer control Hyde, whose actions become increasingly brutal and even murderous, and Jekyll/Hyde's life finally ends in suicide.

Both the *Pall Mall's* "The Maiden Tribute" and *Dr Jekyll and Mr Hyde* were "disturbing" to their readers, but in very different ways. Whereas "The Maiden Tribute" had the simple and straightforward aim of inciting feelings of righteous indignation, *Dr Jekyll and Mr Hyde* carried a subliminal message that the majority of Victorian readers were not yet prepared to acknowledge. Although most apparently recognized the novella's criticism of irresponsible upper-class sexual licence, none seemed able to appreciate either the concomitant critique of moralistic middle-class sexual repression or the overall condemnation of patriarchal power and privilege.

The corollary of that power and repression, the female sex trade, is evoked at the outset of *Dr Jekyll and Mr Hyde* in the description of the setting where Enfield tells Utterson about Hyde's trampling of the young girl. The two men are walking down "a by street in a busy quarter of London," which appears superficially to be a scene of healthy, bustling commercial activity. The implied metaphors, however, evoke a subliminal association with prostitution, the "low end" of capitalist self-promotion.

> The inhabitants were all doing well, it seemed, and all emulously hoping to do better still, and laying out the surplus of their gains in coquetry; so that the shop fronts stood along that thoroughfare with an air of invitation, like rows of smiling saleswomen. Even on Sunday, when it veiled its more florid

charms and lay comparatively empty of passage, the street shone out in contrast to its comparatively dingy neighbourhood, like a fire in a forest; and with its freshly painted shutters, well-polished brasses, and general cleanliness and gaiety of note, instantly caught and pleased the eye of the passenger. (30)

William Veeder has noted that this scene presages Hyde's later abusive treatment of a woman who offers him a "box of lights": "A woman who walks the streets late at night asking men if they need a light is offering quite another type of box. And Jekyll (and Stevenson's readers) know it" ("Children" 141).

Child prostitution in particular is obliquely suggested by Hyde's first act of violence, the trampling of the little girl, and by the manner in which the matter is "settled." Enfield's account (which as William Veeder has shown is considerably compromised by Enfield's inner complicity with Hyde; "Children" 141–42) is that he was returning home at three in the morning from one of his late-night rambles "some place at the end of the world," when he saw Hyde collide with a young girl "of maybe eight or ten," who was apparently running along the street "as hard as she was able" on the way home from fetching a doctor (31). Hyde "trampled calmly over the child's body and left her screaming on the ground." Enfield comments that "it was hellish to see. It wasn't like a man; it was like some damned Juggernaut." The term *Juggernaut,* which was commonly used to refer to something that destroyed anything that lay in its path, suggests a supra-individual force[1] and implies Hyde's symbolic role as the dark side of the male hegemony to which Utterson, Enfield, and Jekyll belong.

A group gathers around the screaming child, and Enfield struggles with the other men to keep the women, who are "wild as harpies," from executing their own form of primitive vengeance on Hyde (a form of justice predating the male-biased law of Victorian England; 32). The men succeed in arranging a more civilized punishment in the form of a pecuniary transaction—one hundred pounds, to be precise—after which agreement the doctor, the child's father, "my friend" Hyde, and Enfield leave the women to spend the rest of the night in Enfield's "chambers" until the banks open. Hyde's check proves "genuine," and the child's father evidently agrees with the rest of the men that one hundred pounds is adequate compensation for what was, in effect, the violation of his daughter's body (32).

Utterson is so disturbed by Enfield's story that he spends most of that night tossing to and fro on his "great, dark bed," replaying the original scene as Enfield related it, "in a scroll of lighted pictures":

He would be aware of the great field of lamps of a nocturnal city; then of the figure of a man walking swiftly; then of a child running from the doctor's; and then these met, and that human Juggernaut trod the child down and passed on regardless of her screams. . . . [I]f at any time he dozed over, it was but to see it . . . move the more swiftly, and still the more swiftly, even to dizziness, through wider labyrinths of lamp-lighted city, and at every street corner crush a child and leave her screaming. (37)

The vision of a crushed and screaming child that haunts Utterson is emblematic of the kind of rape that Stead had recently shown was being committed with impunity by numerous respectable members of Victorian society.

Female prostitution had been recognized as a serious social problem since the late 1850s, but the *Pall Mall* piece had brought it back into the foreground of public awareness. The specific issue of child prostitution had been somewhat obscured by public opposition to the Contagious Diseases Acts requiring mandatory examination of prostitutes for venereal disease, which had been implemented during the 1860s and finally repealed in 1886. A recent controversy over the clandestine exportation of young working-class Englishwomen to licensed Continental brothels had similarly deflected attention from the problems at home.

One episode that might have aroused widespread indignation about child prostitution, had it not been handled so expeditiously by the courts, was an investigation into the local Chelsea brothel of Mrs. Jeffries, a madame who provided "young girls to an upper-class clientele and catered to their sado-masochistic tendencies" (Gorham 360). The brothel "had been in business for twenty years across the road from a police station" (E. Bristow 106). It was also widely reported that among Mrs. Jeffries's customers were some of the very men who had in Parliament opposed raising the age of consent at which sexual congress with a child was legally permissible, from thirteen to sixteen (Gorham 361; also Nield).[2] Mrs. Jeffries's access to masculine power and influence seemed confirmed when at the trial "[b]efore any evidence could be produced, the defence pulled off what must have been a pre-arranged coup. Mrs Jeffries pleaded guilty to keeping a brothel, had her £200 fine paid by a wealthy friend and drove off in a brougham supplied by an earl" (E. Bristow 107).

When the problem was finally exposed in vivid detail in "The Maiden Tribute," however, the public reaction verged on mass hysteria. Although lending libraries such as W. H. Smith's refused to carry the paper, by "the third instalment mobs were rioting at the *PMG* offices in an attempt to obtain copies," and one and a half million reprints of "Maiden Tribute" were sold (E. Bristow 110–11). A number of public protest meetings were held as a direct result of Stead's article, and about six weeks after its publication these culminated in a large gathering, attended by a wide range of groups, including church supporters and radical socialists, at which the National Vigilance Association was formed. The next day, 22 August, an enormous crowd (up to 250,000 has been estimated; E. Bristow 112) gathered in Hyde Park to hear various speakers and demand political reform:

> With white roses for purity; with banners proclaiming 'Protection of Young Girls; Men, Protect the Girls of England; Women of London to the Struggle; War on Vice; Sir, Pity Us; Shame, Shame, Horror'; with tambourines, drums and fifes, ten columns set out for the park. . . . There were wagonloads of young virgins in white flying the pathetic oriflamme, 'The Innocents, Will They Be Slaughtered?' . . . Then there was the hero . . . 'perched on a wagon, proceeding as a conqueror' to shouts of 'Long Live Stead'. (E. Bristow 113)

The mood had all the fervor of an Evangelical revival meeting. An amused French observer recorded that upon Stead's arrival, "suddenly seized by a religious fit, the adepts, grouped around the orator or perched on the same vehicle, intoned a hymn or an anthem on national purity . . . to the role [*sic*] of the tambourines, the beating of the drum and the tune of the fifes, everyone was shaking, gesticulating and seemed suddenly taken up in a St. Vitus dance" (qtd. in E. Bristow 113–14).[3] All the while, however, "[h]awkers had a field day selling the pornographic magazine, *The Devil*" (E. Bristow 114).

Some of the men who had opposed changing the age of consent during the preceding decade had been quite forthright about their reasons for doing so, and their arguments revealed their utter indifference to the needs or concerns of the young working-class prostitutes who serviced them. One member of the House of Lords argued in 1884 that "very few of their Lordships . . . had not, when young men, been guilty of immorality. He hoped they would pause before passing a clause within the range of which their sons might come" (qtd. in Gorham 366).[4] Outside of this elite, however, there was in general a "growing sensitivity to the condition of children," signaled in part by the 1884 foundation of the Society for the Prevention of Cruelty to Children (E. Bristow 92), and Stead's exposé provided the final impetus for overcoming the objections to raising the age of consent. About four months after the Hyde Park demonstration, on 1 January 1886, the Criminal Law Amendment Act, popularly called "Stead's Act," was passed, raising the minimum age of consent to sixteen (Gorham 354).

However, the business of prostitution was not confined to an exclusively aristocratic clientele. For many decades, the self-civilizing spirit had been exceptionally strong in England, and the political and economic influence of a diverse, enterprising middle class was growing. Prostitution was in part stimulated by the "'over-strained prudence' [which] postponed middle-class marriages until such time as increasing requirements of property and social standing were assured" (Nield [iv])[5] There was a "common equation of sexual continence with economic success," but it was generally accepted that this situation necessitated a limited degree of clandestine sexual freedom for men (Nield [iv]). Female prostitution had been one of the great self-contradictions of Victorian life—publicly condemned but tacitly tolerated and even encouraged.

Stead was explicit about the economic inequity that gave rise to the abuses of prostitution, "which [are] nightly levied in London by the vices of the rich upon the necessities of the poor" (2), but as Deborah Gorham has discussed, the majority of reformers tended to focus on the moral rather than the economic context of the problem and failed to recognize how it reflected a profound division of privilege within their social world. This division had been identified much earlier in a well-known passage in Disraeli's *Sybil* (1845), where one of the characters responds to another's declaration that England is "the greatest nation that ever existed," by asserting that it is in fact

> [t]wo nations; between whom there is no intercourse and no sympathy; who are as ignorant of each other's habits, thoughts, and feelings, as if they were dwellers in different zones, or inhabitants of different planets; who are formed by a different breeding, are fed by a different food, are ordered by different manners, and are not governed by the same laws. . . . THE RICH AND THE POOR. (96)

The economic separation between the "haves" and the "have-nots," which continued to be maintained both psychologically[6] and geographically in late Victorian England, was disturbed by the unavoidable fact of prostitution. As Keith Nield describes the situation in London,

> [T]he prostitute was a leading edge of the feared intrusion of the "night side" of the city into fashionable and respectable life. . . . A middle-class demand for casual prostitution, and a predominantly working-class supply of prostitutes, continuously produced relationships which crossed that profound

class barrier, the mutual invisibility which, as Engels observed of Manchester in 1844, was a part of the very physical structure of the town. [iii]

Stead's article revealed how little progress had in fact been made since 1845 in the area of social and economic amelioration, at least as far as it concerned the many women and children trapped in "the sub-culture of chronic urban poverty" (Nield [ii]) where prostitution flourished.

Dr Jekyll and Mr Hyde gives a glimpse of this subculture in the scene where Utterson goes with a policeman to visit Hyde's place in Soho, an area noted for its foreign residents, many of them poor. The fog lifts momentarily to reveal the squalid conditions in which innumerable young children are living: "a dingy street, a gin palace, a low French eating-house, a shop for the retail of penny numbers and two-penny salads, many ragged children huddled in the doorways, and many women of many different nationalities passing out, key in hand, to have a morning glass" (48). The references to the liquor trade may also have suggested to Stevenson's readers the casual prostitution with which it was often tied. As well, the disparity between Jekyll's comfortable affluence and the Soho residents' poverty is emphasized when Utterson reflects that this is the home of Hyde, the heir to Henry Jekyll's "quarter of a million sterling" (48).

The thick fog and intermittency of light from the street lamps impress Utterson as a "mournful reinvasion of darkness," and the "dismal quarter of Soho . . . with its muddy ways, and slatternly passengers" strikes him as "a district of some city in a nightmare" (48).

Hyde belongs to the "night side" of London life with which many Victorian men were actually quite familiar. However monstrous he may seem, he is the shadow self not only of Jekyll, but of Victorian society in general. As the inferior double who embodies and exposes this society's moral deficiencies, Hyde triggers the "awareness of guilt" that Otto Rank describes as "measur[ing] . . . the distance between the ego-ideal and the attained reality" (76). Jekyll, whose repressed sexuality erupts in sadism and brutality and ends in his own self-destruction, epitomizes a collective sense of guilt and concomitant anxiety about the "reinvasion of darkness" into the comfortable, privileged lives of the ascendant professional and merchant classes of English society.

Given the social circumstances surrounding the publication of *Dr Jekyll and Mr Hyde,* it is understandable why the work that Stevenson called his "gothic gnome" (Calder 211)[7] appealed so strongly to the popular imagination. The story was even taken up in the pulpit as an illustration of the dangers of unbridled lust. One anonymous reviewer in the *Rock*, an organ of the Unified Church of England and Ireland, stated that he had deferred writing about *Dr Jekyll and Mr Hyde* until the Lenten season because "the whole question of temptation is so much more appropriately considered at this period of the Christian year, when the thoughts of so many are directed to the temptations of our Lord." The writer felt that the tale could be understood as a parable of the struggle, "common to all," between the "higher and the lower" natures, and that it warned against the dangers of indulging in private lust: "the will, which once was so powerful, [loses] its strength, and . . . the lower nature, which every one should seek to bring into subjection, [gains] the ascendancy" (Maixner 224–27).[8]

An anonymous *Times* review of 25 January 1886, which is said to have marked the beginning of *Dr Jekyll and Mr Hyde*'s popularity, drew a similar moral from the tale: Stevenson "works out the essential power of Evil, which . . . gains ground with each casual yielding to temptation, till the once well-meaning man may actually become a fiend, or at least wear the reflection of the fiend's image" (Maixner 207).

Stevenson himself was impatient with the emphasis many readers placed on the dangers of the sexual impulse itself. He wrote to John Paul Bocock,

> There is no harm in a voluptuary; and none . . . in what prurient fools call 'immorality.' The harm was in Jekyll, because he was a hypocrite— . . . but people are so filled full of folly and inverted lust, that they can think of nothing but sexuality. The hypocrite let out the beast Hyde—who is no more sensual than another, but who is the essence of cruelty and malice, and self-ishness and cowardice: and these are the diabolic in man . . . but the sexual field and the business field are perhaps the two best fitted for the display of cruelty and cowardice and selfishness. That is what people see; and then they confound. (Maixner 231)[9]

Stevenson's scathing comment about the "sexual field" and the "business field" seems to be a fairly clear indication of his feelings about London's flourishing sex trade, where the two fields intersected.

Some readers did seem to understand—or were willing to admit—that the moral hypocrisy and suppression of sexuality so prevalent in Victorian life was the main reason the story was so disturbing and yet fascinating. An anonymous reviewer (said to be Andrew Lang) remarked that a traditional supernatural ghost would be less frightening than the intensely physical Mr. Hyde: "We would welcome a spectre, a ghoul, or even a vampire gladly, rather than meet Mr. Edward Hyde. . . . [S]o every Jekyll among us is haunted by his own Hyde." Implicitly recognizing Hyde's phallic power, the reviewer also noted the uniquely "appalling vitality, and terrible power of growth and increase" of Jekyll's doppelgänger (Maixner 200–01).[10]

Another reviewer, apparently not reading very deeply into Jekyll's confession, asserted that Jekyll's "pleasures [were] of a kind which, while they would bring to many men no sense of shame, and therefore no prompting to concealment, do . . . to him . . . in virtue of their felt inconsistency with the visible tenor of his existence" as an "honourable" man (Maixner 203, 202).[11]

That the story struck uncomfortably close to home for some upper-class gentlemen is indicated in a letter to Stevenson from his friend John Addington Symonds,[12] writer and essayist, who had struggled unsuccessfully against his own homosexual inclinations and had married on the advice of his doctors (Calder 161). Symonds wrote Stevenson that although "the art is burning and intense," he found the book "dreadful because of a certain moral callousness, a want of sympathy, a shutting out of hope. . . . It has left such a deeply painful impression on my heart that I do not know how I am ever to turn to it again." Symonds, like many others, seemed to try to deflect the personal application by dwelling on the universal: "Most of us at some epoch of our lives have been upon the verge of developing a Mr Hyde." Symonds felt the story would have been more uplifting if Jekyll had been reclaimed at the end and "given up Mr Hyde to justice" (Maixner 210–11).[13]

Such generalizing phrases—"most of us," "many men," "the power of Evil," "common to all"—all served a similar purpose for these male readers: to obscure the troubling fact that *Dr Jekyll and Mr Hyde* had called into question the assumption that a gentleman's social status, whether inherited through aristocratic lineage or acquired through individual initiative, exempted him from being morally accountable for his sexual indulgences with the prostitutes, of whatever age, who hailed from the invisible world of the lower classes.

The issue of the sexual abuse of children takes on another dimension in *Dr Jekyll and Mr Hyde*, however, for the hints of sexual exploitation suggest both female and male victims. Only recently have critics begun to notice the homosexual overtones and scatological imagery, which suggest that

Jekyll's "pleasures" may have violated more than one Victorian taboo (Showalter 105–15[14]). Yet as Stevenson surely understood, however taboo the topic may have been in respectable society, Jekyll was not alone in his proclivities.

Stevenson's friend Symonds, although having argued for the legitimacy of adult male homosexuality (Hyde 101–03), condemned the rampant promiscuity and "crude carnality" he witnessed at his old school, Harrow (Grosskurth 32). As Jeffrey Weeks has discussed, "the prevalent schoolboy homosexuality in public schools . . . became a major concern for a number of social-purity advocates from the 1880s onwards. By the mid-nineteenth century, indeed, homosexuality seems to have been institutionalized in some of the major schools" (109). Writing in 1866, Symonds described how one of his cousins removed his sons from Harrow three months after placing them there because of the "enormous" immorality he found there: "He has lived for many years in France and Germany and has had much experience of foreign schools; but he has never met with any *worse* than Harrow among the most corrupt of French academies" (657[15]).

It is now generally recognized that sexually precocious behavior in a child can be an indicator of prior abuse, and the institutionalization of schoolboy homosexuality, as Weeks refers to it, seems to be a clear sign that the abuse was well entrenched.[16] According to Symonds's biographer Phyllis Grosskurth, the boys' sexual activities at Harrow had a pecking order based on age: "It was the common practice for every good-looking boy to be addressed by a female name; he was regarded either as public property or as the 'bitch' of an older boy" (32).

The headmaster of the school during Symonds's time there, the Rev. Charles John Vaughan, publicly condemned this "corruption" but was himself known to sexually exploit his young students. He was forced to resign after Symonds told his father about Vaughan's involvement with one of Symonds's schoolmates. After resigning, Vaughan became vicar of Doncaster, and under continued pressure from Symonds's father was compelled to refuse offers of more important ecclesiastical posts. Years after the death of Symonds senior, Queen Victoria (perhaps unaware of Vaughan's widely rumored reputation as a child molester) offered Vaughan the deanery of St. Paul's. He refused; when he was dying, he stipulated that all his papers be burned and that no biography ever be written about him (Hyde 110–12; Grosskurth 31–37).

Symonds recognized during his later visit to Harrow that removing one adult perpetrator did not remove the problem: "The seeds of vice, sown long ago in this fruitful soil continue to propagate themselves like mushrooms on a dunghill." The brutishness particularly offended him, and he attributed much of that atmosphere to the fact that many of the boys came from merchant and professional families, "from the lower aristocracy and the moneyed classes for the most part, idleness, plethoric wealth, hereditary stupidity and parvenu grossness combining to form a singularly corrupt amalgam" (657).[17]

The character in *Dr Jekyll and Mr Hyde* who is most closely associated with this kind of abuse is the staid lawyer, Mr. Utterson. Utterson twice imagines Hyde's persecution of Jekyll in a visual tableau in which the former comes to the latter's bed. The first time, Utterson is trying to sleep in his own "great, dark bed," but he keeps thinking about the trampling of the child and imagining, from a point of view that comes very close to that of the victim, a threatening figure approaching the victim's bedside:

> [H]e would see a room in a rich house, where his friend lay asleep, dreaming and smiling at his dreams; and then the door of that room would be opened, the curtains of the bed plucked apart, the sleeper recalled, and, lo! there would stand by his side *a figure to whom power was given,* and even at that dead hour *he must rise and do its bidding.* The figure . . . haunted the lawyer all night. (37; my emphasis)

This dream image occurs shortly after a reference to Utterson's public school education. He has just visited his old friend Dr. Lanyon; the two had been "old mates both at school and college" (36).

The haunted Mr. Utterson thence begins to "haunt the door" that Hyde was said to use, in a manner that can only be described as obsessive; morning, noon and night, "by all lights and at all hours of solitude or concourse, the lawyer [is] to be found on his chosen post" (38). After finally meeting Hyde, Utterson "brood[s]" at home "on his own past, groping in all the corners of memory, lest by chance some Jack-in-the-Box of an old iniquity should leap to light there." Although Utterson feels that his past is "fairly blameless," and the narrator assures the reader that "few men could read the rolls of their life with less apprehension," Utterson nevertheless feels "humbled to the dust by the many ill things he had done," and once again he imagines Hyde coming to Jekyll's bed, empathically identifying with Jekyll: "'It turns me quite cold to think of this creature stealing like a thief to Harry's bedside; poor Harry, what a wakening!'" (42).

As an adult, Utterson has cultivated a persona of respectability combined with tolerance, harmlessness, and abstinence; he is "a lover of the sane and customary sides of life" (35). Considering the density of sexual punning in *Dr Jekyll and Mr Hyde* (words such as *rise* and *swell* appear frequently, and the passages quoted above include a number of terms carrying phallic connotations), it would probably not be far-fetched to read in this statement a veiled reference to the "uncustomary" practice of sodomy, as well as an account of how one survivor of childhood abuse coped with the trauma. The fact that the revelation of Hyde's connection with Jekyll is so disturbing to Utterson suggests that it may have aroused latent "repressed memories" of fear and shame. Moreover, the fact that the concept of repressed memory has entered general parlance only since the 1980s may help to explain why the subject would have been treated in such an oblique manner in *Dr Jekyll and Mr Hyde*.

The issue of boy prostitution never received the widespread public attention given to girl prostitution, but given the conditions that apparently prevailed in many of England's public schools (which Stevenson did not attend), it would make sense that there would be a demand for young males, and there is some evidence indicating that this was indeed the case. From the 1860s onward "there was a flourishing trade in male prostitution" generally, particularly in London (Hyde 120), and in 1881 a pornographic work was published under the title of *The Sins of the Cities of the Plain; or the Recollections of a Mary Ann*, which recounted the adventures of a "Mary Ann" or young male prostitute whose actual name was Jack Saul. One passage describes how the writer, a man who paid for Jack's favors, was first attracted to this "effeminate, but very good-looking young fellow," and the boy's youth is further emphasized in a reference to his "fresh looking beardless face" (qtd. in Hyde 121). Jack himself recounts how in the brothel where he worked, "gentlemen" paid a membership fee of one hundred guineas and a "handsome annual subscription and liberal payments for refreshments and the procuration of boys or youths like myself" who would often dress up as women (qtd. in Hyde 122). The author remarks that "the extent to which pederasty is carried on in London between gentlemen and young fellows is little dreamed of by the outside public" (qtd. in Hyde 123).

Another male brothel that catered to an upper-class clientele operated on Cleveland Street, and although the scandal about its activities did not break until the summer of 1889, the place had apparently opened "[t]owards the middle of the 'eighties" (Hyde 123). This establishment made use mainly of telegraph boys who supplemented their meager earnings by prostituting themselves for wealthy clients. According to Montgomery Hyde, there was "more than a hint of blackmail about the place" (123 [and blackmail is the first thing Enfield suspects of Hyde's relationship with Jekyll; 33]). There is no direct evidence indicating that Stevenson knew about the Cleveland Street brothel specifically, but it is difficult to imagine that he was unaware of this particular form of upper-class vice, especially in view of the fact that Parliament was in the process of criminalizing male homosexual activity in early August 1885, during the passage of the Criminal Law Amendment Bill.

The man who proposed adding the decisive clause to the Criminal Law Amendment Bill, Henry Labouchere, apparently intended it to apply only to the protection of youths from adult male interference, but the wording of the clause left the law open to a wide range of interpretation, with the result that mutually consenting adult activity also could be punished. His motion for amendment to the bill was passed on 6 August 1885, one month after the publication of "Maiden Tribute" and two weeks before the Hyde Park demonstration. "Even more than prostitutes or child rapists, whom parliament voted against flogging, homosexuals were to suffer agony from the moral panic" (E. Bristow 115; also see Hyde 134–36), and it seemed that the social purity movement's "campaign to protect innocents could not be kept separate from the urge to punish vice" (E. Bristow 93). Symonds was one of the few outspoken critics of the amendment (Hyde 136–37).[18]

Some textual similarities between "The Maiden Tribute" and *Dr Jekyll and Mr Hyde* suggest that Stevenson had read the article closely and that Stead's account of child victimization in the sex trade had made a deep impression. Stevenson was known for his sympathy toward the more vulnerable members of society, especially women, children, and prostitutes. His father had helped to run a rescue operation for fallen women in Edinburgh (Calder 7), and as a young college student Stevenson had spent a great deal of time lounging and visiting in the inns and brothels of Edinburgh's Old Town, although according to Jenni Calder he could not afford the prostitutes and could hardly afford any drink because his father kept him on such a limited allowance (7–8).

One element featured in both works is the screams of the young victim. In *Dr Jekyll and Mr Hyde* they are mentioned twice by Enfield and twice in Utterson's recollections. Stead's highly sensational argument, based on a number of anonymous interviews, was that there existed in London an extensive traffic in young virgins, "'[o]rphans, daughters of drunken parents, children of prostitutes, girls whose friends are far away'" who would be lured by deception or enticement into houses of ill repute and then raped by any gentleman rich enough to pay the price, usually between ten and twenty pounds (5). He quotes a policeman's reply to his inquiry about whether neighbors or police would not come to the girl's assistance if they heard her screaming from the next house or from the street: the neighbor, the policeman stated, would not do anything because the screams would cease before he had roused himself to do something about it, and the policeman on the beat would not interfere because "'[h]e has no right to interfere, even if he heard anything. Suppose that a constable had a right to force his way into any house where a woman screamed fearfully, policemen would be almost as regular attendants at childbed as doctors'" (3).

A little further on, Stead cites a woman he sarcastically refers to as "a most respectable lady, who keeps a villa in the west of London," saying that "'[i]n [her] house . . . you can enjoy the screams of the girl with the certainty that no one else hears them but yourself.'" Thinking that he was a prospective customer, she then showed him a well-carpeted and insulated room where "'[y]ou lock the door and then you can do as you please. The girl may scream blue murder, but not a sound will be heard'" (5).

To all this, Stead adds the melodramatic observation that "[t]o some men, however, the shriek of torture is the essence of their delight, and they would not silence by a single note the cry of agony over which they gloat" (5). He then goes on to describe the practice of "STRAPPING GIRLS DOWN" (under a separate section with that title): "To oblige a wealthy customer who by riot and excess had impaired his vitality to such an extent that nothing could minister to his jaded senses but very young maidens, an eminently respectable lady undertook that . . . the girl . . . should be strapped down hand and foot to the four posts of the bedstead, so that all resistance save that of unavailing screaming would be impossible" (9). The cries of the young girls that form a central motif in Stead's piece are reiterated in his concluding epigram: "For the child's sob in the darkness curseth deeper / Than the strong man in his wrath" (9).[19]

Even though it is apparent that most young girls who became prostitutes had not been drugged or physically forced into their line of work (Gorham 365), Stead's portrayal of the sadistic strain in upper-class male sexuality may not have been overdrawn, however melodramatic it may appear. As Steven Marcus has shown in his study of Victorian pornography, child prostitutes appealed particularly to the aggressive and violent impulses of some men (most of whom, one could add, were the graduates of an educational system that employed the discipline of flogging on the buttocks). Deflowering young virgins was a thrilling act of transgression for the otherwise respectable gentleman. Marcus notes the "pronounced sadistic tendencies" in one man's written account of his experience with a particular young virgin: "[H]er cry of pain gave me inexpressible pleasure; and saying I would not hurt, yet wishing to hurt her and glorying in it, I thrust with all the violence my buttocks could give. . . . I never had more pleasure in bawdiness than I had in hurting her" (178–79).

Jekyll's confession makes it clear that the "pleasures" he pursued in the "disguise" of Hyde were sadistic in nature. In a comment that would seem to signify innocence but may actually signify early corruption, Jekyll says that initially he could, "like a schoolboy, strip off these lendings and spring headlong into the sea of liberty" (86). His enjoyments were at first merely "undignified," but "in the hands of Edward Hyde they soon began to turn towards the monstrous. . . . I was often plunged into a kind of wonder at my vicarious depravity." Hyde was "malign and villainous"; he drank "pleasure with bestial avidity from any degree of torture to another" (86). Jekyll attempts to rein in Hyde after Hyde's "act of cruelty to a child" (87) almost exposes him/them to the public eye, but when after a period of restraint he finally drinks the potion again, he becomes conscious "of a more unbridled, a more furious propensity to ill," which culminates in his murdering an elderly gentleman: "With a transport of glee, I mauled the unresisting body, tasting delight from every blow" (90).

The transformation of man into beast, a commonplace of Victorian classical tradition, constitutes the pivotal event in *Dr Jekyll and Mr Hyde* and is similarly featured in "The Maiden Tribute." Explaining how the dream inspired the writing of his novella, Stevenson asserted that what "was given [him in his dream] was the matter of three scenes, and the central idea of a voluntary change becoming involuntary" ("Chapter on Dreams" 128), before his wife Fanny, "thinking he was suffering a nightmare, woke him" (Wood 102). Stead similarly invokes the Circean myth when describing his time spent in London's underworld of prostitution:

[A]t the best you wander in a Circe's isle, where the victims of the foul enchantress's wand meet you at every turn. But . . . whereas the enchanted in olden time had the heads and the voices and the bristles of swine, while the heart of a man was in them still, these have not put on in outward form "the inglorious likeness of a beast," but are in semblance as other men, while within there is only the heart of a beast—bestial, ferocious, and filthy beyond the imagination of decent men. (3)

In *Dr Jekyll and Mr Hyde* Stevenson gives a more contemporary signature to the old Circean myth. In the myth, Circe first gave Odysseus's
sailors a drink laced with a drug that would make them forget their native
land; she then transformed them into swine by waving her wand, although
the men retained their human consciousness while trapped within pigs'
bodies. Stevenson dispenses with the magic wand in favor of a modern
chemical experiment, along the lines of the electrical experiment that
brings to life Frankenstein's doppelgänger; the medieval *alchemical* transformation becomes the *all-chemical* transformation of secular science.

Jekyll's drug possesses the same forgetfulness-inducing properties as
Circe's. Like the unfortunate sailors who forget their native land, Jekyll is
enabled to forget his own "culture"; but he does so to an even greater degree, for he loses memory of his very humanity, which to the Victorian
mind especially was defined by the cultivation and the moral constraints
that marked the "civilized" human being. Although in moral terms he does
become a "pig," the actual animal into which he is transformed is an ape—
the creature who, as Darwin had argued fifteen years earlier in *The Descent
of Man* (1871), was "man's" nearest kin.

Utterson's notion that there is "something troglodytic" about Hyde
(40) identifies the prehuman quality that seems to be Hyde's dominant
characteristic, although one can actually place him considerably higher on
the evolutionary scale, with the apes whom Darwin had shown as occupying the evolutionary niche just below the human species. Stevenson's physical descriptions of Mr. Hyde correspond in a number of striking ways with
Darwin's account of the upper primates in *The Descent of Man.*

One of the qualities that observers tend to note about Hyde is his
"dwarfish" stature and his unusual manner of walking, which strongly resemble the stature and movement of the anthropoid apes as described by
Darwin. Darwin had argued that as the "progenitors of man" gradually became more erect or bipedal, they became more successful in obtaining food
and in "defend[ing] themselves with stones or clubs":

> Thus the gorilla runs with a sidelong shambling gait, but more commonly
> progresses by resting on its bent hands. The long-armed apes occasionally
> use their arms like crutches, swinging their bodies forward between them,
> and some kinds of Hylobates, without having been taught, can walk or run
> upright with tolerable quickness; yet they move awkwardly, and much less
> securely than man. (*Descent* 434–35)

Similarly, Hyde, according to Enfield, "stump[s] along . . . at a good walk"
(31), and Poole describes him as having a "quick light way" despite ap-

pearing to be "doubled up" (67). Poole also tells Utterson that Hyde jumped up "like a monkey . . . and whipped into the cabinet" when Poole entered the room without warning. When Poole and Utterson stand outside the theatre, they hear Hyde's footfalls: "The steps fell lightly and oddly, with a certain swing, for all they went so slowly; it was different indeed from the heavy creaking tread of Henry Jekyll." Moreover, when Hyde kills Sir Danvers Carew, he "club[s] him to the earth" with a "heavy cane" and then tramples the man to death with an "ape-like fury" (46–47).

Hyde's facial expressions also have an apelike quality, judging from a description in *The Descent of Man* given by Darwin to make a point about human ancestry. Darwin states that only the males of the anthropomorphous apes have fully developed canine teeth, and that the occasional appearance of large canines in men are simply instances

> of reversion to an ape-like progenitor. He who rejects with scorn the belief that the shape of his own canines, and their occasional great development in other men, are due to our early forefathers having been provided with these formidable weapons, will probably reveal, by sneering, the line of his descent. For though he no longer intends, nor has the power, to use these teeth as weapons, he will unconsciously retract his "snarling muscles" . . . so as to expose them ready for action, like a dog prepared to fight. (425)

When Hyde is confronted by the crowd after running down the young girl, he faces them, as Enfield puts it, "with a kind of black sneering coolness—frightened too, I could see that—but carrying it off" (32). Shortly after, when confronted by Utterson and chastised for his blunt language, he "snarl[s] aloud into a savage laugh" (40).

Another striking feature of Hyde is the rough quality of his voice, a trait that is also consistent with his prehuman or early human character. As Darwin comments, the human species is unique in its "habitual use of articulate language"; yet like the lower animals, "man" also resorts to "inarticulate cries to express his meaning, aided by gestures and the movements of the muscles of the face. This especially holds good with the more simple and vivid feelings, which are but little connected with our higher intelligence." Darwin cites "[o]ur cries of pain, fear, surprise, anger" as examples of vividly expressed emotions (along with "the murmur of a mother to her beloved child"; *Descent* 461).

In Hyde's case, his range of expression throughout the story seems to be limited largely to basic emotional states, and when he does speak, it appears to be with some discomfort. He shrinks back "with a hissing intake of breath" upon being approached by Utterson, and during their exchange

he speaks "a little hoarsely," with a "husky, whispering, and somewhat broken voice" (39, 40). Similarly, when Utterson and Poole start to break
down the door of Jekyll's theatre, they hear a "dismal screech, as of mere
animal terror" (69).

The most consistent response that people have to Hyde seems to be
psychological and emotional rather than logical: they all find him ugly
and repulsive. Darwin records that people tend to feel similarly about
apes: "In the adult male anthropomorphous apes . . . it is the effect on the
skull of the great development of the jaw-muscles that causes it to differ so
greatly in many respects from that of man, and has given to these animals
'a truly frightful physiognomy'" (*Descent* 436). For the Victorian observer
unused to seeing such animals, it would more likely be the unsettling
combination of difference *and* similarity that would be frightful; it might
be a bit like looking at oneself in a fun-house mirror. The felt need to
buffer the shock is apparent in one representation of upper primates that
would have been familiar to Stevenson's readership: an advertisement for
Monkey Brand Soap, which featured a drawing of a humanized, smiling
monkey dressed up in a suit and tie, though without shoes.[20]

London residents had the opportunity to see firsthand some of the
lower primates at the Zoological Gardens at Regent's Park, which had first
opened to the public in 1828 and had since been expanded and developed.
The monkey house, built in the 1830s, had been rebuilt twice during that
period (see Scherren). An 1831 description of some of the primates housed
in the Gardens suggests the combination of "human" appeal and "inhuman" ferocity that their human observers saw in them. The red monkey is
described as "lively and active, but somewhat irascible if disturbed or handled. It is, however, too young to be dangerous. When pleased it dances on
all fours in a peculiar and measured step, which is far from being ungrace-
ful" (Bennett 136). The black ape's "face is broad, rather prominent, slightly
narrowing at the muzzle. . . . The expression of its physiognomy is peculiarly cunning. It seems to be rather violent in its temper, and tyrannizes
not a little over the quiet Gray Gibbon, which is at present confined in the
same cage" (Bennett 190). The Barbary ape in captivity "is generally peculiarly lively, active, intelligent, and, in its youth at least, good tempered. But
these qualities wear off with advancing age, and it becomes sullen, capri-
cious, and in the end unruly, malicious, and dangerous" (Bennett 192; the
possibility that the apes' state of captivity might have contributed to their
irascibility is never raised).

In *Dr Jekyll and Mr Hyde,* many of the characters who encounter
Hyde react with fear and revulsion. Enfield says that when he caught up

with Hyde, the man "gave me one look, so ugly that it brought out the sweat on me like running" (31). Utterson reflects that Hyde "gave an impression of deformity without any namable malformation, he had a displeasing smile" (40). Poole comments that "there was something queer about that gentleman—something that gave a man a turn . . . that you felt in your marrow—kind of cold and thin," at which Utterson admits having felt something similar (68). Dr. Lanyon records that he "was struck . . . with the shocking expression of his face, with his remarkable combination of great muscular activity and great apparent debility of constitution, and . . . with the odd, subjective disturbance caused by his neighbourhood" (77). Dr. Lanyon scientifically notes that his own physical reaction "bore some resemblance to incipient rigor, and was accompanied by a marked sinking of the pulse" (77).

Poole describes the feelings of basic animal fear and superstitious dread incited by Hyde more succinctly: "the hair stood upon my head like quills" (66). In the case of the group described by Enfield at the beginning of the story, the fight reaction is stronger than that of fright: everyone apparently takes a "loathing" to the man, and Enfield says that every time the doctor looked at Hyde "I saw that Sawbones turned sick and white, with the desire to kill him. I knew what was in his mind, just as he knew what was in mine; and killing being out of the question, we did the next best" (31–32).

The atavistic reaction everyone seems to have upon seeing Hyde springs in part from the shock of recognition, from seeing oneself at one remove so to speak, in a more fully instinctual state. This is one reason why Utterson feels "a shudder in his blood" after having seen Hyde face to face: "[T]he face of Hyde sat heavy on his memory; he felt . . . a nausea and a distaste of life; and in the gloom of his spirits, he seemed to read a menace in the flickering of the firelight on the polished cabinets and the uneasy starting of the shadow on the roof" (41). Hyde is the shadow self.

Dr. Lanyon provides the most direct clue to the reason for Hyde's effect on people, when he writes that "I have since had reason to believe the cause [of my reaction] to lie much deeper in the nature of man, and to turn on some nobler hinge than the principle of hatred" (77). The revulsion Lanyon feels at "something abnormal and misbegotten in the very essence of the creature" does not dampen the spirit of scientific inquiry which later proves fatal to him: "[T]o my interest in the man's nature and character there was added a curiosity as to his *origin*, his life, his fortune and status in the world" (78; my emphasis).

In sensing something "abnormal and misbegotten" about Hyde, Lanyon is responding to Hyde's "status" as an instance of biological reversion, which Darwin describes as occurring "[w]hen a structure is arrested in its development, but still continues growing, until it closely resembles a corresponding structure in some lower and adult member of the same group" (422). Lanyon's intuition that "some nobler hinge than . . . hatred" occasions the recoil people feel when confronted by such reversion makes evolutionary sense, for Hyde violates the principle of developmental growth—not simply physical, but also spiritual, intellectual, and moral—which characterizes the human species. It is an indication of how psychologically unbalanced Dr. Jekyll is that the specifically human capacities seem to be more of a burden than a gift to him, and that descending into the more instinct-driven, unconscious condition of Hyde seems like freedom.

While *Dr Jekyll and Mr Hyde* incorporates many of Darwin's observations about the appearance and behavior of apes, it also challenges his notion that "[m]an prompted by his conscience, will through long habit acquire such perfect self-command, that his desires and passions will at last yield instantly and without a struggle to his social sympathies and instincts" (*Descent* 486)—an assumption enthusiastically shared by members of the social purity movement. Stevenson's tale favors the opposite view: the more one trains one's will, the greater the danger of becoming, in C. G. Jung's words, "lost in one-sidedness and deviating further and further from the laws and roots of being. This means, on the one hand, the possibility of human freedom, but on the other it is a source of endless transgressions against one's instincts" ("Child Archetype" 82). Dr. Jekyll, whose frequently mentioned "will" plays a pivotal role in the story, is a prime example of the disciplined, ambitious man who over time has developed the "habit of self-command" to the point that he has become dangerously alienated from the emotional and instinctual elements of his own being.

Jekyll's story is also an indictment of Victorian moral blindness, of the kind of thinking manifested by Darwin himself when he asserted that

> as man gradually advanced in intellectual power . . . his sympathies became more tender and widely diffused, extending to men of all races, to the imbecile, maimed, and other useless members of society, and finally to the lower animals. And it is admitted by moralists of the derivative school and by some intuitionists, that the standard of morality has risen since an early period in the history of man. (493)

Up to a point, the note of self-congratulation here was justified, for the democratizing movement was strong throughout the Victorian period: the vote had been successively expanded, women were being allowed access to educational institutions, and married women's property and child custody rights had been established.

Yet the warning in *Dr Jekyll and Mr Hyde*, which many of its readers were still not ready to recognize, is that this faith in progressive development might be based on a very inadequate understanding of human nature. Stevenson's critique does take aim at the decadence and moral irresponsibility displayed by many upper-class gentlemen of his day, as has been discussed, but its main target is the middle classes' naive expectation that the "desires and passions" could be deferred indefinitely for the sake of upward social mobility. This assumption also underlay the purity reform movement's view that the path to social amelioration lay not in relaxing the severe sexual standards applied to women, but in pressuring men to conform to the same rigid code of behavior (Gorham 357).

Jekyll's double, Mr. Hyde, reveals how savage and uncontrollable the instincts can become when their power and value are denied. Henry Jekyll begins his account of how Edward Hyde was released into the world by confessing to the intense self-division that had characterized his life for many years. He states that his "imperious desire to carry [his] head high" led him to conceal the "pleasures" and "irregularities" into which his "impatient gaiety of disposition" led him. He claims that it was "the exacting nature of [his] aspirations" rather than "any particular degradation in [his] faults" that led him to regard them with "an almost morbid sense of shame." Yet his disclaimer seems to be undercut by his comments that he "laid aside restraint and plunged in shame"[21] during the times that he was not, "in the eye of day," engaged in more productive and useful pursuits (81) and that his "pleasures were (to say the least) undignified" (85). Reading between the lines of Jekyll's decorous language, it seems fairly clear that his "irregularities" were sexual in nature and that some sort of degradation was part of the pleasure he sought, as relief from his impossibly superior persona.

The fact that Jekyll is growing older aggravates his sense of inner discord. He says that when he became engaged in his researches he "was not only well known and highly considered, but growing towards the elderly man," so that the "incoherency of [his] life was daily growing more unwelcome" (85)—as was his growing awareness of declining potency.

Jekyll's personal anxiety about his waning powers reflects a more widespread masculine anxiety, which can also be seen in Darwin's *Descent of Man*. There is a recurring note of uneasiness throughout Darwin's study that belies its general affirmation of European (viz. white male) supremacy. Despite his admission that "[w]e know nothing positively" about Malthus's idea "that the reproductive power is actually less in barbarous, than in civilised races," Darwin goes on at considerable length to prove that there "is great reason to suspect" this to be true (428): "We might, therefore, expect that civilised men, who in one sense are highly domesticated, would be more prolific than wild men. It is also probable that the increased fertility of civilised nations would become, as with our domestic animals, an inherited character: it is at least known that with mankind a tendency to produce twins runs in families" (429). Thus, civilized man compensates for his "highly domesticated" condition with a new access of virility and reproductive power.

One of the arguments made against the idea of natural selection was made by the duke of Argyll, and was based on the observation that "the human frame has diverged from the structure of brutes, in the direction of greater physical helplessness and weakness." Citing the argument (443), Darwin responded by suggesting that the "small strength and speed of man" are counterbalanced by his "intellectual powers," which enable him to form weapons and tools, and by "his social qualities which lead him to give and receive aid from his fellow-men" (444). In this instance, Darwin seems to be arguing that civilization is a form of compensation for declining strength.

There are other places where Darwin openly acknowledges the physical decline that appears to be a component of the civilizing process, evident in the contrast between civilized and primitive people:

> The inferiority of Europeans, in comparison with savages, in eyesight and in the other senses, is no doubt the accumulated and transmitted effect of lessened use during many generations; for Rengger states that he has repeatedly observed Europeans, who had been brought up and spent their whole lives with the wild Indians, who nevertheless did not equal them in the sharpness of their senses. (419)

Darwin does not appear to notice the way this example contradicts his argument that lessened sexual activity in civilized societies results in greater potency. Here he argues that lessened use of eyesight results in weaker, not greater, vision. In Jekyll's case, the ironic solution to this impasse is the invention of a fertility potion, which will restore to him the original vitality that his cultural adaptation has depleted: specifically, the sexual vitality for which male apes were reputed.[22]

Jekyll also attempts to rationalize the problem by universalizing his condition. In an effort to minimize his culpability for leading a life of duplicity, he argues that his divided life was only a more extreme instance of an eternal human dilemma. His exacting aspirations "severed in [him] those provinces of good and ill which divide and compound man's dual nature . . . the hard law of life which lies at the root of religion, and is one of the most plentiful springs of distress" (81). He declares, "[M]an is not truly one, but truly two" and imagines the day when "man will be ultimately known for a mere polity of multifarious, incongruous and independent denizens" (82). There is some truth in Jekyll's statements, that to be human is to know conflict between opposing impulses, which may be termed body and spirit, or nature and culture, and that the human personality can be complex and multifaceted. Yet in presenting himself as simply an extreme example of "the thorough and primitive duality of man" he is being transparently, and unsuccessfully, self-excusing.

A similar and quintessentially Victorian rationalization for duplicitous behavior can be found in *The Descent of Man*. Many of Darwin's comments on the conflict between what may be called "instinctual and social impulses" (which prefigure Freud's views on the conflicts among the id, the ego, and the superego) suffer from similar unresolved contradictions. Darwin notes that a struggle between conflicting instincts or impulses can be found in both animals and humans. Because humans have "emerged from a state of barbarism within a comparatively recent period . . . it is not surprising that there should be a struggle in man between his social instincts, with their derived virtues, and his lower, though momentarily stronger impulses or desires" (494). According to this statement, the impulse which leads one to demonstrate care and concern for others in one's group is on the one hand simply another, although a "higher," form of instinct, while on the other hand it is the source of "derived" or socially acquired "virtues."

Earlier in *The Descent*, Darwin defines these ambiguous "social instincts" that humans share with animals as sociability, sympathy, and care: "The services may be of a definite and evidently instinctive nature; or there may only be a wish and readiness, as with most of the higher social animals, to aid their fellows in certain general ways" (472). He then argues that with physiological changes in brain development leading to increased capacity for memory, "that feeling of dissatisfaction, or even misery, which invariably results . . . from any unsatisfied instinct, would arise, as often as it was perceived that the enduring and always present social instinct had yielded to some other instinct, at the time stronger, but neither enduring in its nature, nor leaving behind it a very vivid impression" (472). Darwin cites hunger as one example of the more fleeting instincts that might move one to antisocial actions, but in this context he does not consider the sexual instinct at all. His next point is that with the acquisition of language, the wishes of the community would be more effectively expressed and that "the common opinion how each member ought to act for the public good, would naturally become in a paramount degree the guide to action." He adds that "however great weight we may attribute to public opinion, our regard for the approbation and disapprobation of our fellows depends on sympathy, which . . . forms an essential part of the social instinct, and is indeed its foundation-stone" (472).

Developing this line of argument, Darwin optimistically speculates that with the progressive development of the moral sense, the "long habit" of "self-command" may even become an inherited trait (486). But he then qualifies his argument that the social instinct is a more "persistent" impulse than "lower" drives for self-gratification and briefly entertains the possibility that the reverse might sometimes be true:

> If any desire or instinct leading to an action opposed to the good of others still appears, when recalled to mind, as strong as, or stronger than, the social instinct, a man will feel no keen regret at having followed it; but he will be conscious that if his conduct were known to his fellows, it would meet with their disapprobation; and few are so destitute of sympathy as not to feel discomfort when this is realised. (486)

Thus, hypocrisy becomes a derived social virtue, justified by human sympathy.

Jekyll's response to his dilemma is not to attempt to resolve or alleviate the conflict between his personal desires and his social aspirations, but literally to sever them. Like Dr. Frankenstein, he embarks upon his research in the hope that it will enable him to remove "the doom and burthen of our life" (83), although his notions about what constitutes this "doom" are rather different from Frankenstein's, and his motives are more patently self-serving:

> I had learned to dwell with pleasure, as a beloved day-dream, on the thought of the separation of these elements. If each, I told myself, could but be housed in separate identities, life would be relieved of all that was unbearable; the unjust might go his way, *delivered from the aspirations and remorse of his upright twin;* and the just could walk steadfastly and secure, on his *upward path,* doing the good things in which he found his pleasure, and no longer exposed to disgrace and penitence by the hands of this extraneous evil. (82; my emphasis)

Jekyll's fantasy of not getting caught was probably a familiar one to a large number of Stevenson's readers, struggling as many of them were to establish a better place in a world of widening opportunities. In Steven Marcus's words, "an immense effort of self-discipline and self-denial, the ability to learn how to defer gratification indefinitely and to persist in the deferral" was required of any individual, man or woman, who wished to pursue self-advancement in Victorian society (149). And as Marcus also adds, the repression that this effort necessitated had its own positive value, for even if it led to the development of a more rigid or less spontaneous personality, it also opened new avenues of living and made possible an expansion of personality and sensibility in other directions. For people in the lower classes especially, it was a path to self-humanization (147–49).

Jekyll's desire to pursue the "upward path" reflects the mood of effort and aspiration that pervaded Victorian life, an attitude shown even in the police officer investigating the murder of Sir Danvers Carew; when the officer learns the identity of the victim, his "eye light[s] up with professional ambition" (47). Jekyll's situation, however, is somewhat different from the one Marcus describes. The first fact Jekyll mentions about himself, after his date of birth, is that he "was born . . . to a large fortune" (81). Since he is not a member of the aristocracy, his family fortune would probably have been acquired through commerce, and it may be that Jekyll feels an obligation to give the family name the social respectability that his father's or grandfather's economic success made possible but did not necessarily guarantee. Jekyll's house is the only one on its square that has not been divided into flats; the rest of the houses are tenanted by "all sorts and conditions of men: map-engravers, architects, shady lawyers, and the agents of obscure enterprises" (40). The "great air of wealth and comfort" of Jekyll's house distinguishes his position of inherited prosperity from the less successful but perhaps no less ambitious enterprises of the professional men who live in his area.

Architectural symbolism, another Gothic feature of Stevenson's tale, conveys the idea that ambition and deferred gratification can have their price, both personally and socially. The back side of Jekyll's house features a "*blind forehead* of discoloured wall . . . and [bears] in every feature the marks of prolonged and sordid negligence" (30; my emphasis). Tramps and children have defaced the door, and "for close on a generation no one had appeared to drive away these random visitors or to repair their ravages" (30). As Enfield says of the door, "It is connected in my mind." Enfield's statement is completed by the words, "added he, 'with a very odd story'" (30–31), but the division of the statement into two parts serves to emphasize the door's symbolic significance as a point of entry to, or division between, different aspects of the psyche. The door, with its sexual and psychological associations, is referred to no less than eight times in the first chapter.

Jekyll overvalues his public persona of upstanding, benevolent citizen to the extent that the "fortress of identity" on which he has come to rely for psychological protection and support soon becomes a "prisonhouse," which he seeks to escape via his magical/scientific potion (83, 85). He notes that the instinctual or "evil" side of his nature had remained in what Jung would call an "archaic, undeveloped" condition from disuse: it "was less robust and less developed than the good which I had just deposed . . . in the course of my life, which had been . . . nine-tenths a life of effort, virtue and control, it had been much less exercised and much less exhausted" (84). Consequently, he feels a great surge of physical vitality and freedom from constraint in his regression to a primitive state: "There was something strange in my sensations, something indescribably new and, from its very novelty, incredibly sweet. I felt younger, lighter, happier in body; within I was conscious of a heady recklessness, a current of disordered sensual images" (83).

When he sees his face reflected in his bedroom mirror, he feels "a leap of welcome" at the sight of the self he had excluded from his surface life for so long: "This, too, was myself. It seemed natural and human. In my eyes it bore a livelier image of the spirit, it seemed more express and single, than the imperfect and divided countenance, I had been hitherto accustomed to call mine" (84–85). But because his instincts with their welcome vitality have now separated so completely from his moral sense, his feeling after his first metamorphosis is that he "knew" himself to be "wicked, tenfold more wicked," than when he was constrained by his Jekyll persona (84). Once he is no longer subject to the pangs of conscience, the reassertion of his instincts is intoxicating to him; the thought of his wickedness "brace[s] and delight[s him] like wine" (84).

One physical effect of the potion which also signifies his loss of conscience is that after the first transformation Jekyll discovers that he has "lost in stature" (84); for he has lost not just in physical, but in moral stature as well. Edward Hyde is a creature entirely devoid of the quality that Darwin postulated as the "foundation-stone" of the moral sense: sympathy for others. Hyde whole-heartedly endorses Utterson's self-confessed inclination for "Cain's heresy" (29). It is doubtful that Stevenson actually believed that apes were incapable of social bonding; more likely he intended Hyde's lack of basic sympathy simply to reflect the atrophy of that capacity in Jekyll himself. Jekyll did engage in deeds of public service, yet his account reveals that his primary concern was not the welfare of others but the enhancement of his own public image. Inveterately narcissistic, he has allowed his instinctual needs some limited satisfaction, while remaining in a state of emotional isolation and retardation.

Once Jekyll loses contact with his moral sense by splitting off into Hyde, degeneration quickly follows, his previously "undignified" pleasures now becoming, as we have seen, "monstrous" and sadistic when acted out by the emotionally undeveloped Hyde (86). Jekyll initially believes that Hyde is dependent on him; as he claims to Utterson, "the moment I choose, I can be rid of Mr Hyde" (44). But after Hyde's trampling of the child, Jekyll begins to become aware of his double's increasing autonomy.

The power of the unconscious becomes evident when Hyde starts returning without being called for. He makes his first appearance while Jekyll is literally unconscious, lying asleep in bed. Jekyll awakes to see his hand transformed; it is "lean, corded, knuckly, of a dusky pallor, and thickly shaded with a swart growth of hair" (88). He sneaks into his "anatomical theatre" (88) to swallow the draught which enables him to change "costume" back into that of a respectable doctor, and reflects upon the apparently increasing strength of his double. He realizes that he now runs the risk of losing "the power of voluntary change" and feels that he must choose between the two (89).

Hyde's role as a representation of a more primitive or rudimentary aspect of the human psyche is suggested when Jekyll observes that his own involvement in Hyde is greater than Hyde's is in him. While Jekyll "projected and shared in the pleasures and adventures of Hyde . . . Hyde was indifferent to Jekyll, or but remembered him as the mountain bandit remembers the cavern in which he conceals himself from pursuit" (89). As Stevenson commented in a letter to John Paul Bocock, "Hyde [is] the younger of the two" (Maixner 231). The fact that Hyde belongs to the pre-human phase of evolutionary development helps to explain why Jekyll can contain Hyde but Hyde cannot contain Jekyll.

In failing to understand the interdependence of his physical, or "primitive," and his moral, or "civilized," natures, Jekyll commits himself to an irreconcilable conflict, relegating his "appetites" exclusively to Hyde and his "aspirations" to his social persona. His decision is an erroneous one, as G. K. Chesterton has observed: "The point of the story is not that a man *can* cut himself off from his conscience, but that he cannot" (72–73). Jekyll makes a decision in favor of his social persona but finds that he no longer has the strength to uphold it (89). He forgoes using the elixir for two months, satisfying himself with the role of "elderly and discontented doctor" and saying "farewell to the liberty, the comparative youth, the light step, leaping pulses and secret pleasures" of Hyde's body, until he begins "to be tortured with throes and longings" and finally succumbs to temptation (90).

What happens next is an exemplary lesson in the dangers of excessive repression: "My devil had been long caged, he came out roaring" (90). Hyde's release carries with it an overwhelming accumulation of unused libidinal energy, a superabundance of aggression that leads to his savage murder of Sir Danvers Carew. Having broken off from Jekyll and the subduing influence of conscience, Hyde's "irrational" instinctual power becomes uncontrollable. Shocked and remorseful, Jekyll attempts to lock his double away, but he soon learns that Hyde can no longer be contained.

Hyde's growing autonomy again becomes evident when, after another period of chaste restraint and increased beneficent social activity, Jekyll starts to feel his "lower side . . . so long indulged, so recently chained down, be[gin] to growl for licence" (92). He confesses, obliquely, that he lapsed once again, but this time "in [his] own person . . . as an ordinary secret sinner." After his indulgence, which appears to have been a visit to a prostitute, he sits in Regent's Park[23] on a "fine, clear January day" in an atmosphere redolent of rebirth in the natural world, "full of winter chirrupings and sweet with Spring odours." He feels physical relief and satisfaction, "the animal within [him] licking the chops of memory" (92). He contentedly assures himself that he is not really "like his neighbours," as his recent action would seem to indicate, because his "active goodwill" outshines "the lazy cruelty of their neglect" (92). This time it is the sleep of conscience, in Jekyll's moment of moral complacency, that enables Hyde to return without being called for. After this incident Hyde gains complete ascendancy, coming unbidden with increasing frequency.

Indulging in "ape-like tricks" and "ape-like spite" (96–97), Hyde acts as Jekyll's ape in more than one sense, for his actions also ape or mimic Jekyll's unacknowledged inner anger. Several critics have noted that the pun in Jekyll's name, "*je* kill," suggests that Hyde acts out Jekyll's homicidal rage (Veeder, "Children" 115, 158 n. 9). The pun also indicates Hyde's function of fulfilling Jekyll's suicidal desire. Underlying Jekyll's wish for self-annihilation is the need to kill off the "I" or ego that has become so rigid and restrictive. In fact, Jekyll's ego is already "dying," for in separating it from his animal nature, Jekyll has deprived it of the very life force that sustains it: "The powers of Hyde seemed to have grown with the sickliness of Jekyll" (95).

The source of Jekyll's anger is suggested when Hyde scrawls blasphemies on the pages of Jekyll's books and destroys the portrait of Jekyll's father. As Veeder has also shown, in the murder of Sir Danvers Carew,

"M.P.," Hyde has moved from hurting the innocent victims of a patriarchal society to the "killing off" of the patriarchy itself, embodied in the legislator and lawmaker Carew ("Children" 126–28). Veeder places the antipatriarchal thrust of *Dr Jekyll and Mr Hyde* within a Freudian context of oedipal rage, in which Hyde can be seen as acting out Jekyll's childhood anger against an all-powerful father.

Significantly, Jekyll mentions only one childhood memory in his account—a fact that also may indicate a lack of integration in his personality—and it comes to his mind after the murder of Sir Danvers. In shame and agony at the murder he has committed via Hyde, Jekyll reviews his life from the time "when I had walked with my father's hand, and through the self-denying toils of my professional life" (91). The price of his patriarchal privilege has been too great, as he dimly understands; it is his rage at this fact that impels him to kill off all aging and "respectable" gentlemen, including himself.

Steven Marcus states that the efflorescence of pornographic and especially sado-masochistic literature during the Victorian period "indicates not merely a general disturbance of sexuality, but what is technically known as a dysfunction" (265). In the personal journals of his gentlemen pornographers, Marcus sees repeated evidence of "emotional deadness" (140) or "anesthesia," a nearly complete lack of feeling or concern for any of their sexual contacts, "severe limitation of the emotions . . . , restricted range of responses to other persons, . . . [and] extremely weak capacities for establishing relations with others" (181). He comments that "this kind of hard, aggressive indifference" both "amused and entertained" the early Victorian writer Anthony Trollope, until "toward the end of his career, [when] he took a look around him and undertook that remarkable reversal which *The Way We Live Now* realizes, [seeing] . . . that a whole class of Englishmen were walking about like zombies" (140). At the other extreme, Marcus mentions the letters of two men, one a clergyman, another an educator, to one of England's first sex education experts, William Acton; both letters "are representative, and what they reveal is a pitiable alienation on the part of a whole class of men from their own sexuality" (18).

Stevenson's novella stresses that Dr. Jekyll's "case" is not a unique one. The lives of the friends in his social circle are all marked by their essential solitariness and lack of emotional engagement. There are no wives, no mistresses, and no children. In Jekyll's account, there is not one direct reference to his mother. The men seem completely alienated from the feminine realm, and aside from occasional, unmentionable visits to prostitutes, they move for the most part—like Lewis's Ambrosio and Shelley's Frankenstein—in an exclusively masculine world, one that is an extreme yet representative instance of the "separate spheres" of male and female activity in Victorian society.

That the tale can be read as a critique of patriarchy and a defence of women and children is further suggested by the dedication of *Dr Jekyll and Mr Hyde* to a woman, Stevenson's cousin and childhood playmate Katherine de Mattos (*neé* Stevenson): "It's ill to loose the bands that God decreed to bind; / Still will we be children of the heather and the wind." As Stephen Heath points out, the story is not about "heather and wind and the broom 'blowing bonnie' . . . but streets and doors and locked rooms; . . . not the Katherine of Louis's childhood, but the immediate assault on the child" (95).

The men have all managed to maintain their status as reputable aging citizens, despite whatever breaches against propriety they may have committed in their younger days. The first description of Dr. Jekyll, offered indirectly by Enfield, is of a man who is "the very pink of the proprieties, celebrated too . . . one of your fellows who do what they call good" (33), and the next reference identifies him as "Dr Jekyll" or "Henry Jekyll, M.D, D.C.L., LL.D, F.R.S., &c." (35). Yet, as has been noted, Enfield immediately assumes the connection between Jekyll and Hyde to be one of blackmail: "an honest man paying through the nose for some of the capers of his youth" (33). Utterson, haunted by knowledge of his own past iniquities, corroborates the fact that Jekyll was "wild when he was young" and similarly thinks that "it must be . . . the ghost of some old sin, the cancer of some concealed disgrace; punishment coming, *pede claudo,* years after memory has forgotten and self-love condoned the fault" (41–42).

The repeated suggestions of unresolved or unatoned guilt suggest the moral and emotional disquiet underlying the men's successful, genteel, yet arid and womanless lives. If power has been given to them, it is also clear that real pleasure has been denied. The social ascent of men of their class has been bought at the price of their moral and spiritual descent. In terms of Otto Rank's analysis, it is precisely the kind of psychological situation that can create "strong tendencies toward self-punishment, which also imply suicide" (76). In Stevenson's "gothic gnome," the destruction of Dr. Jekyll's "fortress of identity" continues the original assault begun by Horace Walpole on the castle of the Father.

CHAPTER SEVEN

The Reptilian Brain at the
Fin de Siècle: Dracula

*I*n keeping with the Gothic practice of retrieving psychically archaic
material for the purpose of cultural commentary, Bram Stoker's
Dracula (1897) revives the vampire myth of folklore and medieval tradition. Like Frankenstein's murderous monster and Jekyll's bestial Hyde,
Dracula signifies a violent return of "buried life."

Although several vampire tales had appeared in the nineteenth century, Stoker's is the first to be placed within a social/historical context of
accelerating technological change. Whereas John Polidori's "Vampyre"
(1819) moved in the rarefied atmosphere of a cosmopolitan Regency aristocracy, and James Malcolm Rymer's (*Varney the Vampyre or, The Feast of
Blood;* 1840, 1847) haunted an old English Abbey in the 1730s,[1] Dracula
enters the bustling metropolis of late-nineteenth-century London. England's late Victorian period was a time of old things passing and new things
coming into being. The *fin de siècle* marked the beginning of the end of
British imperial power, but it was also a time of remarkable social and technological newness, and both these factors come into play during Dracula's
incursions into modern life. What distinguishes *Dracula* from its vampiric
predecessors, then, is its emphasis on the conflict between the modern
world and Dracula's ancient one, and the wide range of psychological and
political issues that this confrontation suggests.

Dracula's long, penetrating canine teeth mark him as an incubus from
medieval nightmare, but his power to drain his victims' life-blood also

153

allies him with the succubus. His strangely ambisexual quality is partly due to the fact that he hails from an even earlier evolutionary stage than does the apelike Hyde: the beginnings of animal life on earth, examined by Darwin in *The Origin of the Species* (1859). Dracula signifies the eruption of the most primitive and elemental instinctual drives related to the struggle for species survival—for food, for safety, and for sexual reproduction—at a time when a rapidly transforming environment was making increasing demands on the human power of adaptation.

The text of *Dracula* is itself a contemporary media pastiche, including clippings from current newspapers such as *The Dailygraph* (95) and *The Pall Mall Gazette* (165). However, the story is told primarily via the journals and letters of the various protagonists. One character's journal is kept in shorthand, and another's "*in phonograph*" (78); one of the chapters is titled "Dr. Seward's Phonograph Diary, Spoken by Van Helsing." The narrative stress on the exchanging and withholding of information (effectively or ineffectively) underscores the idea of interchange or transmission, which is the essence of the vampire situation.[2] In addition, the narrative technique reiterates in literary form the Gothic concern with communication between different psychological areas or domains.

The first four chapters of *Dracula* are transcripts from the journal of Jonathan Harker, a young solicitor who travels to Transylvania on behalf of his employer to arrange Count Dracula's purchase of some property in London. While staying at Dracula's castle he encounters a number of strange incidents, which include his near-seduction by a triad of female vampires; the realization that he is imprisoned in the castle; his discovery of Dracula lying in his coffin on a pile of newly dug earth; and the sight of Dracula crawling face down, along the castle's outer walls. This section ends just as Harker is about to risk his life in an attempt to escape.

The next five chapters are composed mainly of letters between Harker's fiancée, Mina, and her friend Lucy Westenra and of entries from Mina's journal. The latter contains the clipping from the *Dailygraph,* describing a violent storm and seemingly inexplicable shipwreck from which a large, strange dog emerges and escapes onto the land. There are also entries from the ship's log that indicate either that the captain was insane (the reporter's opinion) or that the ship had been subjected to a daemonic assault. As well, Lucy tells Mina about her marriage proposals from three different men who are all friends of one another: an American adventurer,

Quincey Morris; the head of a lunatic asylum, Dr. John Seward; and an aristocratic gentleman, Arthur Holmwood, whom she accepts. Mina takes time off from her work as an assistant schoolmistress and visits her wealthier friend at Whitby, where the storm and shipwreck occur.

Lucy begins sleepwalking and becomes the object of the vampire's attacks. Mina is worried but fails to understand what is happening, although the reader, who has had the privilege of reading Jonathan Harker's account, already recognizes (or at least suspects) that the vampire is responsible. There are also a couple of entries from Seward's diaries, recording his dejection at being refused by Lucy and describing a maniacal patient named Renfield who eats insects. As well, there is an exchange of business letters between a solicitors' firm in Whitby and a cartage company, arranging for the transfer of "goods" to a "partially ruined building," which is "the ancient chapel of the mansion" at Carfax (119). Finally, the connection is made between the first and second sections of the novel when Mina receives word that Jonathan has been recuperating from a "fearful shock," in a convent hospital in "Buda-Pesth" (122–23). Mina travels there, and they marry; she agrees to abide by his request not to read his journal.

In the meantime, Seward notices a big bat outside Renfield's window, Lucy's condition worsens, and Seward calls in his Dutch friend, Abraham Van Helsing, to assist in her recovery. Van Helsing is the only one who understands what is happening, and he attempts to deflect the vampire's attacks with the traditional means of garlic flowers. As Lucy continues to fail, three of the men (first Holmwood, then Seward, and finally Van Helsing) give their blood via transfusions in an unsuccessful effort to save her. Shortly after her death Van Helsing reveals to the others, who are initially resistant to the idea, that Lucy has been transformed into a vampire and is already at work attacking young children. They then enter her tomb and drive a stake through her body in order to release her soul. Shortly thereafter, the connection between Lucy's demise and Jonathan Harker's experience in Transylvania becomes clear to all, after he sees Dracula on the streets of London. Harker's reaction of shock and subsequent denial impel Mina to break her oath and read his diary; she then shares her discovery with Van Helsing.

The group tries to uncover Dracula in his lair at Carfax Abbey, which is adjacent to Seward's insane asylum. Because they have failed to understand Renfield's warnings, Dracula attacks Mina while they are invading the Abbey. Dracula escapes back to Transylvania, and the group, guided by Mina's telepathic access to his whereabouts, follows him. They finally destroy him in a climactic pursuit up the mountainous road to his castle, just before sunset. Jonathan Harker slices the vampire's throat with a Kukri knife, and Quincey Morris stabs him through the heart with a bowie knife. Morris is the only one to die in the conflict, and the Harkers later name their first child after him.

Many reviewers enthused about the story's frightfulness when it first appeared in May 1897, although a few scoffed. A critic writing for the *Daily Mail* saw it as a triumph of the Gothic horror tradition: "In seeking a parallel to this weird, powerful and horrible story, our minds revert to such tales as 'The Mysteries of Udolpho', 'Frankenstein', 'Wuthering Heights', 'The Fall of the House of Usher'. . . . But 'Dracula' is even more appalling in its gloomy fascination than any one of these!" The *Pall Mall Gazette,* perhaps not displeased to see itself mentioned in the novel, announced, "It is horrid and creepy to the last degree. It is also excellent, and one of the best things in the supernatural line that we have been lucky enough to hit upon." *The Lady* reported that *Dracula's* "fascination is so great that it is impossible to lay it aside" (qtd. in Ludlam 107).

A reviewer in *The Athenaeum* was one of the few to remain unmoved, although he acknowledged that "there are better moments that show more power, though even these are never productive of the tremor such subjects evoke under the hand of a master." He complained that *Dracula* "is wanting in the constructive art as well as in the higher literary sense. It reads at times like a mere series of grotesquely incredible events." A reviewer in *The Bookman* seemed to have been intrigued mainly by his own ambivalent response, of being unconsciously drawn to what he consciously rejected: "A summary of the book would shock and disgust; but we must own that, though here and there in the course of the tale we hurried over things with repulsion, we read nearly the whole with attention." This critic claimed to have been most deeply moved by the portrayal of "human skill and courage pitted against inhuman wrong and superhuman strength [rising] to the top" (qtd. in Ludlam 108).

Dracula went through six editions within a two-year period (Ludlam 120), but the tale took longer than either *Frankenstein* or *Dr Jekyll and Mr Hyde* to be disseminated via stage productions, for shortly after the book's first printing Stoker was careful to protect the copyright by staging a limited production at the Lyceum Theatre, where he had worked as manager for many years.[3] It was not until 1924 that the "Dracula industry" began, with a dramatic performance in Derby produced by Hamilton Deane, to whom Stoker's widow had given sole dramatic rights. The play drew packed houses, and when it went to London in 1927, "though it was scorned by the London critics, it captured the imagination of the public and ran for 391 performances after being transferred to two other theatres. . . . One night, twenty-nine people fainted" (Farson 165). Since that time, Dracula, like Frankenstein's monster and Dr. Jekyll/Mr. Hyde, has become a familiar, haunting presence in the twentieth-century horror film.

Perhaps because the tale is set at the end of the Victorian period, critics and film makers have tended to ignore the emphasis on modernity that sets *Dracula* apart from preceding vampire tales.[4] As part of its examination of the Darwinian problem of evolutionary adaptation and species survival,[5] the text includes a great deal of detailed reference to the latest technological extensions of human intelligence, for which several of *Dracula*'s main characters have an enthusiastic regard.[6]

Mina Harker memorizes train schedules and is an efficient typist (like her husband, she also knows shorthand: presumably the most recent system, developed by a German civil servant in 1834). She carries a "'Traveller's' typewriter" (the first manufactured typewriters having first appeared in 1873) into the darker reaches of Transylvania because she "would have felt quite astray" trying to write her journal entries with a pen (416). Dr. John Seward maintains his own journal by dictating into a phonograph recorder (invented in 1877); Mina at one point transcribes the audio recording, typing it out (in triplicate) as she listens (268). As the phonograph is too bulky to carry when tracking down Dracula, Seward must resort to writing with a pen, a task that he finds "irksome" (399). Earlier in the story, Seward and Mina take the "Underground to Fenchurch Street" (first built in 1884) with her typewriter in tow (262). The characters frequently communicate via telegraphs, sometimes with remarkable rapidity; Seward and Abraham Van Helsing receive a message from Mina that Dracula is on his way thirty-five minutes after she first sights him (361–62). A telephone also is used on one occasion (invented in 1876 and just coming into popular use in the 1890s), and Jonathan Harker takes photos of Dracula's London property with a Kodak camera (perfected in 1888).

The characters make use of numerous other advancements besides those in communication and transportation. Quincey Morris, the wealthy Texan, carries along some Winchesters (repeating rifles, first made in 1866) as part of the group's "armament" on the quest to vanquish Dracula (420). The up-to-date medical men refer to "defibrinat[ion]," "trituration," "molecules," "digital pressure," and "hypodermic injection[s]" (149, 151, 323, 156), and Dr. Van Helsing is adept at conducting blood transfusions.[7] Even the first opening of a vampire's coffin is accompanied not by the traditional paraphernalia of stake and cross, but by Van Helsing's fret saw and turnscrew, which he employs in a remarkably methodical manner, considering the gruesome nature of the situation (236–37; screw threads were not standardized until after 1841).[8]

The high visibility of the world of modern conveniences is quantitatively greater than the limited, intermittent visibility of Dracula who, as Leonard Wolf shows in his appendix to *The Annotated Dracula*, appears "onstage" in less than one-sixth of the book's total pages. Qualitatively, however, it seems that Dracula's relatively rare appearances are far more impressive—as if his near-invisibility in itself has endowed him with greater power. As David Seed observes, "Stoker exploits the reader's memory of Section One [the first four chapters devoted to Harker's journal] . . . by keeping Dracula well below the surface of the text once the novel has shifted the setting to England," thus undermining the reader's skeptical resistance to the supernatural (201, 204). This narrative strategy also underscores the idea that Dracula represents the prehistoric, ancestral past, which seems to have disappeared from the modern human psyche but which never really "goes away."

As Jonathan Harker writes in his diary (which he describes as "nineteenth-century up-to-date with a vengeance") after having seen Dracula crawl down the outside of the castle "just as a lizard moves along a wall," "unless my senses deceive me, the old centuries had, and have, powers of their own which mere 'modernity' cannot kill" (47–48, 49). *Dracula*'s publishers evidently were struck by the uncanniness of this scene, which appears on the covers of two of the earliest editions; Dracula creeps face first down the castle wall, his hands (and in the 1901 edition, his feet as well) appropriately long and lizardlike, clinging to the stone.[9]

With his power to subdue wolves and other creatures from the lower orders of the animal kingdom, Dracula signifies the link between the human and animal worlds that modern urban life tends to obscure. Stoker emphasizes the point when he has a reporter from the *Pall Mall Gazette* interview the keeper of the Zoological Gardens about a wolf that recently escaped (shortly after a visit by a strange man whom the reader recognizes as Dracula). The keeper observes philosophically that "there's a deal of the same nature in us as in them there animiles." He also draws an analogy between the reporter's methods of soliciting his cooperation, and his own use of intimidation and reward when dealing with the zoo animals at feeding time; all intimidation is in his opinion a form of "'itten . . . over the 'ead," or evoking the fear of death, and all reward is "food" (166).

Like the lizard, Dracula is actually a very limited being whose activities are almost entirely dominated by his drive for food, safety, and the reproduction of his species;[10] but his power, like that of the apelike Mr. Hyde, is invariably enhanced whenever people fail to recognize his existence. As Richard Wasson observes, "technological progress, having cut humanity off from the old superstitious, dark knowledge, makes itself increasingly vulnerable to the demonic powers like the vampire, for, having written them off as unreal, civilized man has no defense against them" (21). The clever Dr. Seward, for example, takes so long to recognize what is happening that he appears astonishingly stupid to the reader, who is already well aware of the blood-sucking monster at work behind the scenes.

Seward is of course not the only character who resists the truth. The captain of the ship on which Dracula transports himself and his boxes of earth to England also reveals the danger of denying the power of the daemonic. The ship's name, *Demeter*, recalls a myth that dramatizes the powers of the underworld—the "realm of darkness," the shadowy world below the threshold of consciousness and "light."[11] The captain's vulnerability and his literal loss of vision illustrate the psychological consequences of rejecting the supernatural in either its sacred or its daemonic manifestations. After having repudiated the "superstitious fear" that possesses one of the men who had glimpsed Dracula on board the ship, and after his crew has been eliminated one by one, he finds himself surrounded by a thick fog that prevents him from seeing ahead, and he writes in his journal, "We seem to be drifting to some terrible doom" (104, 105). After the death of the last man to perish before him, the captain still refuses to acknowledge the truth and imagines that this one had been the "madman" who had killed all the rest (107).

When he finally sees Dracula "in the dimness of the night," however, his reaction to the daemonic is a sudden intensification of religious feelings of dependence and submission. The previously skeptical captain now prays for divine forgiveness and aid: "God forgive me, but the mate was right to jump overboard. . . . God and the Blessed Virgin and the saints help a poor ignorant soul trying to do his duty" (107). As a Russian Orthodox, an adherent of an older and more "primitive" religion than English Protestantism, the captain has access not only to God but also to the Mother of God and to the protective spirits of the saints. He saves his soul by lashing himself Odysseuslike to the wheel, with his crucifix firmly attached to the ropes; his corpse is found in this state when the ship "as if by a miracle" moves into the harbor (99). The reporter covering the incident for *The Dailygraph* surmises that the captain suffered from "some kind of mania," but the local "folk hold almost universally . . . that the captain is simply a hero" (102, 107).

The captain's experience is replayed in various ways throughout the story, as is the contrast of response between the more sophisticated and skeptical characters who usually occupy some position of social authority, and the less sophisticated but more receptive characters such as the local "folk" of Whitby[12] and the seemingly ignorant Transylvanian peasants who do what they can to warn and protect Jonathan Harker on his first trip to Dracula's castle. Harker records that he felt a bit awkward when one woman gave him her crucifix: "I did not know what to do, for as an English Churchman, I have been taught to regard such things as in some measure idolatrous." Seeing the doubt on his face, the woman puts the rosary around his neck herself, saying in the spirit of her more feminized religion, "For your mother's sake" (13, 14).

Harker's obtuseness about Dracula's real nature is sometimes quite humorous, for the reader is given numerous clues that indicate that the Count is indeed a vampire. After noticing, for example, a number of odd things while staying at the castle—including the remarkable fact that Dracula casts no reflection in a mirror—Harker writes, "It is strange that as yet I have not seen the Count eat or drink. He must be a very peculiar man!" (37, 38). Nor is Harker aware that his crucifix saved his life when he cut himself while shaving, and Dracula, standing nearby, had compulsively moved to feed on his victim.

Later, however, Harker begins to accept the idea that the various charms that the peasants gave to him might be effective, although he still remains somewhat skeptical:

> What meant the giving of the crucifix, of the garlic, of the wild rose, of the mountain ash? Bless that good, good woman who hung the crucifix around my neck! for it is a comfort and a strength to me whenever I touch it. It is odd that a thing which I have been taught to regard with disfavour and as idolatrous should in a time of loneliness and trouble be of help. Is it that there is something in the essence of the thing itself, or that it is a medium, a tangible help, in conveying memories of sympathy and comfort? (40)

That the lack of fear in the modern world may be a sign of its spiritual impoverishment is suggested inversely by the passionate, ecstatic religiosity of the "superstitious" peasants whom Harker sees along his journey through the mountains. After a paragraph of Radcliffean sublimity, he writes that one of the passengers touched him, saying, "'Look! Isten szek!'—'God's seat!'—and he crossed himself reverently" (16). Further along, Harker sees "[h]ere and there . . . a peasant man or woman kneeling before a shrine, who did not even turn round as we approached, but seemed in the self-surrender of devotion to have neither eyes nor ears for the outer world" (17). As Van Helsing later comments in his broken English, "to superstition must we trust at the first; it was man's faith in the early, and it have its root in faith still" (390).

A frequent source of irony in *Dracula* (sometimes pathetic and sometimes humorous) is that Seward, the character who specializes in treating the insane, clearly fails to comprehend the workings of the psyche. Seward's mentor, Van Helsing, understands this deficiency and chastises him: "you are too prejudiced. You do not let your eyes see nor your ears hear, and that which is outside your daily life is not of account to you. . . . Ah, it is the fault of our science that it wants to explain all; and if it explain not, then it say there is nothing to explain" (229). In other words, that which is "outside" Seward's daily life is the inner spiritual sphere, which the scientific psychological research of his time largely ignores. The mad patient Renfield comments with regard to his own taste for flies that "[t]he fly, my dear sir, has one striking feature: its wings are typical of the aerial powers of the psychic faculties. The ancients did well when they typified the soul as a butterfly!" (320). Seward, typically, misinterprets the statement as an indication of developing megalomania—a diagnosis that could more aptly describe his own condition.

Because Renfield is a patient in Seward's asylum, who has indulged in the rather abnormal and repulsive (and reptilian) habit of eating flies, spiders, and even live birds, the doctor dismisses most of his statements as invalid and fails to see the power of the daemonic working through Renfield. Seward is very careful about maintaining his own position of social, moral, and especially *rational* superiority in relation to Renfield; as far as he is concerned, there is nothing Renfield can tell him that he does not already know. Thus, Seward helps to pave the way for Dracula's first assault on Mina, which Renfield unsuccessfully tries to avert.

Seward's rationalistic prejudice is evident in the interview he has with Renfield in the presence of Van Helsing, Quincey Morris, and "Lord"

Goldalming. Renfield moves from a rationality that impresses his keeper to an intense emotionality that Seward interprets as a sign of returning madness. Renfield attempts to win Harker's confidence by first demonstrating, rather verbosely, a comically high level of courtesy, dignity, and informed intelligence:

> What shall any man say of his pleasure at meeting Van Helsing? Sir, I make no apology for dropping all forms of conventional prefix. When an individual has revolutionised therapeutics by his discovery of the continuous evolution of brain-matter, conventional forms are unfitting, since they would seem to limit him to one of a class. Your gentlemen, who by nationality, by heredity, or by the possession of natural gifts, are fitted to hold your respective places in the moving world, I take to witness that I am as sane as at least the majority of men who are in full possession of their liberties. And I am sure that you, Dr Seward, humanitarian and medico-jurist as well as scientist, will deem it a moral duty to deal with me as one to be considered as under exceptional circumstances. (292)

Seward comments that Renfield "made this last appeal with a courtly air of conviction which was not without its own charm."

The question is repeatedly, if obliquely raised, as to whether these men are in fact fitted "to hold [their] respective places in the moving world," which in its largest sense involves protecting the "continuous evolution of brain-matter" by overcoming Dracula—who cannot be defeated if he is allowed to go unrecognized. When Renfield realizes that he will not be allowed out that day, a decision on which Van Helsing concurs with Seward because Renfield will not be specific about the reason for his urgency, the patient collapses into an emotional frenzy that solidifies the doctors' opposition. Seward records that as Renfield "saw that the very excess of his emotion was militating against him, by restoring us more to our old [unequal] relations, he became still more demonstrative," whereupon Seward reasserts his authority over his hostage, much like the zoo keeper with his animals: "I became a little more fixed in my manner, if not more stern." Renfield falls on his knees begging and weeping, "his whole face and form expressive of the deepest emotion" (294).

Renfield's plea echoes Van Helsing's earlier charge against Seward: "Can't you hear me, man? Can't you understand? Will you never learn? don't you know that I am sane and earnest now; that I am no lunatic in a mad fit, but a sane man fighting for his soul? Oh, hear me! hear me! Let me go!" (294). Some time before this episode, Van Helsing attributes Seward's lack of perception regarding "young ladies" to his preoccupation with his profession: "He has his madmans to play with, and to bring them back to happiness and to those that love them" (140). However, it often seems that Seward's intellectual "playing" with psychological theory, classification, and diagnosis is precisely what prevents him from effectively helping his patients.

In his role as the obtuse expert in mental and emotional disturbance, Dr. Seward, like Jonathan Harker, is often an object of humor. Not the least of Seward's weaknesses as a therapist is his tendency toward naive Victorian sentimentalism. After Lucy's body has been laid out in the coffin, with the protective crucifix laid on her lips, Seward notices one of the maids go into the room where the coffin is, and he comments rather effusively, "The sight touched me. Devotion is so rare, and we are so grateful to those who show it unasked to those we love. Here was a poor girl putting aside the terrors which she naturally had of death to go watch alone by the bier of the mistress whom she loved, so that the poor clay might not be lonely till laid to eternal rest" (200). Even when Seward learns almost immediately after this scene that the golden crucifix has been stolen, he has to ask Van Helsing how, and by whom. Next, when Seward reflects on what to him was the unseemly delight of Lucy's mother's lawyer about the ease of settling her will (mother and daughter both having died within a short time of each other), he takes it as "an object-lesson in the limitations of sympathetic understanding" (202). The ironic humor here is inescapable, not only because the expert doctor fails to appreciate the human capacity for ruthless self-interest that Dracula represents, but also because Seward himself is so clearly deficient in "sympathetic understanding" of others.

Van Helsing again takes on the voice of authority when he tries to explain to an uncomprehending Seward the interrelation of humor and horror, after Van Helsing collapsed into hysterics while the two men were leaving Lucy's funeral. Seward records that Van Helsing "gave way to a regular fit of hysterics" as soon as they were alone in the carriage. Van Helsing "insist[s] that it [is] only his sense of humour asserting itself under very terrible conditions." While his mentor laughs and cries, Seward, ever conscious of Victorian propriety, draws down the blinds "lest anyone should see us and misjudge" and tries unsuccessfully to be "stern" with Van Helsing (209–10).

Van Helsing tries to explain to Seward that "true" laughter comes when it will: "[H]e is a king, and he come when and how he like. He ask no person; he choose no time of suitability." Van Helsing says that even as he watched the earth being shoveled onto Lucy's coffin, "King Laugh he come to me and shout and bellow in my ear: 'Here I am! Here I am!' till the blood come dance back and bring some of the sunshine that he carry with him to my cheek" (210).

Laughter for Van Helsing has the apotropaic function it once possessed in medieval ritual, of warding off death and affirming life. In his explanation, "King Laugh" appears as another version of the Grim Reaper in the medieval Dance of Death:

> Oh, friend John, it is a strange world, a sad world, a world full of miseries, and woes, and troubles; and yet when King Laugh come he make them all dance to the tune he play. Bleeding hearts, and dry bones of the churchyard, and tears that burn as they fall—all dance together to the music that he make with that smileless mouth of him. And believe me, friend John, that he is good to come, and kind. Ah, we men and women are like ropes drawn tight with strain that pull us different ways. Then tears come; and, like the rain on the ropes, they brace us up, until perhaps the strain become too great, and we break. But King laugh he come like the sunshine, and he ease off the strain again; and we bear to go on with our labour, what it may be. (211)

Dracula, of course, has no such sense of humor. He has no conception of life's "grim irony" (211) because unlike civilized humans, who are "drawn tight with strain that pulls us different ways," he experiences no tension between conflicting tendencies and aspirations.

Unlike Seward, Van Helsing understands why Dracula should choose London, the heart of the world's most advanced industrial nation and the hope of humanity's increasing immunity from "miseries, and woes, and troubles," to make his appearance. Mina recognizes that the concentration of population in London, "with its teeming millions," makes it an ideal target for the thirsty vampire (215). However, Van Helsing realizes that it is more than a simple matter of population density, for it is the "sceptical, selfish" attitude pervading modern life (226) that makes it intrinsically susceptible to the vampire's assaults. In other words, religious skepticism has led to the loss of a collective sense of the sacred, and economic competition to the breakdown of community. In this world people become like the vampire, who can "do only work selfish and therefore small" (404).

When Seward, avatar of his time, states, "I feel like a novice blundering through a bog in a mist, jumping from one tussock to another in the mere blind effort to move on without knowing where I am going," he is saying more than he realizes (232). Although he thinks that he is referring only to the specific problem of understanding what Van Helsing is trying to tell him, he is actually describing the condition of his own life. Like the initially skeptical captain of *The Demeter*, Seward is spiritually adrift.

Van Helsing's response to his young friend's perplexity is simply to ask him "to believe" (232).

Notwithstanding its critique of the modern secular/scientific temper, however, *Dracula* includes several references to recent neurological research or "brain science," about which Seward is well informed and which shed some light on the vampire syndrome (see 88, 90, 230).[13] Nineteenth-century "brain science" was one of those areas where the difficulties of the tension between spirituality and science were most painfully apparent. Surgeon Thomas Pettigrew, whose 1844 study of the relation between superstition and various mental states was part of Stoker's library, argued that to regard brain research simply as a branch of physiology was to ignore important questions concerning the "nature and essence of mind" (qtd. in Leatherdale, *Origins* 181).

Stoker looked into both the metaphysical[14] and the physical lines of enquiry in his research for *Dracula.* Three of his brothers were medical doctors (Ludlam 41), and his notes reveal that he "learned the symptoms and treatment of specific head injuries" from his surgeon brother, William (Leatherdale, *Dracula* 88). As well, one of Seward's first direct references to current neurological research is to the work of David Ferrier (1808–1864), whose "brain-knowledge" Seward imagines he might one day outstrip (90). Seward is tempted to complete the "experiment" with Renfield, who has just eaten a live bird, by supplying the lunatic with the cat he has requested. Seward thinks that such a move might be justified on scientific grounds: "Men sneered at vivisection, and yet look at its results today!"

Ferrier's *Functions of the Brain* (1886) examines the brain's division of labor into different areas and hemispheres and includes numerous illustrations of the brains of humans, human embryos, and various animals, including monkeys, fish, frogs, pigeons, rabbits, cats, and dogs. His study also refers several times to the work of P. Broca, and so it seems quite likely that Stoker would have been aware of Broca's discovery in 1878 of the phylogenetically older section of the brain beneath the neocortical mantle, which he named the "limbic lode." Like Ferrier, Broca was concerned with the physical commonalities and differences in the brains of humans and animals. He focused on the physiological—and by extension instinctual—basis of human behavior, or, one could say, the material foundation of "the continuous evolution of brain-matter."

Broca emphasized two aspects of the limbic lode: its connection with the olfactory apparatus and, what is more important, "its presence as a common denominator among the brains of mammals" (Isaacson 1–2). The more recent term *limbic system* is derived from Broca's research.[15] Contemporary neuroscientists have further divided the brain's structure into three main parts, labelled "reptilian," "paleomammalian" (or limbic system), and "neomammalian." The "R-complex" located at the base of the forebrain in reptiles, birds, and mammals is said to be "essential for genetically constituted forms of behavior" (MacLean, "Cerebral" 140).

Current research suggests that the R-complex is the area related to instinctually derived behavior and also may be "a repository of ancestrally learned behavior . . . a storage mechanism for parroting learned forms of emotional and intellective behavior acquired through the participation of limbic and neocortical systems" (MacLean, "Cerebral" 140, 145). Thus, it appears to be the reptilian brain that makes us creatures of habit. Research has further demonstrated that the intermediate limbic system, the seat of much emotional response, acts to suppress or intensify the established responses of the reptilian brain, according to the varying pressures of changes in the environment. According to Robert L. Isaacson, this limbic activity enables the innovative paleomammalian neocortex to do its adaptive work of quickly and efficiently "processing . . . information which has too many fine details to be easily handled by the mechanisms in the lower brain regions" (237). As he also explains,

> [t]he protoreptilian brain looks to the past. It learns and remembers but is poor at forgetting. The neocortical brain looks to the future, either to tomorrow, next week, next year, or to heavenly rewards. The neocortex is the brain of anticipation. It prepares for, anticipates, and predicts the future. . . . The sin of excessive "attachment" to things, places, even roles, is excoriated in the wisdom of East and West alike. In the triune brain metaphor, this means that the graven images of the protoreptilian brain must be overcome. (243)

Such ideas about the nature of the reptilian brain bear a striking correspondence to Van Helsing's analyses of the vampire's psychic disposition, its capacities, and its motivations. One work that has been cited as a source for *Dracula* is Sarah Lee's *Anecdotes of Habits and Instincts of Birds, Reptiles and Fishes* (1853; Leatherdale 238; *Origins* 153), although Clive Leatherdale has suggested that the more likely work would have been Lee's earlier book, *Anecdotes of Habits and Instincts of Animals* (1852; *Origins* 153), which contains a chapter on the mammalian bats. However, there is good reason to think that Stoker may have read the section on reptiles in the later work, for there are several respects in which Dracula's behavior seems more reptilian than batlike.

An essential difference between reptiles and mammals is in care of the young, which in the case of mammals is extended by nursing. Few reptiles care for their young, and some species cannibalize them (MacLean, *Triune* 136), as do the vampires in *Dracula*. Lee recounts that male alligators eat the newly hatched young; she also tells the story of a pregnant python who sat coiled over her fifteen eggs for fifty-six days, but as soon as they were born "left them to themselves" (*Birds* 250, 286). Lee also notes the apparent callousness of reptiles, illustrated during an alligator hunt in which the alligators who escaped the hunters' bullets paid "no attention to the death of their companions" (*Birds* 252). Lee states that reptiles' reputation for "murder and rapacity" is generally well deserved (*Birds* 253). She also stresses their "sluggish[ness]," noting their ability to lie buried in sand or earth for long periods of time without eating or drinking (*Birds* 241, 249, 320, 340).

Another similarity between reptiles and vampires is in their mating behavior: they do not form sexual bonds, and biting is a common preliminary of reptilian intercourse (MacLean, *Triune* 103, 110–11). As well, reptiles lack the mammalian capacity for play, a fact that may help to explain why vampire sex is such a deadly business. As Dracula confesses, "my heart . . . is not attuned to mirth" (35). Reptiles' incapacity for play also can be related to their reliance on rigid behavioral routines, a quality that Abraham Van Helsing notes is one of the vampire's greatest weaknesses.

It is also possible that Stoker gained some of his insight into reptilian behavior during his note-taking visits to London's Zoological Gardens (Leatherdale, *Dracula* 86[16]), where there was a reptile house (as well as a monkey house, where the bats were lodged; Wolf 128). The apocryphal story about Stoker "dreaming up" Dracula one night after a dinner of dressed crab also seems highly appropriate; one can easily imagine the author going to bed at night meditating on lower life forms after having consumed one of them for dinner, and then later meeting them in his dreams.[17]

In any case, Stoker's knowledge is relayed through his namesake, Abraham Van Helsing, the local expert on the vampire's reptilian character. Van Helsing informs the others that the vampire is a creature of "more than mortal [cunning] for [its] cunning be the growth of ages."[18] The vampire's knowledge is prehuman, for it is part of the world that existed before human life appeared (the lizard in particular is the reptile that scientists believe probably bears the closest resemblance to the long-extinct mammal-like reptiles; MacLean, *Triune* 16). Its power lies within this elemental world; according to Van Helsing, it can change form and "within [its] range, direct the elements: the storm, the fog, the thunder; [it] can command all the meaner things": rat, owl, bat, moth, fox, wolf (283).

Developmentally, however, the vampire is a rudimentary being. As Van Helsing puts it, "[it] is brute, and more than brute; [it] is devil in callous, and the heart of [it] is not" (283). As the "devil [is] callous," the vampire is the enemy of God, and of human sympathy and conscience. To become a vampire is to lose all "heart or conscience," to become a "foul thin[g] of the night"—when the vampire who can see in the dark is at its strongest (284, 286). Despite all its magical powers, the vampire "is not free. . . . [It] cannot go where [it] lists; [it] is not of nature . . . [and yet must] obey some of nature's laws." Its powers wax and wane with the cycles of the day (287).

The vampire casts neither shadow nor reflection because it has no soul. As Otto Rank has shown, the shadow, as well as its later correlative the mirror, was interpreted from very early times as an indication of the soul (49–68). Another reason that the vampire casts no reflection is that "the face of the vampire is the hidden side of the human character" (Senf, "*Dracula*" 101), or the human capacity for degenerating into an inhuman, soulless condition. It is, as Van Helsing describes it, the "evil thing . . . rooted deep in all good" (288).

Van Helsing repeatedly describes Dracula's mind not merely as rudimentary but also as being developmentally stunted: a "child-brain" in contrast to the "man-brains" pitted against him: "I have hope that our man-brains, that have been of man so long and that have not lost the grace of God, will come higher than his child-brain that lie in his tomb for centuries, that grow not yet to our stature, and that do only work selfish and therefore small" (404). The doctor further compares the mind of Dracula with that of the criminal, the sort "who seems predestinate to crime":

> This criminal has not full man-brain. He is clever and cunning and resourceful; but he be not of man-stature as to brain. He be of child-brain in much. . . . The little bird, the little fish, the little animal learn not by principle, but empirically; and when he learn to do, then there is to him the ground to start from to do more. . . . To do once, is the fulcrum whereby child-brain become man-brain; and until he have the purpose to do more, he continue to do the same again every time, just as he have done before! . . .
>
> The Count is a criminal and of criminal type. . . . [H]e is of imperfectly formed mind. Thus, in a difficulty he has to seek resource in habit. (405–06)[19]

As Van Helsing understands, Dracula's inability to adapt quickly to changing conditions is his greatest weakness. Obeying the dictates of habitual response, he returns to his "lair," where the group, aided by Van Helsing's knowledge and Mina's insight, tracks him down.

The human equivalent of this automatic flight response is demonstrated by Jonathan Harker, when he discovers that he is a prisoner in Dracula's castle: "a sort of wild feeling came over me. I rushed up and down the stairs, trying every door and peering out of every window I could find; but after a little the conviction of my helplessness overpowered all other things. When I look back . . . I think I must have been mad for the time, for I behaved much as a rat does in a trap" (39). In neuroscientific terms, Harker's initial reptilian reaction is finally overcome when he sits "down quietly" and allows the neocortical activity to take over. He begins "to think over what is best to be done" and after some consideration decides that for the present the best course to follow is that of secrecy, silence, and cautious observation (39).

Harker's panicked reaction also shows the humorous side of human behavior that is directed by the reptilian brain. Charlie Chaplin arouses laughter when he keeps coming back to get hit on the head because it takes him so long to figure out how to do things differently; he shows us in stark relief our own human difficulty in learning new behavior. This is one reason why the Dracula film tradition has had such a strong tendency toward "campiness," why Dracula's compulsiveness often seems both funny and horrific,[20] and why Stoker's *Dracula* is distinguished by its dark wit.

The mingling of humor and horror first occurs when Dracula welcomes Harker to the castle with the traditional folk expression, "Welcome to my house. Come freely. Go safely. And leave something of the happiness you bring" (26)—for the reader already suspects, if Jonathan does not, that happiness for Dracula is a pint or more of warm human blood. We experience a similar jolt of grim humor when the never-too-subtle Van Helsing requests in his fractured English permission from Lucy's fiancé—who still thinks that she died a natural death—to interfere with her remains: "May I cut off the head of dead Miss Lucy?" (247). There is also the terrible but unmistakable pun when Mina, who has been infected by Dracula and runs the risk of becoming a full-fledged vampire, declares that her "soul is at stake" (392).

Particularly, the reader is frequently invited to laugh at the pretensions and delusions of men like Harker and Seward. As Harker recounts his strange and uncanny night journey to Dracula's castle, he pauses in the midst of describing himself waiting at the great door late at night with no-one answering, to comment on his professional status back in England: "Was this a customary incident in the life of a solicitor's clerk sent out to explain the purchase of a London estate to a foreigner? Solicitor's clerk! Mina would not like that. Solicitor—for just before leaving London I got world that my examination was successful; and I am now a full-blown so-licitor!" (25). In addition to being a "full-blown solicitor," Jonathan Harker also seems to possess a full-blown sense of his own importance, in a place where his newly elevated status makes no difference.

In his famous essay on laughter, Henri Bergson has examined how such deflation of pretension and rejection of the inflexible behavior that he terms "mechanical inelasticity" (10) are key elements in the response of laughter. Bergson argues that laughter is as much a social as an aesthetic gesture, in that it serves as a "corrective" to the "rigidity of body, mind and character, that society would still like to get rid of in order to obtain from its members the greatest possible degree of elasticity and sociability" (20–21). Although one may question Bergson's assumption that "society" invariably values elasticity over rigidity of behavior, as well as his equation of inelasticity (both mental and corporeal) with "eccentricity" (19), his dis-cussion of the connection between the qualities of flexibility and graceful-ness, and those of "imagination" and "soul," is poetically persuasive and brings to mind the contrast drawn in *Dracula* between the compulsiveness of the soulless vampires and the more flexible responses of their human op-ponents. According to Bergson,

> [I]n every human form [our imagination] sees the effort of a soul which is shaping matter, a soul which is infinitely supple and perpetually in motion, subject to no law of gravitation, for it is not the earth that attracts it. This soul imparts a portion of its winged lightness to the body it animates: the immateriality which thus passes into matter is what is called gracefulness. Matter, however, is obstinate and resists. . . . Where matter . . . succeeds in dulling the outward life of the soul, in petrifying its movements and thwart-ing its gracefulness, it achieves, at the expense of the body, an effect that is comic. (28–29)

Additionally, Bergson identifies repetition as a basic principle of humor on the dramatic stage, something with which Stoker was undoubtedly famil-iar in his capacity as manager of the Lyceum Theatre: "*In a comic repetition of words we generally find two terms: a repressed feeling which goes off like a spring, and an idea that delights in repressing the feeling anew*" (73; Bergson's italics). We laugh, then, at all unthinking, uncreative, "knee-jerk" responses because we wish to repudiate them. But we also laugh because we recognize our own complicity in such behavior; in turn, the laughter serves to ease or dissolve the tension and rigidity that characterize the "reptilian" response to experience. As Van Helsing understands, even in the midst of horror, "King Laugh" is a uniquely human adaptive device.

The peculiar "lizard fashion" with which Dracula scales the castle walls (47, 48, 64) and the fact that Harker first meets the vampire on St. George's Day (13) indicate that the battle against Dracula is an archetypal fight with the dragon. Lee records that some lizards "retain the old and fabulous name of Dragons; and their appearance justifies the appellation, for they have wings, and some have crests" (*Birds* 263). As well, the Romanian word for dragon is *Dracul,* which, according to an article that Stoker consulted at the Whitby library, in the Wallachian language means "devil" (Leatherdale, *Dracula* 90, 97).

The struggle against the dragon is a struggle against the domination of instinctual impulses, and one that can ultimately result, in Erich Neumann's words, in "positive development and transformation" (*Great Mother* 38); but Dracula's opponents' chances of winning the fight are seriously hampered by their initial failure to recognize Dracula, as well as by their underestimation of Mina. In failing to see Dracula's connection with the dehumanized Renfield, and regarding Mina as an ethereal Victorian maiden who is "too precious" to risk joining them on their first foray into Dracula's abode (289), they make two major tactical errors, which enable Dracula to visit her unhindered on the same night that Renfield's request for freedom is denied.

Mina agrees to be excluded from the men's activities, but her reservations about doing so are astute: "[I]t did not seem to me good that they should brave danger and, perhaps, lessen their safety" (289). She feels it is "a bitter pill . . . to swallow" yet accepts "their chivalrous care" without protest, partly because she fears that if she were a "drag or hindrance to their work, they might even leave [her] out of their counsels altogether" (290). In fact, they decide to do just that, as her well-meaning but blind and condescending husband notes upon returning from their venture. Finding Mina asleep and pale after Dracula's secret visit, Harker writes, "She looks paler than usual. I hope the meeting to-night has not upset her. I am truly thankful that she is to be left out of our future work, and even of our deliberations. It is too great a strain for a woman to bear" (303).

Relegated to the role of dependent child, Mina is literally "sent to bed" twice by the men, who assume the role of responsible adults. She leaves them the first time so that they can arrange their excursion. The second time, she records that "they sent me to bed, and all went off to smoke together, as they said, but I knew that they wanted to tell each other of what had occurred to each during the day" (290, 310). When they all later realize that Mina has been infected by Dracula, they abandon the "separate spheres" arrangement and increasingly begin to rely on her fortitude and insights. When the group loses track of Dracula near the end of their journey into Transylvania, Mina presents to the men her analysis of the situation and her recommendation about how to proceed. Van Helsing responds with a courteous yet wholly sincere eulogy: "Our dear Madam Mina is once more our teacher. Her eyes have seen where we were blinded" (420).

Mina herself is part of the newness of the radically changing modern world that the vampire invades, although she is somewhat uncomfortable about the challenges currently being made to traditional notions about women's social identity. As a highly resourceful and intelligent individual who is justifiably rather proud of her own accomplishments, she deserves the epithet of *New Woman*—the new and controversial champion of greater social equality between the sexes. Yet Mina has reservations about this movement. After having "a capital 'severe tea'" at an "old-fashioned inn" with Lucy, Mina comments, "I believe we should have shocked the 'New Woman' with our appetites. Men are more tolerant, bless them!" (110). Although this observation reflects a rather conservative attitude to women's emancipation, as some feminist critics have argued,[21] it is later corrected by the devastating consequences of the "blessed" men's decision to exclude Mina from the fight against the vampire. As Nina Auerbach suggests, "it seems more plausible to read the novel as a fin-de-siècle myth of newly empowered womanhood" than to see *Dracula* as "an emanation of Victorian sexual repression" (24).

A major source of Mina's strength is her willingness to accept herself as a creature of appetite and pleasure. Her comment seems to suggest that the New Woman ideology itself is based on an inadequate and overly idealistic understanding of human nature and that it actually participates in the lingering Victorian desire to desexualize women. The plot of *Dracula* appears to endorse the movement toward female emancipation that was undermining the bastions of traditional male privilege, for Mina is exposed to the danger of becoming a vampire mainly because she has been denied active participation in the men's "moving world." Viewed symbolically, her situation reflects that of women whose intellectual and emotional powers remain undeveloped, who become parasitic in their personal relations because they have been prevented from exercising their nondomestic skills and talents.

This may be one reason why Lucy is more susceptible than Mina is to the vampire's attacks. Auerbach believes that both Mina and Lucy are "violently transformed from victims to instigators of their story" (24), whereas I would argue that only Mina achieves this transformation. Lucy is the weaker character largely because she has led a more privileged and less demanding life than her friend. Mina was born an orphan (190) and apparently overcame her disadvantaged social position through education, becoming a companion/teacher for young girls such as Lucy (207, 130) and finally marrying an industrious and upwardly mobile young man. Mina and Jonathan achieve a measure of security and affluence after his senior partner dies; when Mina is at home, she no longer answers the door herself but waits for her servant Mary to do it (218).

Lucy, in contrast, has never known anything but comfort and security; the fact that she can marry a man who will one day possess a hereditary title gives one indication of her superior social status. Lucy is a beautiful and charming *femme fatale,* capable of uttering the "heresy" that she would not mind marrying all three of the men who proposed to her one day (76). Yet like Mina she is also a generous and kind-hearted woman who extends her sympathy to old and young alike. Mina writes of one of their outings that Lucy "is so sweet with old people; I think they all fell in love with her on the spot" (82). Lucy nevertheless appears rather childish in comparison to Mina, and her letters and diary (which she begins in imitation of Mina) suggest a more limited range of observation and reflection. Thus, in a sense, she is less "armored" against the vampire than her more disciplined and purposeful friend is. The same can be said of Lucy's mother, a typical domestic Victorian matron, who through her ignorance repeatedly allows Dracula entry into Lucy's bedroom.

According to some feminist critics, Lucy (and to some extent Mina) is punished for expressing overt sexual desire,[22] but what needs more consideration is Stoker's emphasis on the hard, impersonal, almost reptilian quality of her desire, which gives the impression of being more predatory than amorous. The vampire conflates the act of feeding on another's blood, or killing one's prey, with the act of species reproduction (as do serial rapist/killers, whose actions one might say are directed by the reptilian brain). Although one can also draw a connection between vampiric and intrauterine sustenance, the analogy is limited by the fact that the fetus does not kill the life that feeds it. The vampire's impulse for sexual congress is indiscriminate and compulsive, demonstrating neither the playful rituals of courtship found in many higher mammals nor the specifically human blending of emotional nurturing and physical passion.

As has been mentioned, the identification of vampires with lower life forms is suggested more than once in the story, when female vampires are seen feeding on the young. Such indifference about the welfare of the young would not normally be found in higher mammals, who engage in extended nurturing of their offspring. The scenes where Dracula throws down his bag of prey containing a child for the female vampires to consume and where Lucy as vampire flings "to the ground, callous as a devil, the child that up to now she had clutched strenuously to her breast, growling over it as a dog growls over a bone," are equally horrific (53, 253). From an evolutionary perspective, these scenes vividly reveal the overthrow of the more recently evolved or "higher" instincts. From a mythical perspective, they show the Earth Goddess in her destructive aspect, and the closing off of future possibility symbolized by the child (as in Hansel and Gretel, or Red Riding Hood, mentioned in *Dracula*, 170, 234).

Seward's description of Lucy's appearance when she throws the child onto the ground conveys its archetypal impact: "The beautiful colour [of her skin] became livid, the eyes seemed to throw out sparks of hell-fire, the brows were wrinkled as though the folds of the flesh were the coils of Medusa's snakes, and the lovely, blood-stained mouth grew to an open square, as in the passion masks of the Greeks and Japanese. If ever a face meant death—if looks could kill—we saw it at that moment" (254). The image evoked here is the *vagina dentata* of the life-giving and life-devouring Earth Goddess, which can be found, as Seward's comparisons suggest, throughout primitive religious art. As Erich Neumann has shown, this is the negative, destructive face of the otherwise "generative and nourishing, protecting and warming Femininity" that represents "world, life, nature, and soul" in the mythic imagination: "[T]he black, abysmal side of life and the human psyche . . . [is] also perceived in the image of the Feminine; death and destruction, danger and distress, hunger and nakedness, appear as helplessness in the presence of the Dark and Terrible Mother. . . . [She expresses] man's experience of life as a female exacting blood" (*Great Mother* 149).[23]

Despite its terrifying effect, the vampire is also an extremely seductive creature. Its allure is based on the appeal of sinking into an elementary instinctual state and forgoing the tensions arising from the desires of the individual will or from care or concern for others. But because the vampire lacks a developed sense of futurity and knows only the impulses of appetite and self-protective flight, to succumb to its charms is to find oneself in an even more defenseless condition and subject to a more intense and immediate anxiety.

Thus, Jonathan Harker, an extremely fastidious fellow, feels an "agony of delightful anticipation" at his impending dissolution into sheer physicality as the three "vamps" approach him (51). He feels the experience as an intensification of heat and tactility:

> [I] could feel the hot breath on my neck. Then the skin of my throat began to tingle as one's flesh does when the hand that is to tickle it approaches nearer—nearer. I could feel the soft, shivering touch of the lips on the supersensitive skin of my throat, and the hard dents of two sharp teeth, just touching and pausing there. I closed my eyes in a languorous ecstasy and waited—waited with a beating heart. (52)

The overt sensuousness of this description encourages the reader to attribute the beating of Jonathan's heart to erotic arousal; more subliminally, however, what is evoked is the reaction of a frightened animal facing imminent death. Aside from the sexual connotations suggested by the conceit of orgasm as "dying," his description also indicates that the threat he is facing is his own spiritual death. Mina similarly admits that when Dracula made the assault on her that the men interrupted, she "strangely enough . . . did not want to hinder him," although when he began to feed on her, she felt her "strength fading away" (342, 344). Whenever Lucy moves into a less than fully conscious state, she too cooperates with Dracula by removing the obstacles that prevent him from reaching her; but her diary also testifies to the deathlike quality of his spell: "I have a dim half-remembrance of long, anxious times of waiting and fearing; darkness in which there was not the pain of hope to make present distress more poignant; and then long spells of oblivion, and the rising back to life as a diver coming up through a great press of water" (164).

Lucy experiences her return from unconsciousness to consciousness as an emergence from what Neumann would call the underwater "embrace of the primordial uroboric dragon" (*Origins* 105). Her transitions between human and vampire states are often described as fluctuations between consciousness and unconsciousness. During one of the nights in which Seward acts as her guard, he notes that "the moment she became conscious she pressed the garlic flowers close" and that whenever she moved into "that lethargic state" in which her breathing became labored, she put them away from her (192–93). When her fiancé, Arthur, comes into the room, Lucy opens her eyes and addresses him lovingly, but then her eyes close, and she "sinks" again into sleep and labored breathing. Seward's observations make it clear that when she next opens her eyes she is still in the grip of the vampire: "In a sort of sleep-waking, vague, unconscious way she opened her eyes, which were now *dull and hard* at once, and said in a soft voluptuous voice, such as I had never heard from her lips:—'Arthur! Oh, my love, I am so glad you have come! Kiss me!'" (194; my emphasis).

At this point, Van Helsing, noticing the discrepancy between her expression of love and the siren tone of her voice, intercepts Arthur before he can kiss her, whereupon "a spasm as of rage flit[s] like a shadow over her face; the sharp teeth champ together," and her eyes close again. She returns one last time to full consciousness. She thanks Van Helsing for protecting Arthur, asks the doctor to continue guarding him, and finally "dies," to join the ranks of the living dead (194–95).

The vampire's powers increase with the setting of the sun because it belongs to the darkness of the unconscious. Mina discovers that the best moments for gaining access to Dracula are sunset and dawn, when she is under hypnosis. She does not arrive at the idea through conscious reflection or analysis but says it "must have come in the night, and matured without my knowing it" (370)—which once again suggests that the unconscious becomes a life-threatening force only when it is alienated from consciousness. Psychologically speaking, sunset and dawn correspond to those liminal moments of falling asleep and waking, when the dream world of the unconscious meets and mingles with the flow of conscious thought. In Jungian therapy, such "hypnagogic states," as they are called, are induced with the aim of making unconscious images more visible to conscious perception.

Mina earlier identifies this condition when she describes her experience the night of Dracula's first visit to her. She remembers it as a dream in which Jonathan was bending over her: "My dream was very peculiar, and was almost typical of the way that waking thoughts become merged in, or continued in, dreams" (308). Seward carefully notes a similar process during the times that Van Helsing hypnotizes Mina:

> [S]unrise and sunset are to her times of peculiar freedom, when her old self can be manifested without any controlling force subduing or restraining her, or inciting her to action. This mood or condition begins some half-hour or more before actual sunrise or sunset. . . . At first there is a sort of negative

condition, as if some tie were loosened, and then the absolute freedom quickly follows; when, however, the freedom ceases the change-back or relapse comes quickly. (391–92)

Dracula's careful delineation of the shifting relations between conscious and unconscious mental activity accords with the Gothic practice of bringing unconscious elements to "light." It also indirectly criticizes the materialistic and rationalistic orientation of "mad doctors" such as Seward, who fail to recognize the nature and the power of the unconscious, and thus fail to address effectively the conflicts between conscious and unconscious impulses. In this respect, Seward himself can be seen as a type of vampire who drains the life of others. The fact that Dracula chooses an old ruined abbey next to Seward's modern insane asylum for his lair suggests that the emergence of psychoanalysis in the late nineteenth century may be one of the contemporary developments that have disturbed and reawakened the vampire.[24]

Other factors that unleash the vampire at the end of the nineteenth century are Britain's declining international influence and the concomitant breakdown in international relations that would come to dominate much of the twentieth century. In the words of Erich Neumann, upon the breakdown of the old values that once held the social world together, when there is no inner "compensatory movement" toward "transpersonal experience," the psychological effect can be "a shrinking of world horizons, and the loss of all certainty and meaning in life" (*Origins* 390). A recurrent motif in *Dracula* is the exhaustion of masculine (or patriarchal) energy and an accompanying sense of debility, fear, and confusion.

Although none of the men in this story is ever successfully attacked by a vampire, all are subject to a feeling of being drained in some vital way. While monitoring Lucy's decline, Seward records that although he is keeping up his diary, he is feeling "too miserable, too low-spirited, too sick of the world and all in it, including life itself," to do so with any enthusiasm (191). Arthur, called "Lord Godalming" after his father dies, appears to Seward as if "his stalwart manhood [had] shrunk under the strain of his much-tried emotions" (202).

In the past, these two had indulged their nostalgia for the ancient hunting/warring life by going off with Quincey Morris on expeditions to remote and uncivilized corners of the earth, but in their present circumstances, their stalwart manhood seems rather fragile. That these excursions, or regressions, could not provide adequate compensation for the men's deracinated urban existence is suggested in Dracula's comment to Jonathan Harker: "[Y]ou dwellers in the city cannot enter into the feelings of the hunter" (29).

Jonathan Harker also becomes, according to Leonard Wolf, "increasingly more supine as Dracula grows more active" (266). Wolf sees this debility as deriving from Dracula's sexual usurpation of Mina, but Harker's emotional collapse occurs at the outset of the story, long before his wife is attacked by the vampire. Mina writes to Lucy that after Jonathan's "violent brain fever" (as it has been explained to her; 122), he "is only a wreck of himself" (127). After she returns to England with her husband, Mina writes that he still "wants looking after" and that he has been having bad dreams (186–87). Then, after the death of his senior partner and father figure, which leaves them "with a fortune which to people of our modest bringing up is wealth beyond the dream of avarice," she writes that Jonathan "says the amount of responsibility which it puts upon him makes him nervous. He begins to doubt himself" (190). Mina becomes another Ophelia, lamenting the decline of her modern-day Hamlet trapped in emotional paralysis: "Oh, it is too hard that a sweet, simple, noble, strong nature such as his—a nature which enabled him, by our dear, good friend's aid, to rise from clerk to master in a few years—should be so injured that the very essence of its strength is gone" (190–91).

Harker continues to be subject to spells of lassitude until he stops trying to reject the evidence of his own experience and accepts the necessity of battling Dracula. Jonathan's adventure at Castle Dracula remains literally a closed book between him and Mina until he sees Dracula on the streets of London. Because the vampire is so focused on his prey that he does not see the couple, Mina is able to describe his subhuman appearance minutely: "His face was not a good face; it was hard, and cruel, and sensual, and his big white teeth, that looked all the whiter because his lips were so red, were pointed like an animal's" (207). Jonathan stares at Dracula in terror, and then Mina leads her husband away to a bench, where they sit down and he falls quietly asleep "with his head on [her] shoulder" (208).

Seeing that Jonathan, upon awakening, has completely erased from his consciousness the memory of seeing Dracula, Mina becomes concerned about "this lapsing into forgetfulness" and decides that it is time to break her promise and read his journal. After she confronts her husband, he writes that the mutual revelation "seems to have made a new man of me. It was the doubt as to the reality of the whole thing that knocked me over. I felt impotent, and in the dark, and distrustful. But, now that I *know,* I am not afraid" (225).

The quality of declining vitality characterizes all the European men, including the aging Van Helsing, who admits, "My life is a barren and lonely one, and so full of work that I have not had much time for friendships" (222), and whose appearance after Lucy's funeral leads Seward to wonder whether "the strain of the past week has broken down even his iron strength" (209). The one man who seems to be exempt from this weakness is Quincey Morris, the rough-and-tumble American, perhaps because he hails from a more recently civilized society that is more in contact with the natural world.[25] As Seward reflects in the same journal entry, Quincey "bore himself through [the funeral] like a moral Viking. If America can go on breeding men like that, she will be a power in the world indeed" (209).

The contrast between Quincey's robust energy and the faltering strength of the other men points to the shift in international power from England to America that was beginning to be evident at the end of the nineteenth century. Renfield also asserts the growing predominance of the United States when he courteously addresses Morris:

> Mr Morris, you should be proud of your great state. Its reception into the Union was a precedent which may have far-reaching effects hereafter, when the Pole and the Tropics may hold allegiance to the Stars and Stripes. The power of Treaty may yet prove a vast engine of enlargement, when the Monroe doctrine [of European noninterference in the Americas] takes its true place as a political fable. (291)

Renfield's comments also serve as a reminder that *Dracula* itself is a form of "political fable."

Although "at first sight" Britain still appeared "imposing" as a center of world power at the *fin de siècle,* and its output in established industries such as coal, textiles, and ironware was still increasing, its "relative share of world production steadily diminished [between 1885 and 1918]; and in the newer and increasingly more important industries such as steel, chemicals, machine tools, and electrical goods, Britain soon lost what early lead it possessed" (Kennedy 224, 228). Part of the breakdown in traditional lines of international military and economic force was due to the "global trading and communications network—telegraphs, steamships, railways, modern printing presses," that receive so much attention in *Dracula* and that made possible increasingly rapid intercontinental transmission of other technological breakthroughs (Kennedy 198).

The narrative of *Dracula* is suffused with images of decline and potential disaster, lurking behind the brighter picture of busy modern life: Dracula's castle is located "on the very edge of a terrible precipice" (38); the ship *Demeter*, like the ship of state, seems to be "drifting to some terrible doom" (105); when Dracula comes to London, he lodges in a "partially ruined building" "surrounded by a high wall, of ancient structure . . . [that had] not been repaired for years" and where Jonathan first noticed the "dilapidated notice that the place was for sale" (119, 34). There are also a number of references to historical invasions of more sophisticated cultures by savage barbarians: Dracula is proud of his descent from Attila the Hun, and there are several allusions to the invading Viking hordes with their battle-frenzied Berserkers (41, 166, 286). Also, of course, the argument has been made that Stoker's Dracula was inspired by accounts of the fifteenth-century Wallachian leader, Vlad the Impaler, who inflicted sadistic torture on his enemies during one of those periods of territorial conflict that seem endemic to the Balkan countries.[26]

According to Paul Kennedy, although at the turn of the century many people were mainly "concerned about domestic, social issues . . . and clung to the liberal, laissez-faire ideals of peaceful cooperation," "there existed in governing elites, military circles, and imperialist organizations a prevailing view of the world order which stressed struggle, change, competition, the use of force, and the organization of national resources to enhance state power" (196). Increasingly influencing the direction of world affairs was the "worship of the 'beast'"—Erich Neumann's phrase—the attitude that "prevails wherever one-sidedness, push, and moral blindness are applauded, i.e., wherever the aggravating complexities of civilized behavior are swept away in favor of bestial rapacity" (*Origins* 391). The voice that was gaining ascendancy was the voice of Dracula, who scornfully declares to Jonathan Harker, "Blood is too precious a thing in these days of dishonourable peace" (42). In England particularly, the "debate concerning the political, economic and moral validity of imperial expansionism . . . reached a crescendo when the voices of Chamberlain, Curson, Lord Roseberry and Rhodes, proclaiming the doctrines of unlimited expansionism . . . almost . . . drowned the voices of the doubters" (Garnett 33).

The modern world portrayed in *Dracula* clearly has its share of evil rooted in good, as Van Helsing says. The spirit of modern commerce is implicitly criticized when Harker reassures Dracula that his desire for secrecy in his affairs is legitimate: "[S]uch is often done by men of business, who do not like the whole of their affairs to be known by any one person" (44). Despite all its impressive advancements, the modern world appears in

Dracula to be the site of severe moral and cultural decline, ruled primarily by the reptilian brain's directives to defend territory and ruthlessly eliminate competition: "[T]he whole place [is] becoming alive with rats" (301).

Two members of Bram Stoker's family had experienced firsthand the breakdown of community in the face of a desperate struggle for survival. One was his mother, during the 1832 cholera epidemic in Sligo. Charlotte Stoker had described her experiences to Bram when he was a young child and, years later, she recorded her memories at his request. She recalled one traveler who had been taken ill a few miles out of town who was buried alive by some of the townspeople; they pushed him with long poles into the pit they had dug. Corpses were thrown into large trenches that would hold forty or fifty bodies, and premature burials were not uncommon; one man rescued his wife from such a grave, and she survived to live a long life. Another man was roused from his deathlike stupor when the men who were laying him away tried to break his legs with a big hammer in order to make him fit into the coffin. One can easily see how Bram, having heard these tales from a very young age, would have developed a fascination with the myth of the living dead.

Charlotte's own family was met with "a mob of men armed with sticks, scythes and pitchforks" (Ludlam 29) when they traveled to Ballyshannon to seek shelter with friends there. They were forced to keep traveling, and at the next town their luggage was torn from them and piled in the center of the town square, "and a cry went out, 'Fire to burn the cholera people!'" (Ludlam 30). Their lives were saved by the officer in command of the regiment quartered in the town. They finally managed to sneak back to their friends' home in Ballyshannon, and when it was proven that they did not have cholera, they were allowed to stay. When they returned to Sligo after the epidemic, five-eighths of the population was dead (Ludlam 25–31).

Stoker's brother George witnessed similar social breakdown during the Russo-Turkish war in the late 1870s, when he had worked as a doctor for the Turkish Army and encountered the horrific sight of bodies, dead and dying intermingled, lying so thickly in the streets of one town of the war-torn area that they had become impassable. Many of the soldiers "had been struck in the head and were rolling about in the mud, groaning and shrieking, covered with filth and gore," while more carts arrived "every minute with more loads of pitifully crying men" (Ludlam 49). Like

Charlotte, George was encouraged by Bram to write down his experiences, which were published under the title *With the Unspeakables* in 1878.

Despite the rather bleak prognostication of world affairs that can be discerned in *Dracula,* Stoker's Gothic novel nevertheless affirms that "man" remains "a noble piece of work" (at different points in the story, each of the main characters is described by another as being noble). The group expedition to track down and kill Dracula is motivated by altruism; the men feel impelled to protect both Mina Harker (whose name I take to mean "my heart,"[27] in that she represents the human capacity for feeling and sympathy) and the civilized world from possession by the vampire.

The killing of Dracula is also, as Leonard Wolf comments, a moment of great international and intercultural cooperation (or cooperative imperialism; 330). Jonathan beheads the vampire with his great Kukri knife, "the preferred combat weapon of the Gurkhas of Nepal, [who were] famous fighting troops in the British army in preindependence India" (Wolf 270); Quincey Morris stabs Dracula through the heart with his bowie knife, developed by the American James Bowie, who died of knife wounds while fighting the Mexicans at the Alamo in 1836 (Wolf 330); and they all use their Winchester rifles to threaten the peasants who attempt to protect Dracula's coffin.

Significantly, however, Quincey Morris is the only member of the group to be killed in the confrontation; he is stabbed by the peasants as he rushes through them toward the coffin. The high-hearted Quincey may have greater energy than the other men, but he is deficient in subtlety and discrimination, as he himself almost admits after trying, frontier-style, to shoot at "a bat" with a pistol and inadvertently shattering the window of the room where his friends are talking. The bullet ricochets from the embrasure and lands in the far wall, and then Quincey confesses that "it was an idiotic thing of me to do" (289). Thus, it seems that the implications of Quincey's status as the American leader of the future may be less than optimistic. The same can be said of the fact that the other main character to die, and the only one to succumb to the vampire's curse, is Lucy Westenra, the "Light of the West."

While their triumph over Dracula enables John Seward, Lord Arthur Godalming, and Jonathan Harker to go on to live (presumably) happily married and fruitful lives, Van Helsing's comments on the vampire remind us that Dracula is only one of an ever-recurring species and that the modern world should never consider itself immune from its threat:

> [H]e is known everywhere that men have been. In old Greece, in old Rome; he flourish in Germany all over, in France, in India. . . . The vampire live

on, and cannot die by mere passing of the time; he can flourish when that
he can fatten on the blood of the living. . . . [H]is vital faculties grow stren-
uous, and seem as though they refresh themselves when his special pabulum
is plenty. (285–86)

Being intricately connected with what Mina identifies as human "blood,
and pain, and trouble" (341), Dracula's fictional invasion of London was
a warning of the "ruin and desolation" that would soon prevail in Europe
(Kennedy 195). Less than two decades after the publication of *Dracula,*
an assassination in a Balkan state precipitated the outbreak of the first
"Great War."

CHAPTER EIGHT

*American Gothic: Historical
and Psychological Critique
in Stephen King's* The Shining

The Shining first appeared in 1977, in the aftermath of two major political crises. Three years earlier, President Richard Nixon had resigned under threat of impeachment in the Watergate scandal, and four years earlier American troops began their withdrawal from Vietnam, after twenty years of American intervention and a decade of war, which had come to be seen as a national "political, diplomatic, psychological, and moral disaster" for the United States (Nevins and Commager 571). Faith had been shaken, both in America's imperialist ideology and in its domestic political process. In response to this national "identity crisis," American readers and film goers developed a keen "appetite for the . . . horrible" (Scott, *Heart* 13), and there was a growing audience for tales of terror in both film and literature—especially in the Gothic horror novels of Stephen King.[1]

The Shining is a "hair-raising" tale about a family of three who spend the winter as caretakers and sole occupants of a deserted hotel located in a remote, mountainous area of Colorado. In the summers, the Overlook Hotel is a posh resort that caters to a wealthy clientele, but in the winters, as the Torrance family discovers, it is haunted by terrifying, malevolent supernatural forces. The father, an aspiring writer, is psychologically unstable; he had been victimized as a child by a brutal, alcoholic father and is constantly struggling against his own alcoholism and violent impulses. For this reason, he is the one who succumbs to the spell of the Overlook, and he attempts to murder his wife and son. His son, however, has telepathic abilities (the "shining") and "calls" for help from the hotel's cook, who is spending the winter in Florida. On the same night that the cook returns to the Overlook, struggling through a severe snow storm, the wife battles against the insane father. Finally, in a confrontation between the father and son (the mother lying wounded on another floor), the father—or the spirits who have taken over his body—is defeated, and the hotel explodes because its defective boiler has been left untended. The cook helps the wife and son return to the nearest town. In the last chapter, or "Epilogue," the two are resting and trying to recuperate at another summer resort, where the cook has found employment.

Because the nightmare images of Gothic fiction are in a sense the harbingers of a new awareness, it is characteristic of reader response that initially people will react very strongly to a Gothic novel without fully understanding why they do so. This gap between reaction and comprehension is one of the main reasons why *The Shining,* when it first appeared, was generally regarded as a light but highly effective form of popular entertainment (another reason being the academic tendency to dismiss popular fiction as critically insignificant).

The quotations from reviews included at the beginning of the Signet edition indicate how powerful an effect of superstitious dread *The Shining* created: "harrowing and all but unbearable tension" (*Worcester Telegram*); "stiffens the hairs on your neck" (*Triad Magazine*); "will curl your hair and chill your blood" (*Chatanaooga Times*); "makes your flesh creep" (*Dallas Times Herald*); "deliciously shivery reading" (*Austin American-Statesman*); "Will have your heart pounding" (*The Marlboro Daily Enterprise*); "back-prickling" (*Kirkus Review*); "sends chills down your spine" (*Rochester Democrat and Chronicle*). However, none of the reviewers seemed able to identify precisely what it was that came back to haunt the Torrance family during their winter sojourn in the Overlook Hotel.

King has said that "everything we do has a history. No matter where you come in on any situation, you are not coming in at the beginning" (Winter 21). This sense of history is strong in *The Shining,* not only in its numerous allusions to the Gothic literary tradition[2] but also in a subtext that traces the formation and history of the United States up until the time of the book's publication. As one recent critic has noted, most of King's fiction is "politically charged" with contemporary social criticism (Magistrale, *Landscape* 24), and in *The Shining* this critique includes a careful examination of the historical background of the malaise that has become increasingly evident in the post-Vietnam era of American public and private life.

The Shining merges the literary traditions of American Gothic and American jeremiad, presenting a severe indictment of American political history and a warning to the nation about the perils of continuing in its present path. This conjunction of an apocalyptic warning and a tale of terror is, moreover, also in itself an American tradition. As one critic has mused, perhaps the distinction of being the first American horror writer should go to Michael Wigglesworth, whose "turgid Calvinist doggerel" in his long poem *The Day of Doom* (1662) "achieved great popularity in Massachusetts as a warning to the elect of the consequences of religious backsliding" (Docherty 1).

The Shining's Overlook Hotel functions as the traditional Gothic symbol of a haunted past; its climactic explosion and dissolution recalls Walpole's Castle of Otranto, Poe's House of Usher, and many other disintegrating Gothic structures. One theory about the Overlook's cultural significance is developed in *The Shining* by the father, Jack Torrance. In a phone call to his friend Al Shockley, who is a majority owner of the Overlook, Jack threatens to write an exposé of the place based on the information about corruption he has found in the basement: "I do think this place forms an index of the whole post-World War II American character" (187).

Although Jack's reading is somewhat flawed by its short-sightedness, his claim is astute, as far as it goes. The hotel, built between 1907 and 1909, was purchased after World War II by Horace Derwent—a sort of Howard Hughes "millionaire inventor, pilot, film producer, and entrepreneur"—when it became a locus of corporate and political power, and as Jack later discovers, of organized crime. When the manager, Stuart Ullman, briefs Jack for the job of winter caretaker, Ullman tells Jack that "Vanderbilts have stayed here, and Rockefellers, and Astors, and Du Ponts. Four Presidents have stayed in the Presidential Suite. Wilson, Harding, Roosevelt, and Nixon" (6).

Assuming that Ullman is listing the presidential guests chronologically, and means Franklin D. rather than Teddy Roosevelt (who was in office when the Overlook was built), the order of the names does suggest a certain cyclical oscillation between idealism and corruption in American political life; as Jack comments, "I wouldn't be too proud of Harding and Nixon" (6). In the case of Woodrow Wilson of course, the idealism was at times misguided; he played an active role in the Versailles Treaty, which ensured Germany's economic devastation after World War I. The post-World War I presidencies following Wilson—of Warren G. Harding, Calvin Coolidge, and Herbert Hoover—have been described as "dull, bourgeois, and ruthless." The slogan for Harding's administration was Normalcy, yet it was characterized by

> spectacular scandals. . . . In the two and a half years of his tenure of office his easygoing acquiescence in the exploitation of government by big business and his tolerance of gross corruption amply justified the expectations of those who looked for an end to idealism. . . . Government withdrew from business, but business moved in and shaped most government policies. (Nevins and Commager 410, 408, 406).

The hotel's connection with political scandal is underscored when Watson, the Overlook's maintenance man, says to Jack, "Any big hotels have got scandals. . . . Just like every big hotel has got a ghost" (22).

The mention of both Roosevelt and "Tricky Dick" Nixon suggests the sense of decline in the public trust that accompanied the increasing concentrations of private and corporate wealth in post-World War II America. The country's growing economic inequity is also hinted at in several references to the corporate lawyers who have frequented the hotel, one of them married to the woman who became the withered old hag that keeps emerging as a rotting corpse from the bathtub of room 217.

In keeping with the theme of political/economic corruption, it is appropriate that the devil who lures Jack into the Faustian bargain appears as a powerful CEO who will give him the "world" in exchange for his soul. As the ghostly Grady tells him, "the manager" might reward his co-operation ("bringing" them his son and eliminating his wife), by promoting Jack "in the Overlook's organizational structure. Perhaps . . . to the very top" (344, 381, 351).

The entire family receives hints of the hotel's unsavory past in glimpses and traces of the parties that took place there, and when Jack falls under its spell, he sees in some detail the sexual perversions and moral degradation that the hotel has witnessed. Danny sees in one of his visions blood and grey brain matter spattered all over the wall of the Presidential Suite—psychic evidence of a gangland murder committed there in 1966 (93–94, 164, 248). At one point before Danny learns to read, he thinks his father referred to one of his trances as a "Ha Loo *Sin Nation*" (28; my emphasis), a linguistic mistake that also indicates the symbolic connection between the crimes at the Overlook and America's sinful past.

The culmination of this political and social history is the nightmare of nuclear war, manifested in *The Shining* by the final explosive destruction of the Overlook Hotel. Numerous references are made throughout the novel to the aggressive military history of the United States, especially since World War II. Its interference in Third World countries in the interests of American private enterprise is commented on by the woman sitting beside the Overlook's summer chef, Dick Hallorann, when he is flying from Miami to Colorado to rescue Danny. She notices his startled reaction to a telepathic message from Danny, and Hallorann lies to her that it was just due to the vibration during take-off of a steel plate in his head: "From Korea." She bristles in reply, "It is the soldier who ultimately pays for any military intervention," and declares, "This country must swear off its dirty little wars. The CIA has been at the root of every dirty little war America has fought in this century. The CIA and dollar diplomacy" (339). She later tells him that she has "seen the horrors" of one of those wars, next to which concern for her personal safety "pales into insignificance." After landing, she flashes him the peace sign popularized during the anti-Vietnam War protests of the sixties (in which Jack participated after his brother, Brett, was killed in battle; 225), and Hallorann, on picking up her "shine," regrets having lied to her (357, 360).

The phrase *dollar diplomacy* goes back to the pre-World War I presidency of "Teddy" Roosevelt and the policies of his appointed successor W. H. Taft. The United States's first major foreign intervention occurred during this period when Roosevelt, an exponent of the "big stick" approach that recurs throughout *The Shining,* bypassed formal diplomatic procedures and "took" (his word) from Colombia the strip of land through which the Panama Canal was built. The orchestration of this event included a "revolt" by the Panamanians ostensibly quelled by American soldiers, which actually never occurred, although it was reported by the American newspapers (Nevins and Commager 370–73, 390). The date of the Overlook's construction—one year after the first official visit made by an American president outside the United States, when Roosevelt visited the Canal Zone in 1906[3]—also connects the hotel symbolically with American transgressions in international relations during the twentieth century.

More significant historical moments are unearthed when Jack scrounges through the papers in the basement of the Overlook. The first item he finds is an old order for four hundred cases of toilet tissue—an apt symbol for all the "dirty business" that has been expelled from America's idea of itself. The second is a newspaper headline dated 19 December, 1963, about the "ORDERLY TRANSITION" Lyndon Johnson promised after John F. Kennedy was assassinated (153). Then when Jack is about to leave the basement, he discovers an old invitation, with an engraving of the Overlook lit up at night by Japanese lanterns, to a masked ball being held August 29, 1945—the month that World War II ended after the American bombing of Hiroshima and Nagasaki. This is the same masked ball that keeps returning in ghostly fashion to terrorize the Torrance family.

One detail that serves as a reminder that cold war anxiety was still a disturbing part of American life when *The Shining* first appeared is the "Cossack" fur hat worn by the first policeman Dick Hallorann meets after his flight (360). There is also reference to Jack's and Danny's fondness for the television shows "Secret Agent Man" and "The Avengers," in which the heroes and heroine wage mock battles against evil KGB agents (285). The Nixon-Ford administration had built up American military "protection" against the Soviet "threat" in an effort to recover national credibility after the international humiliation caused by the fiasco of Vietnam. Ford, who believed "that the chief executive should be a caretaker, not a leader," urged "'fiscal discipline' in his veto of the 1976 Education Appropriation Act, [and] . . . in the same year, requested an eleven billion dollar increase in military spending" (Nevins and Commager 596–97). The arms build-up continued during and after the publication of *The Shining* because "the forces supporting the Cold War were no longer susceptible to logic" (Nevins and Commager 612; President Carter, elected in 1976, initiated some minor arms reduction treaties with the Soviet Union, but his efforts for peace were largely unsuccessful).

The nuclear threat is also evoked in *The Shining* when Jack is about to give Danny the nest of the wasps he exterminated by means of the Overlook's "bug bomb." His wife, Wendy, asks him if he is sure it is safe, and he replies, "I followed the directions on the bomb" (120). Later, when more wasps mysteriously emerge from the nest and sting Danny, Jack begins to suspect that following the directions will not necessarily ensure safety. He insists that the wasps' resurgence must have been due to a defect in the bomb and says he will sue the manufacturer, but when he sees the multitude of wasps that have come out of the nest (now under a clear Pyrex bowl), he thinks, "*How had it happened? How in God's name?*" (134, 136).

Because Jack underestimates the Overlook's symbolic significance, he cannot begin to answer that question. The Overlook on its lofty mountain peak not only represents the failure of the American Dream since World War II, but it also represents the failure of the original promise of the City on the Hill, the dream of America's Puritan forefathers. The Puritan faction that emerged dominant in the conflicts of the New England settlements justified the ruthless genocide of American Indians with the rationale that the new settlers were fulfilling God's providential promise,[4] and faith in an overruling Providence continued to be a cornerstone of Jeffersonian democracy.

The cultural imprint of this originating delusion is suggested in Jack's memory of the time he and Al Shockley were driving in Al's Jaguar (an updated Gatsby death car, of which there are many in *The Shining*),[5] both extremely drunk. They collided with a bicycle lying in the middle of the road but "Providentially," in Al's words, no one was killed. Jack also thought later that "some queer providence . . . had kept the cops away" (39, 40). The analogue is clear: the hotel's greatest weakness, the defective boiler, can be located in its basement, its foundation—just as the nation's greatest weakness can be found in the original premises upon which it was built.

Like the classic Gothic villain, American society is haunted by its own past crimes, from which its victims rise up as ghosts. Danny remembers seeing a child's puzzle that said, "(*Can you see the Indians in this picture?*)," and later, three days after Thanksgiving, he thinks of that question again when the hedge animals are about to attack him (193, 287). During their stay in Boulder, the Torrance family resides on Arapahoe [*sic*] Street (13, 33, 56), named after an Indian tribe whose members, with a larger group of Cheyennes, suffered a savage massacre at the hands of some "ill-trained and drunken militia" on 28 November 1864 at Sand Creek in Colorado (Hoxie 163). The victims of this "infamous" event were "mostly women and children, who thought they had been granted peace and military protection" (Washburn, *Handbook* 168). Similarly, Wendy and Danny discover that the man who has taken them to an apparently peaceful mountain retreat, where they hope to find refuge from the family's financial troubles, becomes a drunken, violent, murderous maniac. Jack's attempt to kill his own wife and child, which culminates in the final destruction of the Overlook, occurs four days after the anniversary of the Sand Creek slaughter (306, 310).[6]

Jack tries to kill Wendy and Danny only after he has succumbed to the spell of the Overlook; in effect, his personal family violence has been endorsed and encouraged by the national tradition of inter-racial violence that the Overlook represents. In the case of the Arapaho, their annihilation was undertaken "with full knowledge and consent" of Governor John Evans and his superior officers, to whom the Cheyenne and Arapaho had previously given most of their guns, keeping only enough for hunting, as part of their agreement to maintain peace. The natives' trust was further violated when the Indian villagers first saw the soldiers on the river bluffs above them and the chief bought out an American flag and a smaller white one to signify their truce, but to no avail. As six Indian warriors rode to greet the troops, the seven hundred armed men, led by the "bloodthirsty" Colonel Chivington, a former Methodist minister, attacked:

> Women with their children clustered around them begged for mercy, but they were shot, stabbed, and many were scalped before death overtook them. The screams of the dying and wounded brought no halt to the bloody attack. . . . Before the fight was over, four twelve-pound howitzers were brought into action and blew the remaining defenders to pieces.
>
> The few remaining survivors, mostly children, found hidden in the lodges were butchered in cold blood. . . . From the "hell" of Sand Creek, [the soldiers] brought out over 100 scalps which were later displayed between acts at the Denver Opera House. Three small bewildered Indian children were also exhibited as proof of this "great victory" over the Cheyenne. (Peithmann 64–69)

Four years later a congressional inquiry was held, whose final report condemned the "barbarity" of the massacre, which had already inflamed relations between whites and Indians to the point that peaceful resolution of their conflicts had become impossible. Of course, this was neither the first nor the last time that English and American soldiers distinguished themselves by their savagery; earlier there was the Pequot slaughter of 1637 and the Great Swamp Fight of 1675, and later there was the My Lai massacre of 1969.[7]

The Overlook Hotel occupies land to which the Arapaho, one of the last nomadic tribes to submit to reservation life, once had free access. Not until 1875, their arms removed and their leaders dispatched to a Florida prison, did they capitulate to the demands of the American government— demands that constituted, in effect, a less blatant but equally devastating policy of cultural genocide. "Pacified" and "demoralized," the Southern Plains Indians "settled down to the routines of reservation life," and over the next sixty years witnessed an almost continuous violation of the original territorial agreements in repeated reductions of their reservation land (Washburn 4: 224–27).

As in Danny's puzzle, the Indians have become virtually invisible in the "picture" of modern American life, but their old animistic world revives into an intense hostility when the Overlook is left alone in the mountain wilderness for the winter, with the fierce wind "whooping" and "scream[ing]" around it (210, 213, 245). At one point it sounds like a "womanish shriek" (212), and later it reminds Wendy of "a woman fleeing a murderer in a cheap melodrama" (392). When Dick Hallorann approaches the Overlook, he feels "surrounded by a red force of immense power that might have been memory. He was drowning in instinct" (389). Native spirits "come back" like the wasps Jack thought he had exterminated (136), to the hotel that is in King's words a "symbol of unexpiated sin" (*Danse* 253).[8] Danny says to his mother, "The Bad Stuff. . . There was none of it here before, was there?" and she replies "No. The hotel put it here" (371). Specifically, Danny and Wendy are referring to the alcohol that Jack has evidently consumed, but their comments also can be applied more generally to the effect that "civilized" European Americans had on the life of America's original human inhabitants.

The opening epigraph in *The Shining*, from Poe's "The Masque of the Red Death," can also be connected with the "Red Death" wreaked upon the remaining native Americans during the years of the frontier movement. This movement is alluded to at the beginning of *The Shining* when Danny examines some maps as a way of passing time while waiting in the car for his father. He thinks, "Colorado, Nebraska, Utah, Wyoming, New Mexico. . . . As far as he was concerned, new maps were the best part of moving West" (35). But this later wave of the original Errand into the Wilderness[9] became yet another monumental Error in the Wilderness, as the white man continued to follow the genocidal policy established by the first settlers in the New World.

In *The Shining*, the psychic shock experienced by the westward-moving settlers as they discovered America's "untamed" frontier is registered by Wendy. She finds herself thinking repeatedly about the Donner party, the group that resorted to cannibalism when stranded in the Sierra Nevada: "The mountains did not forgive many mistakes"[10] (62, 63, 73, 92, 199). Jack hears "Home on the Range" as part of the kaleidoscope of sound at the "party" in the Colorado lounge (348), and earlier when Danny asks him about REDRUM, Jack, thinking of "red drum," comments that it "sounds like something an Indian might take on the warpath" (128).

It has been argued that the idea of "Manifest Destiny," which fuelled the westward movement, has extended to the more recent American military involvement in Asia, and the interplay of allusions in *The Shining* does seem to convey this historical momentum. More bombs were dropped on Vietnam by the American military during the Eisenhower, Kennedy, Johnson, and Nixon administrations than were dropped by all the allied forces during World War II, and there were an estimated one and one-half million Vietnamese civilian casualties (Nevins and Commager 569). At the beginning of the seemingly enlightened administration of Jack Kennedy, American military involvement in Vietnam expanded to include "defoliation operations, and population removal . . . which forced the peasants to resettle and thus destroyed traditional village life" (Nevins and Commager 565).[11] When Jack Torrance throws rotted shingles off the roof of the hotel, he calls out a warning that also can be applied to the excessive military aggression of the United States: "Bombs away" (106).[12] As Jack's father once said to him, "turning to Jacky with a smile," after smoking out a wasps' nest the way that his own father had showed him, "Fire will kill anything" (329)—an unsettling observation, to a generation of readers who have witnessed photo-documentary coverage of napalm's effects.[13]

One of King's strategies for "bringing home" the horrors of America's interracial and international violence is to ally them with domestic violence. At one point, Danny remembers his father reading the folktale "Bluebeard" to him when Jack was drunk and Danny was only three years old. Danny remembers the "ghastly, loving detail" with which the old fairy tale book illustrated the young wife's discovery, when she disobeyed Bluebeard's order not to unlock the door of the forbidden room:

> The image was burned on Danny's mind. The severed heads of *Bluebeard's* seven previous wives were in the room, each one on its own pedestal, the eyes turned up to whites, the mouths unhinged and gaping in silent screams. They were somehow balanced on necks ragged from the broadsword's decapitating swing, and there was blood running down the pedestals. Terrified, she had turned to flee from the room and the castle, only to discover *Bluebeard* standing in the doorway, his terrible eyes blazing. "I told you not to enter this room," *Bluebeard* said, unsheathing his sword. (170)

Danny recognizes that although the tale was titled "Bluebeard," it was actually about Bluebeard's wife, a lady whose corn-colored hair reminds him of his mother. Danny also notices the similarity between Bluebeard's "big and ominous castle" and the Overlook (169). His connecting the story to his own family circumstances indirectly suggests the persistence of patriarchal privilege and the silencing of the feminine voice in a modern American family such as the Torrances. The tacit agreement between Jack and Wendy is that he possesses the superior intellect and is entitled to indulge in the patronizing tone he uses so frequently when explaining things to her.

There are repeated reminders in *The Shining* of how pervasive family violence has become in contemporary American life. At the outset of the novel, Ullman tells Jack about the Overlook's previous caretaker Grady, who killed his little girls with an axe, and his wife and himself with a shotgun (9). Shortly thereafter, Wendy thinks about the couple living above their Boulder apartment suite who engage in drunken weekend battles where the woman ends up crying, "Don't, Tom. Please don't. Please don't" (9, 11). Later, Danny remembers a friend whose "daddy had punched his mom right in the eye and knocked her down" when doing the "Bad Thing" (i.e., drinking; 27).

As well, it is possible that in focusing on domestic violence in *The Shining*, King may have been influenced by the first American Gothic novel, Charles Brockden Brown's *Wieland*,[14] also a tale about a man's attempt (in this case successful) to murder his wife and children, and also a highly political fable. Printed in 1798, the fictional setting of *Wieland* is Pennsylvania in the 1760s, the period preceding the formation of the United States as an independent territory, "between the conclusion of the French and the beginning of the Revolutionary War" (Brown, "Advertisement" to *Wieland* 24). Like Jack Torrance, Theodore Wieland hears a voice commanding him to kill his family. He suffers the delusion that the voice is God's and believes he has received a divine injunction to demonstrate his faith and obedience through this act (184–87). The political import of this seemingly apolitical story is suggested by the fact that the first thing Brown did after writing it was to send a copy to Thomas Jefferson, then vice president of the United States.

As Jane Tompkins has demonstrated, *Wieland* appeared during an anxious and unsettled post-Revolutionary period, entering into "a dialogue that had engaged civic-minded men and women since the age of Locke and Rousseau over the nature of man, the proper form of civic representation, and the right of citizens to overthrow their government" (47). Tompkins argues that the deracinated Wieland family presents "a direct refutation of the Republican faith in men's capacity to govern themselves without the supports and constraints of an established social order" (49). Wieland, who admits to having "thirsted for the knowledge of [God's] will" (*Wieland* 184), "fills the vacuum of authority by inventing a source of authority outside himself whose 'commands' he feels bound to obey" (Tompkins 53–54). It is Wieland, "the devout, well-educated farmer, the very epitome of the man on whom Jeffersonians staked their vision of Republican order," who collapses morally and psychologically, and "his 'Transformation' from sturdy yeoman to homicidal maniac is intended, as Brown's subtitles tell us, as a prototypically 'American Tale'" (Tompkins 53, 58).

Tompkins asserts that "*Wieland* is a patriotic novel: its main action, in an attempt to alert people to the dangers of mob rule, realizes the Federalist nightmare" (58). King's work similarly evidences a skeptical attitude toward American democracy; Tony Magistrale has commented that in *The Dead Zone,* for example, King's depiction of how one character succeeds in becoming president indicates the author's "tacit agreement with Alexis De Tocqueville's derisive warning in *Democracy in America* against the tendency toward collective misjudgment inherent in the American political system" (*Landscape* 35). However, the warning in *The Shining* is more specific, for it points to the dangerous consequences of both maintaining an aggressive military policy and failing to acknowledge historical guilt.

In *The Shining,* as in *Wieland,* there is some speculation about the ontological status of the supernatural, although in Brown's novel the mad father believes himself to be acting under divine injunction, while in King's he appears to be under the influence of daemonic forces. Whereas in *Wieland* the debate is expressed in terms of the late eighteenth-century opposition between Enlightenment rationalism and "Gothic superstition," in *The Shining* it is presented as a contrast between Freudian and Jungian psychological perspectives—a contrast that forms an important component of the novel's critique of contemporary attitudes.

Debate about the paranormal in *The Shining* focuses initially on the issue of the apparent telepathic powers of Danny, the five-year-old protagonist: specifically, his abilities to "pick up" other people's thoughts, to find lost objects with no prior knowledge of their location, and to foretell future events, usually with the assistance of his invisible friend "Tony" (Danny's full name is Daniel Anthony Torrance). Concerned about Danny's "trances" and worried that his physical and emotional condition seems to have declined since the family moved into the Overlook Hotel, his parents take him to the physician in nearby Sidewinder, "Dr. ('Just call me Bill') Edmonds" (137).

Dr. Edmonds offers the Torrances an admittedly "oversimplified" Freudian interpretation of the problem. After examining Danny, he tells Jack and Wendy that their son is simply "too imaginative" and that Danny has been suffering from the emotional trauma of the recent family dislocations:

> From what Danny told me, his "invisible friend" was truly a friend until you folks moved out here from New England. Tony has only become a threatening figure since that move. The pleasant interludes have become nightmarish, even more frightening to your son because he can't remember

exactly what the nightmares are about. That's common enough. We all remember our pleasant dreams more clearly than the scary ones. There seems
to be a buffer somewhere between the conscious and the subconscious, and
one hell of a bluenose lives in there. This censor only lets through a small
amount, and often what does come through is *only symbolic.* That's oversimplified Freud, but it does pretty much describe what we know of the
mind's interaction with itself. (151; my emphasis)

Dr. Edmonds's explanation refers to Freud's insight about how unconscious
material can undergo a process of revision before it is registered by the conscious mind. But the doctor's excremental (or toilet) metaphor in his statement that Danny is now "flushing [Tony] out of his system" (150) reveals
a failure to appreciate either the potential value of the unconscious or the
idea that the unconscious "speaks" in a symbolic language that one can
learn to read. Dr. Edmonds is simply revealing his own ignorance when he
asserts that his explanation sums up "what we know of the mind's interaction with itself." The well-meaning doctor also literally shrugs off Danny's
telepathic ability as simply a product of "[w]ish fulfillment plus a lucky coincidence" (148).

Dr. Edmonds also betrays a tendency to dismiss any information that
does not tally with his theory. During the examination, when Wendy is
waiting in a room outside, Danny says that he knows his mother is thinking about her sister, who was killed by a van at the age of six. At the end of
the visit, Dr. Edmonds asks Wendy if Danny had ever been told about the
circumstances of the sister's death. Although she replies negatively, Edmonds does not consider this information (nor Danny's mention of the
anagram *redrum,* nor his use of the word *shining*) to be significant enough
to warrant any revision of his assessment (150–51).

Wendy and Jack initially demonstrate the unquestioning acquies-
cence of the anxious client who longs to rely on the security that the doctor's authority seems to afford. When Wendy tries to suggest that Danny
might have "second sight," Dr. Edmond's reassuring smile becomes "a
good, hearty laugh," which leads them to smile as well, both "amazed at
how easy" it is; "Danny's occasional 'lucky guesses' about things was something else they had not discussed much" (146–47). Relieved by the fact that
during their own discussion with Dr. Edmonds the issues of divorce, alcoholism, and child beating have been brought into the open for the first
time, Wendy and Jack momentarily accept his interpretation of Danny's
"problem." Yet at the same time Wendy is dissatisfied; the doctor's

explanation strikes her as "glib" and tasting "more like margarine than but-
ter" (148). Back at the Overlook some time later, when the dangers of their
situation are becoming more apparent, she declares unequivocally to Jack,
"The doctor was full of shit and we both know it. We've known all the
time" (247).

The enlightened, scientific view of such matters offered by Dr. Edmonds can offer only temporary comfort to Danny's parents, and their
dilemma illustrates the limitations of a theory that rejects the possibility of
a transpersonal dimension to the psyche. Dr. Edmonds's quick dismissal of
any facts that might upset his views also exposes the fallacy of his supposed
scientific objectivity.

Freud himself was continually revising his own theories, but he generally espoused the superiority of the scientific viewpoint. In *Totem and
Taboo,* he states that because human views about the universe have pro-
gressed from the animistic to the religious to the final, scientific stage (13:
90), superstition in a civilized individual may be regarded as a sign of obsessional neurosis (13: 86). When discussing how even in the closest human relationships feelings are never pure or unmixed, he also makes the
argument that in primitive societies malevolent ghosts are simply "projec-
tions of [repressed] hostile feelings harboured by the survivors against the
dead" (13: 62).

Danny has some appreciation of the dangerous power of scien-
tific/psychoanalytic authority with regard to the question of telepathic ability. He initially refrains from telling his parents about the unsettling things
he thinks he sees at the Overlook because he does not want them to think
he is "LOSING HIS MARBLES." He fears that he could be taken to a
"BUGHOUSE or a SANNYTARIUM"; "THE MEN IN THE WHITE
COATS . . . took you away from your family and made you live in a room
with soft walls. And if you wanted to write home, you had to do it with
Crayolas" (194, 195).

In "The Uncanny," Freud suggests that some people are still susceptible to any apparent confirmation of "old, discarded beliefs" because they
do not "feel quite sure" about their new beliefs, and this experience gives
rise to a sense of the uncanny, or "*unheimlich,*" which in his definition is
"that class of the frightening which leads back to what is known of old and
long familiar" (17: 220). Freud asserts that "anyone who has completely
and finally *rid himself* of animistic beliefs will be insensible to this type of
uncanny . . . none of these things will disconcert him. . . . [It is] purely an
affair of 'reality-testing,' a question of the material reality of the phenomena" (17: 248; my emphasis).

Although Freud had some interest in the occult, his scientific framework does not admit any transpersonal or immaterial dimension to the human psyche, as he explains in one discussion on dreams:

> During the epoch which may be described as pre-scientific, men had no difficulty in finding an explanation of dreams. When they remembered a dream after waking up, they regarded it as either a favourable or a hostile manifestation by higher powers, daemonic and divine. When modes of thought belonging to natural science began to flourish, all this ingenious mythology was transformed into psychology, and to-day only a small minority of educated people doubt that dreams are a product of the dreamer's own mind. (5: 633)

His own ingenious explanation of one patient's premonitory dream is similar to Dr. Edmonds's explanation of Danny's sensitivity, in that it stresses the role of coincidence and emphasizes censorship and revision, of both an unacceptable memory and the original dream. Freud insists that when his patient Frau B. ("an estimable woman who moreover possesses a critical sense" [5: 623]) thought that she had dreamed of seeing an old friend shortly before running into him in the same place she had dreamt about, she must have substituted the figure of this friend for that of an old lover with a similar name. Freud further argues that she must have recast the locale of her dream in order to allow it entry into consciousness. In other words, she never dreamed the dream she thought she had dreamed. "Thus the creation of a dream after the event, which alone makes prophetic dreams possible, is nothing other than a form of censoring, thanks to which the dream is able to make its way through into consciousness" (5: 625).

In contrast to Frau B., Danny does receive some affirmation that he can trust his telepathic powers. When he talks to Dick Hallorann, who is about to leave for his winter vacation, the cook seems to adopt the Jungian view that there is a collective dimension to the human psyche that operates outside the normal space/time framework of conscious thought: "What you got, son, I call it shinin on, the Bible calls it having visions, and there's scientists that call it precognition. I've read up on it, son. I've studied on it. They all mean seeing the future" (85). When Danny observes to his mother that the doctor did not believe in Tony, she assures him that she does, despite the fact that she does not "know what he is or who he is, if he's a part of you [Danny] that's special or if he comes from . . . somewhere outside." She also expresses her willingness to heed Tony's advice (200).

Dick's later journey to rescue Danny also brings up the epistemological problem of "shining." The Colorado park ranger whom Dick phones from the Miami airport is skeptical about Dick's worry that there might be trouble at the Overlook, asking, "May I ask how you've come by this information, sir?" (337). Then again, when Dick is driving through a blizzard to Sidewinder, the man who tows him out of a snowdrift asks the same thing, in response to Dick's assertion that Danny is in trouble: "How would you know that?" (386). Dick's temper snaps at this point, but a little later on the man helping him muses, "Ain't no way you could know someone's in trouble up there . . . But I believe you. Sometimes I get feelins" (388).

The idea that this information may be relied on, even though it has no rational basis and cannot be fully understood, comes up in Wendy's response to the uncanny events happening at the Overlook. She clearly appreciates the menace and thinks that it does not matter at this point how one interprets what is happening, whether "(*Real psychic phenomena or group hypnosis?*). . . . [It] was just as deadly either way" (391).

Dick suggests in his conversation with Danny that although not all people seem to have the capacity for shining, it may nevertheless have a universal, instinctual component; "I think all mothers shine a little, you know, at least until their kids grow up enough to watch out for themselves" (88). His comment can be related to another critical theoretical difference between Jung and Freud, with regard to the role of instinct, its relation to the conscious mind, and the dynamics of instinctual repression.

In *Totem and Taboo,* Freud argues that repression of the instincts may be regarded as "a measure of the level of civilization that has been reached" (13: 97). Although he does acknowledge that children and primitive people seem to possess a "fullness and delicacy of feeling" that may be underestimated (13: 99), his model for both individual and human cultural development is one of successive and discrete stages, in which one stage "surmounts" another and the success of the final stage depends on the degree to which the instinctual impulses of the lower stages are resisted. Because such impulses can only be repressed and not abolished by cultural prohibitions, the relation between prohibition and instinct, or conscious and unconscious aims, is frequently one of "continuing conflict" (13: 29). This constant censorship battle often can be draining, as Freud himself recognized: "[W]e men, with the high claims of our civilization and under the pressure of our repressions, find reality generally quite unsatisfactory and so keep up a life of fancy in which we love to compensate for what is lacking in the sphere of reality by the production of wish-fulfillments" ("Origin of Psychoanalysis" 31). He then identifies neurosis and artistic creation as the negative and positive methods of evading reality by producing such wish fulfillment.

Freud's analysis provides an apt description of Jack, a deeply miserable and unhappy man who has failed to confront the sources of his own rage and anger; he consequently fails both in his struggle to repress those feelings and in his aspiration to become a great writer. Wendy's hopeful thoughts about Jack's current writing project suggest the elements of repression and personal wish fulfillment that are involved in it: "[H]er husband seemed to be slowly closing a huge door on a roomful of monsters. He had his shoulder to that door for a long time now, but at last it was swinging shut" (121). Jack's personal agenda and his increasing identification with the abuser also become evident in his changing attitude to the characters in the play he is writing. He originally conceived of the play's primary theme as "the abuse of power" in a private school, but he later begins to see it as depicting the "destruction of a kindly old teacher" (259).

The futility of Jack's response to his inner demons suggests the limitations of a strictly Freudian approach. Perhaps the major weakness in Freud's theory is its reliance on a basically static model that fails to account adequately either for the dynamics of the conflict he is proposing or for its therapeutic and creative possibilities. Jung, in contrast, dissatisfied with Freud's "mechanistic" view, developed his own "energic" model in which transformation of the conscious attitude becomes possible through an exchange of energy with the unconscious. While not disputing the idea that consciousness tends to put up an "extraordinary resistance" against the unconscious, Jung maintains that the unconscious acts in a "compensatory or complementary manner towards the conscious" and that the distinction between conscious and unconscious material should not be imagined as a fixed boundary but rather as a "threshold [of] intensity," which elements must attain before they become apparent to the conscious mind (*Structure* 112, 69).

From the Jungian perspective, Jack's emotional difficulties can be viewed as symptomatic of the civilized "man" for whom, Jung argues, "the rationalism of consciousness, otherwise so useful to him, proves to be a most formidable obstacle to the frictionless transformation of energy" (*Structure* 24). Jung compares the conscious mind's evasion tactics to that of a man who "hears a suspicious noise in the attic and thereupon dashes down into the cellar, in order to assure himself that no burglar has broken in and that the noise was mere imagination. In reality he has simply not dared to go up into the attic" (*Structure* 99).

A similar idea is suggested at the outset of *The Shining*, via the traditional Gothic analogy between castle/church (or hotel) architecture and the human psyche, when Jack and his new employer, Stuart Ullman, look over the floor plans of the hotel. Ullman informs Jack that there is nothing in the attic but bric-a-brac because "each successive manager has put everything they don't want up in the attic" (4). Ullman instructs Jack to put rat traps and poison bait up there because "[s]ome of the third-floor chambermaids say they have heard rustling noises," even though he himself does not "believe it." (4). He later comments that the basement, with its boiler that must be carefully maintained by the caretaker, is "[w]here the action is" (5). As Jack gradually succumbs to his own psychological and emotional disintegration, he does in fact spend more and more time in the basement, attempting to piece together the history of the Overlook Hotel from the old newspapers and records he finds down there. But "the vital clues, the connections that would make everything clear," elude him (326).

With his own personal history of family violence, Jack, like the defective boiler, is always in danger of "blowing." His alcoholic father physically abused his wife and children, and although one of Jack's most vivid memories is of the time his father cracked his mother's skull by smashing a cane on it, Jack nevertheless can recall feelings of deep affection and attachment for the man. His bond with his mother, a "good," passive Catholic woman (who somehow survived the attack and outlived her husband), was comparatively weak, but as Jack collapses emotionally, his violent thoughts about Wendy clearly indicate not only the emotional imprint made by the abusive father but also a great deal of unconscious rage at the ineffectual mother who failed to defend her children against the father's excesses. At one point, Jack remembers a published short story of his in which he explored the family background of a child molester, "the father a beater as his own father had been, the mother a limp and silent dishrag as his mother had been" (258).

Jack's method of dealing with his family history is summed up in his recollection of his father's death and funeral: "[T]he man who had dominated Jacky's life, the irrational white ghost-god, was under ground" (226). However, his attempt to bury family history proves to be fruitless, for the ghost returns when Jack eventually becomes possessed by his own fury and finds himself compelled to externalize that history by re-enacting it.

Ironically, in trying to resist the promptings of his unconscious mind by relying increasingly on a rationalistic perspective, Jack only makes himself more vulnerable to possession by the unconscious. Even when he is already experiencing his own daemonic visions, he attempts to deny both his own and Danny's experiences by dismissing them as merely hallucinations. After Danny's near-fatal encounter with the zombie in Room 217, Jack goes to investigate the room; in a chapter titled "The Verdict," he lies that he found nothing there (256). Afraid that he himself is "cracking up" (255), he tries to convince both himself and Wendy that the ghost was simply a subconscious projection of Danny's and that their son may be suffering a "limited type" of schizophrenia (266–67). When Jack speculates to Wendy about the probable subjective nature of Danny's visions, his associative train of thought reveals the weakening of his own reasoning powers:

> If precognitive trances are possible, they're probably functions of the subconscious mind. Freud said that the subconscious never speaks to us in literal language. Only in symbols. . . . Games, little games. Conscious on one side of the net, subconscious on the other, serving some cockamamie image back and forth. Same with mental illness, with hunches, all of that. Why should precognition be any different? Maybe Danny really did see blood all over the walls of the Presidential Suite. To a kid his age, the image of blood and the concept of death are nearly interchangeable. To kids, the image is always more accessible than the concept, anyway. William Carlos Williams knew that, he was a pediatrician. (264–65)

Like Dr. Edmonds, Jack both underestimates the significance of the symbol-making activity of the "subconscious" and overestimates the difficulty of comprehending that activity.

His comments once again point to a significant difference between Jung and Freud, this time regarding the nature and function of images in dreams. In Freud's view, images are "hallucinations" that "replace thoughts" (*Interpretation* 82); the *a priori* verbal form "is replaced" by the image, which invariably has been stimulated by a previous sensory impression: "[N]ot only representability, but the interests of condensation and the censorship as well, can be the gainers from this exchange" (*Interpretation* 375). A consistent pattern in Freud's interpretation of patients' dreams is that of translating the delusive visual images into a "true" verbal description of the dreamer's personal dilemma.

Jung's disagreement with Freud on this issue is directly related to Jung's contentions that the human psyche includes a collective aspect and that intensification of unconscious activity may indicate not only the need to change the conscious attitude but also the means of changing it. Jung allows for the personal component in unconscious image making, as well as for an impersonal component, in the archetypal image. The shadow, the wise old man, the anima, the divine child, and a multitude of symbols of transformation are some of the archetypes he explores. Jung does not share Freud's assumption about the primacy of the verbal component and argues that all ideas are "founded on primordial archetypal forms whose concreteness dates from a time when consciousness did not *think,* but only *perceived*" (*Archetypes* 33). When one learns to read these images symbolically rather than semiotically, as "the best possible expression for a complex fact not yet apprehended by consciousness" rather than merely "a sign for elementary instinctual processes" (*Structure* 75), one can begin to benefit from the way "the unconscious 'thinks' and paves the way for solutions" (*Archetypes* 33).

Several comments throughout *The Shining* suggest the idea that human story-telling, from folk tale to Gothic tale, may work in a manner similar to the one Jung attributes to individual dreams, making similar use of images to identify collective problems. When Danny remembers his father reading "Bluebeard" to him, what he thinks of are the images: "It seemed vaguely to Danny that the story had had a happy ending, but that had paled to insignificance beside the two dominant images: the taunting, maddening locked door with some great secret behind it, and the grisly secret itself, repeated more than half a dozen times. The locked door and behind it the heads, the severed heads" (170). Whereas on the social level the tale points to the issue of domestic violence, on the psychological level the image also exposes civilized man's "grisly secret"—the sheer savagery of which he is still capable. The irresistibility of the urge to unlock the secret, on the part of both Danny and Bluebeard's wife, also indicates the tremendous pressure exerted by the old forgotten or ignored contents of the unconscious to make themselves known. This is a major impulse behind Gothic fiction: not simply to indulge in wish fulfillment of unacceptable instinctual impulses, but to unlock such doors and to reveal a fuller view of human nature than is generally held.

Wendy and Jack are both a great deal more resistant to the dark truths lurking in the Overlook Hotel than Danny is, and Danny is well aware of their reason for denying a phenomenon such as "Tony" as a valid source of information: "Because it was frightening, they swept it quickly from their minds" (30). Yet Wendy's denial is never as vehement as Jack's, partly because her family background was not as physically violent and partly because her intellectual defenses against the truth are not as great as his. That Wendy is less intellectually oriented than Jack is suggested by the details that she studied sociology (as opposed to English literature) in college and reads Victoria Holt novels (47, 61). Jack continues to rationalize what is happening to them at the Overlook long after Wendy recognizes the danger they are in, and it is Jack, as he himself realizes at one point, who is the "weak link" in the chain that should protect them from the daemonic forces threatening to overwhelm them (278–79).

Jack's susceptibility illustrates Jung's argument about the dangers of excessive reliance on conscious will and intellect:

> The psyche of civilized man is no longer a self-regulating system but could rather be compared to a machine whose speed-regulation is so insensitive that it can continue to function to the point of self-injury.

> *In the intensity of the emotional disturbance itself* [i.e. regression] *lies the value, the energy which he should have at his disposal in order to remedy the state of reduced adaption. Nothing is achieved by repressing this state or by devaluing it rationally.* (*Structure* 79, 82)

In his discussion of psychic self-regulation, Jung also uses the biblical example of Nebuchadnezzar and Daniel, who correctly read the warning in Nebuchadnezzar's dream; but the tyrant, who never heard the warning, subsequently "fell victim to a psychosis that contained the very counteraction he had sought to escape: he, the lord of the earth, was degraded to an animal" (*Structure* 80–81). It is not difficult here to draw a connection between the biblical Nebuchadnezzar and Jack, who ignores the warnings offered by his visionary son, Daniel.

Jack, too, degenerates into a bestial state, but unlike Nebuchadnezzar he is too hopelessly entrapped in his delusions to ever emerge from it. While the winter storm "howl[s]" around the hotel (364), Wendy and Danny fight for their lives against him. He cries that Wendy should be "chastised" and "punished," and "cuff[s] Danny . . . with a snarl," crying, "I'll show you who is boss around here!" When they drag him into the cooler, he gets up "on his hands and knees" (like Blake's engraving of Nebuchadnezzar in *The Marriage of Heaven and Hell*),[15] "his hair hanging in his eyes, like some heavy animal. A large dog . . . or a lion" (368, 369, 374). As they shut the door on him, he "leap[s]" at them, having become one with the menacing natural world represented by the vengeful hedge animals (bushes surrounding the hotel that have been shaped by human topiary ingenuity into dogs, lions, a rabbit, and a buffalo). During the night, his screams mingle with that of the surrounding storm as he "breaks down" into an increasingly elemental condition (374, 377).

The frequent foreshadowing of Jack's inevitable surrender to an atavistic state contributes to the narrative anticipation of the impending catastrophe. This technique directly involves the reader in Danny's experience of being presented with information that carries some unmistakably ominous, frightening significance yet whose precise meaning is frustratingly obscure. When the family is first left alone at the Overlook after all the other staff have departed, Jack feels "as if his life had dwindled to a mere spark while the hotel and the grounds had suddenly doubled in size and become sinister, dwarfing them with sullen inanimate power" (101)—a power that he eventually recognizes is not inanimate, but malevolently animate. Later, when he is up on the roof doing repairs and thinking about how to revise his play, he is bitten by a wasp, which "put[s] an end to cogitation" (106). He feels

> his hand and his whole arm consumed by holy, righteous fire, destroying conscious thought, making the concept of civilized behavior obsolete. . . . [When] the brown, furious cloud rose out of the hole in the fabric of things . . . [w]hen you unwittingly stuck your hand into the wasps' nest, you hadn't made a covenant with the devil to give up your civilized self with its trappings of love and respect and honor. It just happened to you. . . . [Y]ou ceased to be a creature of the mind and became a creature of the nerve endings; from college-educated man to wailing ape in five easy seconds. (110)

Jack eventually does become that Hydelike ape, wielding his club against his wife and son. Uncovering the wasps' nest and gazing at them going slowly about "their instinctual business" of killing all but the hibernating queen, he identifies the wasp's sting with his own experience of life—his violent father and his own consequent violent and hostile behavior, which included an uncontrolled attack on a former student that cost him his teaching job at a private school (109–16). But Jack fails to note the significance of these associational connections, and as Bernadette Lynn Bosky has shown, his reaction is typical of many of King's well-educated male characters who pride themselves on their reasonability and fail to heed their intuition.

Another typically Gothic narrative "trick" that King performs in *The Shining* was earlier identified by Sir Walter Scott, in his review of *The Castle of Otranto:* the writer of Gothic fiction, when successful, "wind[s] up the feelings of his reader till they bec[o]me for a moment identified with those of a ruder age" in which belief in the supernatural was still strong (93). In King's novel it is the "ruder age" of powerful native magic that is vividly recreated, along with an even more ancient and frightening prehuman time.

King effects the psychological movement down from a seemingly safe and civilized world to a more primitive condition in a number of ways. For one thing, he undermines reader objectivity and distance by making five-year-old Danny the emotional focus of the story, and by conveying the experience of the other main characters with a stream-of-consciousness technique (involving italics, capital letters, ellipses, dashes, broken sentence structures, and parentheses) that creates a strong sense of emotional immediacy.

As well, the cultural/psychological threshold is lowered at the beginning of the novel with the humorous, if politically incorrect, obscenities of Watson (the maintenance man whose grandfather built the Overlook). Watson compares Ullman to an overbred, domesticated dog: "I hate that little fucker. Yap-yap-yap, all the livelong day, he's just like one a those little dogs that bites you on the ankle then run around an pee all over the rug . . . . It's a pity the things you see when you ain't got a gun" (19).

The downward movement continues with the increasing evocation of the sense of smell. The hotel with its "smelly reputation" (400) becomes the locus of a life-and-death struggle between the devouring primeval swamp and the civilized human who has emerged from it. Danny describes his encounter with the hag in Room 217 in these terms: "[S]he wanted me. . . . She wasn't even thinking, not the way you and Daddy think. It was black . . . it was hurt-think . . . like the wasps that night in my room! . . . [S]he started to choke me . . . I could smell her . . . *I could smell how dead she was*" (249). The recurring references to an "insectile" buzzing sound, whether from the wasps or the fluorescent lights or the voices of the Overlook, also reinforce the atmosphere of ancient prehuman life.

Yet the fact that the smell of oranges always precedes Dick Hallorann's visions seems to suggest that when one connects with this original life force, there is a possibility that individual and social identity may be enhanced and not necessarily destroyed. This is a recognition which Gothic fiction stimulates: the conscious ego is only a portion of the total self. From a Jungian perspective, such a recognition brings both emotional relief and an expanded awareness. Because Jack, who is so confident at the beginning of the story that his superior intellect will protect him from cabin fever (9) and who has battled his alcoholism through a supreme effort of will, craves this relief so desperately, he runs a much greater risk of "drowning in instinct" (389) than does Dick, who is more comfortable with the collective aspect of his identity and is "used to following his hunches" (311).

Thus, in keeping with the ameliorative aims of the jeremiad, defined by Sacvan Bercovitch as "a ritual designed to join social criticism to spiritual renewal, public to private identity, the shifting 'signs of the times' to certain traditional metaphors, themes, and symbols" (xi), *The Shining* joins its condemnation with a movement toward regeneration. There are three characters who serve as symbolic agents of cultural and spiritual renewal or redemption in *The Shining:* the black man, the child, and the mother. Along with the image of Christ, which appears at significant moments in the plot, they constitute, in Jungian terms, symbols of transformation.

Dick Hallorann, the black man, acts as a savior in his journey back to the Overlook to rescue Danny, just as he also represents the shadow side of the American psyche. He embodies the emotional force and the physical ease for which African-Americans are noted, and often stereotyped, that has been historically suppressed by white society, both in the form of the brutal treatment of black people before and after slavery was abolished and in the dominant society's lingering puritanical unease about bodily pleasure. The shadow in Jung's terminology represents that aspect of the self that is deemed unacceptable or unworthy and so is rejected or denied. But because the healthy psyche is self-regulating, the shadow cannot be permanently submerged; it must find expression in order to restore psychic balance.

Jack's imbalance is underscored by the way he succumbs to a prejudicial hatred of "niggers" during his breakdown, but Dick's actual saving grace is indicated by Danny's vision of Dick dressed in kitchen whites (although Danny never actually saw him in them) that endow his image with a numinous quality (304).

Dick himself must overcome his own self-hatred and rage at the white man before he can enter the Overlook to attempt to rescue Danny; as he is approaching the hotel he tunes in on its

heavy . . . hateful, murderous/ thought-force:
(GET OUT OF HERE YOU DIRTY NIGGER THIS IS NONE OF YOUR BUSINESS YOU NIGGER TURN AROUND OR WE'LL KILL YOU HANG YOU UP FROM A TREE LIMB YOU FUCKING JUNGLE-BUNNY COON AND THEN BURN THE BODY THAT'S WHAT WE DO WITH NIGGERS SO TURN AROUND NOW). (389)

After the explosion, when Dick enters the adjoining shed to get gas for the snowmobile ride down to Sidewinder, he is tempted by the spirit of the place, with its thick accumulation of hatred, to murder Danny and Wendy. When Danny calls to him to come out, Dick hears a voice saying "(*'Come on out now nigguh de massa callin youall."*) . . . (. . . *Do it, you weak-kneed no-balls nigger! Kill them!* . . .)" (439). But Dick overcomes the pressure, as well as his increasing sense of identification with Jack, the power-mad white man, and he drives the two to shelter.

Dick succeeds in his heroic journey, and the final scene of *The Shining* is appropriately symbolic of a healing cultural and psychic *rapprochement:* he is sitting on a dock at the Red Arrow Lodge in Maine, with his arm around Danny, and with Wendy beside them, "reel[ing] the fish in, little by little" from the watery depths of the lake. Dick notes that Danny is "gettin brown," and Wendy responds, "Yes. Very brown" (447, 443). Danny's tan is taken by the two adults as a sign of his growing health, but in a larger sense, his darkening skin color implies that for the nation, desegregation is a necessary step toward a "healthier" future.

When Jung first came to America on a speaking engagement with Freud in 1909, he was deeply impressed by what he considered evidence of the "psychic imprint" of African and native Americans on Americans of European descent. Jung was so intrigued by America that he quickly made a second visit, whereas Freud diagnosed the country as a "gigantic mistake" and never returned (Stern 97; King would undoubtedly appreciate both reactions). Jung also visited an American Pueblo Indian community and traveled to Africa.[16] Even before Jung visited the United States, however, he was struck by the role of native and black Americans in the dreams of his American patients: "[T]he black man regularly embodied the 'shadow,' the unlived life-potential, while the red man symbolized the ego-ideal, the idealistic aspirations of Americans" (Stern 126). This idea seems to be at work in *The Shining,* where Dick Hallorann acts as the agent of a renewed "life-potential" succeeding the collapse of the Overlook.

A second agent of renewal is Danny, who functions symbolically as the archetypal "Divine Child": the collective soul-bearer of the race, the "mediator, bringer of healing," signifying futurity, possibility, and spiritual wholeness. In myth, the child is "delivered helpless into the power of terrible enemies and in continual danger of extinction, [yet he] possesses powers far exceeding those of ordinary humanity" because he represents the human impulse for self-realization (Jung 83, 89). Danny may have clear perception, but he has not yet grown into understanding; he cries to Dick in frustration, "But I don't *understand* things! . . . People . . . they feel things and I feel them, but I don't know what I'm feeling! . . . I wish I could read. Sometimes Tony shows me signs and I can hardly read any of them" (85).

With his unfulfilled potential, he represents the new life that will follow upon the destruction of the old.

In order to defend her son, Wendy, like Dick, must overcome personal weakness and social conditioning. Wendy lacks self-confidence, but with her blond hair, which Danny compares to corn and wheat, she is also a Ceres figure, goddess of the self-replenishing earth. Her matriarchal character is evoked when Danny, warned by Tony that his mother is in mortal danger, thinks panic-stricken that she must not die because "she satisfied his childish definition of eternity" (419). Wendy is unsure whether she has enough of the "primal mother" in her to protect her offspring against the ravages of the father (364). Her own upbringing with a "devouring mother" (Danny imagined that Wendy's mother wanted to eat her; 201) has left her unsure about herself and her own capacities, but unlike Walpole's meek Hippolita, Wendy succeeds in opposing Jack with tenacious force, although at great cost to herself. She also demonstrates a real ferocity in defending Danny from Jack's outbursts, at one point threatening to kill Jack if he ever hurts Danny again (232). She reverses Jack's family history as well by bashing him over the head with an empty wine bottle, as Jack's father had done to his wife with a cane (369). Ultimately, she puts "self-preservation after son-preservation" (233). Even the ghostly Grady grudgingly admits that "she appears to be . . . somewhat stronger than we had imagined. Somewhat more resourceful" (381).

All the adult characters regress during the course of their struggles to a religious state of awareness, an intensifying sense of "superstitious dread" (52, 135) signified in part by their increasing use of expletives invoking God and Christ. Wendy's and Dick's oaths are uttered in tones of prayerful supplication, thanks, and promise, whereas Jack's are most often blasphemous. There are also two visions of Christ that appear: one when Danny confronts what is left of Jack in their final encounter and sees the depth of suffering in his father's face; and another when Jack recalls a gestalt puzzle shown to his class by their teacher, a nun. Jack remembers the puzzle at the moment he realizes that he is the "weak link" the hotel is working on. He had been the only child left in his class who failed to recognize the image and finally lied that he saw it; later when alone in the classroom he did recognize the "sad . . . wise. . . . careworn" face, but only after muttering "Shitfire-hellfire-shitfire" under his breath. This memory feeds into Jack's sense of being damned and defeated and in turn leads him into succumbing to the Overlook's spell by throwing away the magneto for the snowmobile, their only vehicle for escape (278–82).

The Christ image appears again, via Jack, at the climax of the action, when Danny faces down the powers of evil working through his father. He "sees through" their lie and states, "[Y]ou'll never get what you want from me." Then "suddenly his daddy *was* there, looking at him in mortal agony, and a sorrow so great that Danny's heart flamed within his chest." Jack tells Danny to "remember how much" he loves him and begs him "for God's sake" to run away, but Danny refuses to move, taking one of his father's "bloody hands" and kissing it, saying, "It's almost over" (Wendy repeats this gesture with Dick at the end of the story; 444). Danny for the first time in his life has "an adult thought, an adult feeling" in the realization that he is alone, that no one else can help him. At this point, what is left of Jack turns the mallet with which he has been threatening Danny against himself (427–28). One critic has referred to this scene as another instance of the "sacral parody" that is typical of King's fiction (Egan 138); yet when one considers the elements of recognition, crucifixion, sacrifice, and self-annihilation from an archetypal perspective, one can see that it enacts what Jung has called the "realization of the shadow . . . [which has] the meaning of a suffering and a passion which implicate the whole man" (208).

The reader's sense of the pathos of Jack's failure is intensified by the knowledge that the bond between father and son has been such a close one. Wendy has occasional feelings of jealousy in her recognition that "Danny had been Jack's for the asking, almost from the first." When Danny was a baby, Jack helped to tend him with care and patience, feeding him and burping him and soothing his stomach aches, frequently with more success than Wendy. Jack "hadn't minded changing diapers, even those he called the special deliveries" (53). His assumption of the role of Gothic villain becomes all the more horrific in the light of his obvious love for his child.

As Danny watches what is left of his father disintegrate, he finally recalls something that had been nagging at his memory: the boiler has been left untended and will soon blow the whole thing up. In terms of the novel's architectural symbolism, the repeated suggestions that the son must remember what the father has forgotten (or "overlooked") point to the need for a deeper understanding of the historical foundations of American life. As bastion of a cultural identity that is no longer viable, the Overlook must self-destruct, but the child who is "gettin brown" represents the hope—or at least the possibility—of the future.

Wendy and Dick both try to reassure each other that despite the grief and horror of losing Jack, she and Danny will "be okay," but the tone of the final section is tentative rather than confident. There is the disturbing information that the person helping Wendy to find employment in

Maryland is "Uncle Al" Shockley (443–44), who with his inherited wealth and power is very much involved in the dirty corporate world of Uncle Sam and who admits to full knowledge of the Overlook's seamy history (187). Also, it is a "Chamber of Commerce brochure" that persuades Wendy that the place might be a "nice town to raise a kid in" (444). Although the American Gothic nightmare seems to be behind them, there is an uneasy sense that its warning may not have been fully understood. The future still holds its dangers, and there is no final assurance that the horror will not return.

Attempting to explain the reasons for the rise of the horror film and novel in America in the seventies and early eighties (as well as for his own enormous popular success), King has identified the change as part of a major shift in the general attitude which could also be detected in "the rise of such things as Rolfing, primal screaming, and hot-tubbing" (*Danse* 267). Outside of his fiction, King gives few hints about his work's political import. However, given the severe critique of American history and society offered in *The Shining*, it is not difficult to see why, near the end of the twentieth century, the biggest national producer of Gothic nightmares should no longer be England but the United States, the country with the biggest "ego" so to speak, which currently occupies, rather uneasily, the position of world leader in the nuclear age.

Epilogue: Alien *and the Future of Gothic*

*T*he Gothic novel connects the present with the past in order to provide a guide to the future. It serves to modify prevailing attitudes
by effecting an imaginative temporal displacement that allows for the expression of otherwise taboo material. In Stephen King's words, the horror
novel "says, in a symbolic way, things we would be afraid to say right out
straight . . . it offers us a chance to exercise . . . emotions which society demands we keep closely in hand" (*Danse* 21–23). From the beginning,
Gothic novels have taken aim at cultural "blind spots" and worked against
whatever form of censorship their societies have imposed, whether psychological, social, historical, or literary. The first Gothic novels of the late
eighteenth century utilized a quasimedieval setting in order to create the
displacement effect, and although the later Gothic novelists generally dis-
pensed with the explicit use of a medieval setting, they nevertheless continued to evoke a medieval or pre-Reformation atmosphere and a more
primitive psychological ambience, which allowed the "return of the repressed" into their social worlds. Thus *Dr Jekyll and Mr Hyde, Dracula,* and
The Shining all make use of contemporary settings, while at the same time
evoking "primitive" or "uncivilized" states of emotion and awareness.

Similarly, many science fiction novels and films—although they
make use of futuristic landscapes and technology—also indirectly reflect
current conditions and tendencies, while stimulating an archaic sense of
"superstitious dread" that warns and admonishes.[1] As Brian Aldiss states,
speaking of Shelley's *Frankenstein,* "Science fiction was born from the
Gothic mode, is hardly free of it now" (18).[2] Another reason that the

Gothic tradition has adapted so well into film is the importance of the visual or imagistic component in conveying psychological symbolism and powerful emotional effects. An illuminating example of how contemporary science fiction maintains Gothic conventions can be found in Ridley Scott's film *Alien*, which drew a large popular audience when it appeared in 1979, continues to be viewed widely via the video rental market, and has been followed by a series of three more films, the most recent of which appeared in 1997.

The film concerns a commercial spaceship that has been sent, without its crew's knowledge, on a dangerous mission to obtain some material from a planet far beyond the solar system. On the first exploratory foray after the landing, a crew member enters a large, dark, cavernous structure that appears to be composed of fossilized organic matter. He discovers what appear to be living organisms in a valley or depression of the structure, and when he descends to examine them one attacks him. The captain admits the victim back onto the ship despite the rules prohibiting such action and against the objections of the heroine, Ripley, that the captain is running the risk of infecting the ship with antagonistic life forms. The victim seems to recover after the parasitic alien has been separated from his body, but before he has finished his first meal, he begins to retch violently, and his body suddenly erupts, releasing the monstrous, metamorphic life form into the ship, where it eventually destroys every human member of the crew except Ripley. She finally escapes on a shuttle craft as the ship explodes behind her.

Alien recalls Shelley's *Frankenstein*, in its stress on the distinction between the manufactured and the organic; but whereas the danger in *Frankenstein*'s monster lies in its manufactured or mechanical aspect, the threat in *Alien* comes from the organic. *Frankenstein*, appearing in the wake of the social ravages attending the Industrial Revolution, presented a warning about the growing dominion of the scientific, experimental attitude and pointed to the possibility that the seemingly marvelous inventions of human technological ingenuity could rise up against their creators. *Alien*, in contrast, appears in a period haunted by the threat of environmental collapse, and presents the organic as the daemonic, overwhelming force that rises up against humanity and its relatively puny constructions. However, what both works have in common is a concern with the antagonistic attitude to nature that has prevailed since the Industrial Revolution.

In *Alien*, certain images draw a sharp contrast between the mechanical and the organic realms, conveying the impression of a rift or an antithetical opposition between the two. The film opens with a long sequence showing the seemingly empty ship silently moving on its own through the vast reaches of outer space. The ship is impressively huge, but ugly, dirty, and clumsy-looking, possessing none of the streamlined grace of earlier cinematic rocket ships and flying saucers (including Kubrick's *2001*). When the crew members wake up from their interstellar sleep, the camera angle draws attention to the plastic diaperlike pants they have been wearing, and the scene quickly shifts to one where they are eating and drinking. The members of the crew are also frequently shown carrying cups of hot coffee and other beverages. Taken all together, these images serve as a subliminal reminder that humans have evolved from an extremely simple life form that was no more than a digestive tube, consuming and excreting—only slightly less complex than the wormlike, dripping, breeding, devouring monster that is bent on destroying them.

The power of the organic is also underscored in the first sight of the alien lair, where the straight lines and sharp corners of an apparently mechanical artifact seem to have been absorbed into the enormous curves and hollows of an organic fossil. The ship's scientist analyzes the atmosphere of the alien's planet and concludes that it is "almost primordial," and the regession to a state preceding human consciousness is suggested by the standard Gothic technique of reducing vision, both in the intermittency of the image transmitted to the ship's video screen and in the darkness surrounding the investigative crew. One team member complains that she "can't see a goddam thing," and the expletive is repeated by the man who descends into the "cave" or lower layer, which symbolizes the steamy beginnings of life on earth: "It's like the goddam tropics in here." In addition, the walls of the entry passage to the lair are curved and covered with riblike shapes, creating the impression that the crew has entered the dark "belly of the whale," an effect that is intensified in the lower layer, where they discover that what they have found is not a dead fossil after all, but a lethally potent living force aroused from its long-dormant state.

The ribs also establish the castle/edifice/body identification that is a feature of Gothic fiction. To enter the lower layer is also to penetrate the inner body and to regress to the beginning of human life in the womb. The monster's breeding ground is emphatically female and reminds viewers of the bloodiness and messiness of human birth. When closed, the pod is egg-shaped, and its top resembles a cervix, which in response to human warmth opens suddenly, first revealing its inner organs with their tracery of white blood vessels, and then releasing its hideous, slimy progeny. The background sound of a human heartbeat during encounters with the monster, both in the lair and later on the ship, does more than emphasize the crew members' fright; it recreates the ambience of life in the womb, a state of union with, and dependency on, one's "host." The audience's horror at the sudden appearances of the monster is compounded by the intermittence of sight itself. The sequences in the ship's passageways, like those in the alien's lair, take the audience "underground" to the disorienting darkness of an unconscious or preconscious state.

After the incubating creature has penetrated the body orifices, death comes in an explosion of the stomach and intestines—a violent sundering of what Bakhtin has named the intact, self-contained "classical" body and a reassertion of the interpenetrative "grotesque" body dominated by the lower regions. In the case of the full-fledged monster, the feature that is highlighted is the "vagina dentata"—with a vengeance—a copiously salivating, gaping maw that exposes not one but two and three sets of fangs.

Alien exploits what Camille Paglia has called our "evolutionary revulsion from slime, our site of biologic origins"; and it has done so more successfully than many other current horror films, whose makers "[blunder] about, seeking, without realizing it, the chthonian swamp of generation, the female matrix" (11, 269). *Alien* identifies precisely what terrifies and fascinates a late-twentieth-century urban audience, cocooned in a relatively safe, highly technologized world: the sudden, shocking intrusion of all things dark and oozy.

As *Alien* also suggests, perhaps the most notable shift in Gothic fictions over the last two hundred and thirty years has been in their manner of presenting the supernatural; the ghosts have become increasingly more material, and the idea of ancestry has deepened. Ghostly apparitions of the dead have given way to eruptions of subhuman and prehuman life forms, and the movement seems to be proceeding steadily downward, in evolutionary terms: from the apelike Hyde, to the reptilian Dracula, to the "insectile" primordial life that invades the Overlook, to the indeterminate yet rudimentary breeding monster of *Alien,* which at times resembles the inner flesh of an oyster or clam. In a largely urban, secular culture that excludes a great deal of the natural physical world and at the same time rejects the metaphysical, the organic has become a primary symbol of transpersonal reality, manifested as daemonic energy.

Alien also registers cultural anxiety about the current world-wide transition to a global corporate economy, or corporate "feudalism" as it is sometimes called. The ship *Nostromo* is identified at the outset of the film as a commercial vehicle carrying twenty million tons of mineral ore for refinery processing. The corporation evidently uses some profit-sharing incentives, but two of the crew members, workmen who have "contracted" for a smaller return than the others, argue that "the bonus situation has never been on an equitable level." Ripley affirms that "the law" will protect their interests, but her confidence is thrown into question by the later revelation that the crew has been sent without its knowledge or consent on a potentially fatal mission, in which the aim of acquiring the powers of the unknown entity is primary and the lives of the crew members secondary. One of the crew observes that the company ("they") "must have wanted the alien for the weapons division," drawing a specifically twentieth-century connection between war and corporate profit. The appellation of "Mother" given to the company and its ship is clearly euphemistic, for contracts and law notwithstanding, the corporation functions as an impersonal, heartlessly aggressive force. Its oppressive, monolithic power is emphasized visually by frequent shots from beneath the moving ship, which appears to threaten to take over the entire screen.

The theme is a familiar one, though not an exclusive one, to Gothic fiction. As in Conrad's *Nostromo*, after which the ship is named, and in Mary Shelley's tale of human over-reaching, as well as in King's *The Shining*, where the Overlook's monster "grin[s] with broken-toothed greed" (429), actions motivated by pride, greed, and ambition—whether their own or someone else's—are the protagonists' undoing.

The characteristically Gothic conjunction of the moral and the grotesque occurs in *Alien*'s destruction of the only thoroughly evil character on the ship, who turns out to be an android—a cerebral agent of corporate greed and a monstrous parody of scientific curiosity disconnected from human feeling (like Frankenstein and Jekyll before him). After the remaining crew members succeed in destroying him when he attempts to kill the heroine, they re-animate only his head to obtain information from him and finally disconnect him altogether. With one exception, all the crew members suffer gruesome deaths as well, but it is significant that the first death, which receives the most extended visual attention, occurs to the one who has rejected the cautionary advice of another (female) crewmate and insisted on exploring the interior of the strange edifice they discover. In a period of oil spills and nuclear accidents, the warning is simple and unmistakable, and not greatly different from *Frankenstein*'s: hasty and irreverent assaults on female Nature will not go unretaliated.

We also see in *Alien* the Gothic affirmation of heroic values, as well as the interrogation of sexual politics, which forms the social dimension of Gothic fiction's archetypal and psychological concern with the feminine principle. The heroine is a lean, mean Amazon who possesses courage, moral integrity, and what eighteenth-century readers would have called "benevolence," or concern for others. She is the one who points out that the remaining crew members must stay and fight together rather than flee on the ship's shuttle, because it "won't take four." Her judgement is clearer than her well-meaning but weak (and white, male) captain's, yet she maintains a strong sense of creature feeling. She has a strong attachment to the ship's cat (whom curiosity did *not* kill) and in the second movie of the series, *Aliens* (1986), to a young, defenceless girl, both of whom she succeeds in rescuing from the "bitch" monster moments before the final catastrophe (the second film also features a woman dressed as a Nicaraguan guerilla fighter, who dies courageously defending her crew). The heroine is an integrating figure: like Stoker's Mina and King's Wendy, she is a modern woman who reaffirms the power of the primal mother without sinking back into chthonic oblivion. The other hero in *Alien* is also a figure from the underside of Western culture, a black man like King's Dick Hallorann; he "talks dirty," but when the crisis comes, he sacrifices his own life in a failed attempt to rescue his sensitive but weak partner, who has been too paralyzed by fear to defend herself.

The significance of the heroine's courage is not primarily ethical, however, for she enacts an archetypal night journey of descent and return from a confrontation with the monsters of the deep.[3] As we have seen, the battle between the civilized and the metamorphic prehuman forces takes place mainly in a space age equivalent of the old Gothic castles' and monasteries' underground tunnels. The monster moves about in the ship's arterial air ducts, and the nightmarish confrontations usually occur in the narrow, dark passageways connecting different parts of the ship, where the only light comes from the crew's archaic fire torches.

Alien thus demonstrates in a multiplicity of ways how science fiction can express the Gothic impulse: alerting us, through a process of regression, to dangers that lie ahead, and responding to the loss of the sacred in a secular and scientific age by evoking the daemonic. Given the close affinity between works such as *Alien* and the Gothic literary tradition, it is not difficult to see why such films should be so popular and how they too can provide "equipment for living."

NOTES

INTRODUCTION. WHAT GOTHIC NIGHTMARES DO

1. Tompkins is citing Joseph Fox, apparently from his preface to his novel *Santa-Maria; or the Mysterious Pregnancy* (1797).

2. Hardy's phrase comes from his *Tess of the d'Urbervilles* (123); it is Angel Clare's expression for Tess's attempt to describe her sense of the "hobble of being alive" (122). Hardy's concern with the depletion of vitality in modern life is more carefully explored in *The Return of the Native,* especially in his characterization of Clym Yeobright, whose appearance shows that "thought is a disease of the flesh" (124).

Lawrence shared Hardy's conviction that modern life lacks "that zest for existence which was so intense in early civilizations" (Hardy, *Return* 151). He uses the phrase *talking heads* in *St. Mawr* to describe Rico. While Lawrence is apparently referring to a current expression for expressive, aesthetically pleasing physiognomies, his preceding description of Rico indicates Lawrence's more ironic use of the term: "If his head had been cut off, like John the Baptist's, it would have been a thing complete in itself, would not have missed the body in the least" (18).

3. Peter Brooks similarly observes that a Gothic work such as M. G. Lewis's *The Monk* is a reaction to the Age of Reason and a reassertion of the sacred in its most primitive form (249). Brooks comments that *The Monk* explodes both "an excessively rationalist world view and the traditional eighteenth-century novel's framework of 'manners'" (253). Syndy McMillen Conger also examines how the "'pre-religious' or primitive" impulse in Walpole's *The Castle of Otranto* reflects dissatisfaction with established Protestantism and stresses "superstitious dread of ancestral spirits, of taboo, and of interdiction" ("Faith" 57).

4. Not all nightmares work in this manner—as psychic guides. Repetitive trauma-induced nightmares may in fact aggravate a problem rather than show the

means to its solution. For an informative study of dream analysis which includes Freudian, Jungian, "content analysis," and "gestalt" approaches, see Ann Faraday.

5. See Keith Thomas for a discussion of how the Reformation undermined the traditional "notion of society as a community uniting the dead and the living." Thomas points out that the unprecedented "violence of the Reformation, the destruction of the abbeys and chantries, and the violation of the testaments of so many dead persons" signified the beginning of "a more atomistic conception of the relationship in which members of society stood to each other," an attitudinal shift that he argues has led to the contemporary "lack of a modern ritual adequate to deal with the crisis of death" (720–22).

Also see J. Paul Hunter, who discusses the rise of the novel as a response to the widespread sense of temporal and social dislocation in a rapidly urbanizing eighteenth-century England: "[T]he novel depends . . . on a sense of successive moments with accumulating value and, crucially, on a sense that every moment has a meaningful past. . . . [T]he novel offers individuals an alternative activity—even an alternative consciousness—for solitude, providing intellectual and spiritual companionship, though only for a limited time" (134–35).

6. R. L. Isaacson, following Paul MacLean, describes the brain as a kind of gating system, in which the neocortex functions to block "the habits and memories of the past" so that the thinking brain can function unhindered by the signals from the limbic system (emotional brain) and the visceral (reptilian) brain (242).

7. Some critics do not differentiate between the awesome and the mystifying. See for example Terry Heller's *The Delights of Terror: An Aesthetics of the Tale of Terror*, which traces the complex ways in which narrative design affects reader response, and includes a chapter on James's *The Turn of the Screw*. Heller does not confine his examination to the Gothic canon, however, but includes a number of works categorized roughly according to Tzvetan Todorov's divisions: marvelous, uncanny, fantastic, and fantasy modes.

8. In another essay, Kahane suggests that the "uncanny mother of infancy" which dominates the Female Gothic struggle is strictly a social construct which "will continue to haunt us as long as women remain, on the one hand, the sole custodians of infantile identity, and on the other, on the margin of social power" ("Gothic" 351).

Margaret Anne Doody (1977) has shown how the dream imagery of earlier eighteenth-century fictional heroines—"mountain, forest, ghost, desert, cavern, lake, troubled waters, ruined building with tottering roof, subterraneous cavern," etc.—became incorporated into the Gothic novel to articulate the conviction that "the true nightmare . . . is history." Doody argues that "[i]t is in the Gothic novel that women writers could first accuse the 'real world' of falsehood and deep disorder" ("Deserts" 554, 562, 560).

Sandra Gilbert and Susan Gubar have emphasized women's struggle against the literary precedents of men, to articulate their own experience, and more recently Kate Ferguson Ellis (1989) has examined the way women's Gothic fiction subverts the ideology of bourgeois domesticity.

9. Rosemary Jackson, for example, combines Todorov's approach with some linguistic/psychoanalytic theory from Freud, Lacan, and others, along with a consideration of the cultural context of fantasy fiction. Franco Moretti uses both Marxist and psychoanalytic theory in his analysis but fails to integrate them, treating the two approaches in separate sections of his discussion: "I do not propose here to reconstruct the many missing links that might connect socio-economic structures and sexual-psychological in a single conceptual chain" (104).

Two critics whose works bridge some of the gaps between Marxist and psychoanalytic theory are Punter and Baldick. More recently, Martin Tropp's informative study signals a shift toward a broader cultural perspective than that offered heretofore by particular theoretical approaches. Tropp's views on the social significance of *Frankenstein, Dr Jekyll and Mr Hyde,* and *Dracula* correspond in a number of ways with my own. As well, the third and fourth chapters of his study, "The City Imagined" and "Beneath the Crystal Palace" offer a thought-provoking analysis of the 1851 Great Exhibition in London, in relation to Charles Dicken's Victorian Gothic, *Bleak House* (1852-53) and Henry Mayhew's study *London Labour and the London Poor* (1851).

10. T. E. Apter has suggested that (Freudian) psychoanalysis itself is a form of fantasy, that "fantasy can explore and test reality in much the same manner as psychoanalysis," and that fantasy literature exposes "general limitations in perception and knowledge" (130–51, 7, 11).

11. For a discussion of how Jungian literary criticism is engaged in "rethinking the possible boundaries of literary criticism," see Richard P. Sugg's Introduction to *Jungian Literary Criticism*, 1–6 (3).

12. Leslie Fiedler's essay, "Archetype and Signature," clarifies the important distinction between the immemorial or atemporal patterns of human experience—the archetype—and their particular historical expressions in art—the signature.

CHAPTER 1. PRECEDENTS FOR "GOTHIC" FEAR: MEDIEVAL LIFE, JACOBEAN DRAMA, AND EIGHTEENTH-CENTURY ATTITUDES

1. For an account of how Warton in his *History of English Poetry* (1774) and Thomas Percy in his *Reliques of Ancient English Poetry* (1765) altered and even mistranslated the heroic romances, while (in Warton's case at least) "regarding [them]

as historical documents which provided accurate descriptions of ancient manners and times, with exception being taken only to their accounts of the fabulous," see Joseph M. P. Donatelli (443).

2. See Kenneth Clark on the eighteenth-century vogue for resuscitating the "Gothic" spirit in architecture and then in literature.

Also see Wilhelm Worringer for an analysis of the "will to form" or the world view that gives rise to Gothic art and architecture, and Paul Frankl on the historical shifts in understanding and appreciation of Gothic form over eight centuries. Frankl points out that around 1750, England was "overwhelmed by a flood of Gothic" architecture and design and that although a "Chinese wave swept over the English imagination at the same time . . . the Chinese wave ebbed away, whereas the Gothic settled and grew clear" (386).

3. See Nicolas Kiessling for a brief discussion of the incubus figure in Judaeo-Christian, early Germanic, and Celtic traditions, as well as in early and romantic British literature.

4. In the words of Mircea Eliade, the primitive ritual for regeneration of the world "unfolds not only in a consecrated space (i.e., one different in essence from profane space) but also in a 'sacred time'"; "every consecrated space coincides with the center of the world"; and the center "is pre-eminently the zone of the sacred, the zone of absolute reality" (21, 20, 17)—a zone that the Protestant churches no longer provided.

5. Two early essays by Clara F. McIntyre (1921 and 1925) focus on the influence of Elizabethan tragedy on Gothic fiction, but there has been little critical interest shown in the subject over the last few decades.

6. Also see Judith Weil's chapter, "The Tragical Folly of Dr Faustus," where she argues that in the course of the play Faustus moves from being a learned fool, to being "the best actor on a stage of fools," to achieving an "intellectual" recognition of the "good he once denied," which finally endows him with tragic stature (50–81). In a note, Weil comments on the theological debate and "intellectual ferment of Marlowe's Cambridge"; she suggests that while the play exhibits "tension between Calvinist and moderate Anglican positions," it does not support "the hero's own Calvinist attitude" (191 n. 9).

7. For a fascinating account of the legal, medical, and religious conflict about witchcraft in this time, see Michael MacDonald's description of the investigative flurry around one Elizabeth Jackson's trial for witchcraft. Jackson was accused of uttering a curse against a teenage girl, Mary Glover, who went into convulsions and displayed other bizarre physical symptoms whenever Jackson was present.

MacDonald convincingly argues that Edward Jorden's investigation, titled *A Briefe Discourse of a Disease Called the Suffocation of the Mother,* which put forward a natural rather than supernatural explanation of Mary's troubles, was motivated partly by Jorden's desire to "advance a political religious cause and to win the favour of powerful men" (liv). Some of those powerful men were actively seeking to enlist the sympathies of the future King James I, who "switched . . . rapidly from an enthusiasm for demonology to limited scepticism" after he ascended the English throne (xlix). "At the very least," says Macdonald, "Jorden helped foster the King's newly cautious attitude to witchcraft" (l).

MacDonald also notes that after this episode, confidence in the evidence presented to convict witches was eroded, and the "practice of exorcism by prayer and fasting was also officially forbidden as a result of the case" (li).

8. Robert Mayo, using the *Lady's Magazine* as a reasonably reliable index of the popularity of tales of terror, says that in terms of "sheer bulk" Gothic stories comprised 52% of the magazine's output from 1791 to 1798, 62% from 1799 to 1802, 23% in 1803, and 72% from 1804 to 1806. After 1806 a decline set in, and "during 1813 and 1814 Gothic stories disappear entirely." Mayo suggests that although the Gothic vogue was over by 1814, its "appeal was still fresh in the public mind" (61–62, 64).

Important Gothic works did appear within the next decade—Shelley's innovative *Frankenstein* in 1818, Charles Maturin's *Melmoth the Wanderer* in 1820, and James Hoggs's *Private Memoirs and Confessions of a Justified Sinner* in 1824, along with some of Walter Scott's adaptations of Gothic romance—but these were part of the last "trickle" that occurred between the final defeat of Napoleon in 1815 and the expansion of the franchise in the first Reform Bill of 1832.

9. On the influence of the popular Gothic novel on "realistic" writers such as Jane Austen and George Eliot, see Judith Wilt.

10. Because the first phase of major novels was realistic in its orientation, Ian Watt has argued in *The Rise of the Novel* that this is the dominant mode of all subsequent fictional forms of any critical significance. Watt dismisses the later eighteenth-century sentimental and Gothic novels as "fugitive literary tendencies . . . [with] little merit" (290).

11. Northrop Frye rejects the conventional notion that "the age of sensibility was the time when poetry moved from a reptilian Classicism, all cold and dry reason, to a mammalian Romanticism, all warm and wet feeling" (130). He suggests instead that the shift was from a conception of poetry as "product" to one of poetry as "process." Where the emphasis is on the former, "the qualities of consciousness take the lead: a regular metre, clarity of syntax, epigram and wit, repetition of sense in antithesis and balance rather than of sound." Where the emphasis is on the latter, "the qualities of subconscious association take the lead, and the poetry becomes hypnotically repetitive, oracular, incantatory, dreamlike and in the original sense of the word charming" (133). It is not difficult to see how some of these qualities also found expression in the Gothic fiction of the 1790s.

12. Sir Walter Scott draws attention to the oral and traditional sources of certain types of fiction in the first chapter of his most "Gothic" work, *The Bride of Lammermoor* (1819). The narrator recounts that he is simply the editor of a story given to him in the form of rough notes from his friend Dick Tinto, who had heard it while staying at a farmhouse in the mountains of Lammermoor, from the "aged goodwife" who presided there (26).

13. Clery's study focuses on the dissemination of Gothic superstition as a consumer commodity. He argues that the comic spoofing of the Cock Lane sensation on the stage at Drury Lane signals "the wrestling of the invisible world from the sphere of religious doctrine, and its incongruous, hilarious embrace by the fashion system of the city." The ghost becomes "available to be processed, reproduced, packaged, marketed and distributed by the engines of cultural production" (17). For a fuller account of the Cock Lane episode, see D. Grant.

CHAPTER 2. SEXUAL VIOLENCE AND WOMAN'S PLACE: *THE CASTLE OF OTRANTO*

1. From Gray's letter of 30 December 1764.

2. From Williams' letter to George Selwyn, 19 March 1765.

3. The *Critical* issues are January 1765, xix, 50–1 and June 1765, xix, 469.

4. The *Monthly Review*, February 1765, xxxii, 97–99, and May 1765, xxxii, 394.

5. From *Historical and Literary Memoirs and Anecdotes Selected from the correspondence of Baron de Grimm . . . Between the Years 1753 and 1769* (1814), ii, 292–94.

6. Kallich is citing Walpole's *A Catalogue of Royal and Noble Authors,* first published in 1758, from volumes one and two of the five-volume edition of Walpole's *Works.* For an informative discussion of Walpole's libertarian views and lingering aristocratic sympathies, see Kallich's chapter "The Whig Politician" (34–63). Walpole hated tyranny of any sort; he was "among the first of his age to disapprove of slavery on moral grounds" (Kallich 1). He also later opposed the bloody tyranny of the masses in the French Revolution.

7. The subject has remained largely an "unspeakable" one until well into the twentieth century, as Jeffrey Masson has revealed in his study of Freud's theory of hysteria. Masson shows that Freud initially treated seriously his female patients' stories about being sexually abused as children and young teenagers, by fathers, uncles, and other adult men who were sufficiently close to the family circle to take advantage of them. When Freud realized that persisting in his views would make

him a pariah in the psychoanalytic community, he changed them, deciding that the women's stories were delusive symptoms of their hysterical need for attention. Masson also argues that Freud developed his theory of hysteria to evade his guilt feelings about the suffering of a female patient who almost bled to death when undergoing surgical "treatment" endorsed by Freud.

8. Dole is citing Walpole's *Historic Doubts on the Life and Reign of King Richard the Third,* 114–116.

9. For accounts of Walpole's childhood relationship with his mother, see Ketton-Cremer (6–16), Gwynn (11–22), and Kallich (8–9).

10. Gwynn endorses the idea that Horace was not Sir Robert's natural son, while Ketton-Cremer and Kallich are skeptical; the latter two both point out that the notion first seems to have arisen in early-nineteenth-century gossip, and was based on the opinion of Lady Mary Wortley Montague, who had been friendly with Sir Robert Walpole's mistress (Ketton-Cremer 10–11; Kallich 8–9).

11. Walpole was not alone in his voyeuristic taste. See Peter Wagner's "Trial Reports as a Genre of Eighteenth-Century Erotica."

CHAPTER 3. SENTIMENT VERSUS HORROR: GENERIC AMBIVALENCE IN FEMALE GOTHIC AND ANN RADCLIFFE'S *A SICILIAN ROMANCE*

1. For a recent study of women fiction writers in their changing social conditions from 1660 to 1800, see Janet Todd.

2. I have relied here mainly on Louis I. Bredvold, pp. 8–26. Bredvold cites Shaftesbury's *Characteristics* (1: 86).

3. Also see the first chapter of Mary Poovey's study, in which she traces the progressive "idealization of female nature" that occurred in the first half of the eighteenth century and was stimulated by the seventeenth-century Puritan legacy of "the elevated and spiritually significant position of the home." When "separation between the home and the workplace became the middle-class rule rather than the exception" by the early decades of the eighteenth century, women, as guardians of the home, "could even take pride in sacrificing their sexual desires for this 'higher' cause" (8).

4. There has been considerable variety of opinion about the tradition of sensibility and Richardson's relation to it. Erica Harth stresses the problem of class conflict in *Pamela,* where the servant girl succeeds in marrying her master. Harth sees the novel's resolution as a form of social/psychological wish fulfillment: "love both overcomes and respects social boundaries" (150). Pamela's struggle occurs

within an economic context where her "'jewel' of chastity" is the sole signifier of her exchange value (149). Thus Pamela's virtue is rewarded not just morally and emotionally but materially as well. Stephen D. Cox, in contrast, sees a more straightforward humanizing impulse at work in the novel: "Richardson stresses the idea that self-knowledge usually comes from one's experience of other people and one's sensibility to them" (67).

5. Poovey is citing James Boswell, p. 250. She gives a fuller discussion of some of the social and economic changes that contributed to transforming the "lewde" woman of the Renaissance into the "proper lady" of the late eighteenth century in *The Proper Lady*, pp. 5–15.

6. Tompkins is citing a 1770 work titled *Female Friendship*.

7. Wollstonecraft had borne an illegitimate child by a former lover and had attempted suicide from despair over the relationship.

8. For a discussion of the aesthetic and intellectual status of the novel in the late eighteenth century, see Ioan Williams' Introduction to *Novel and Romance*, especially pp. 23–24.

9. In Book XIX of Homer's *Odyssey*, Penelope is confused as to whether a dream she has had bodes well or not, and she states:

> Dreams . . . are awkward and confusing things: not all that people see in them comes true. For there are two gates through which these insubstantial visions reach us; one is of horn and the other of ivory. Those that come through the ivory gate cheat us with empty promises that never see fulfilment; while those that issue from the gate of burnished horn inform the dreamer what will really happen. (302)

10. Robert Donald Spector has used this term in his bibliographical study of Gothic fiction; he deals with the works of Charlotte Smith and Ann Radcliffe under the chapter heading "Sentimental Gothicism." William Emmet Coleman has also used a similar term, "Gothicism of Sensibility," to designate a particular variety of Gothic fiction, but he bases this category on a different set of distinctions than I am concerned with here; he includes both Ann Radcliffe's novels and Lewis's *Monk* in this group.

11. Two unlabeled volumes are included in one book in the Arno Press edition. In the parenthetical references to the text, the volume will be listed first.

12. For a discussion of Radcliffe's engagement with the issue of established, institutional, arbitrary power in general—"that prime political fact of the modern state"—see Kim Ian Michasiw (329).

13. Napier is citing Radcliffe's *A Journey Made in the Summer of 1794*, ii. 250.

14. Tompkins is citing Sergeant Talfourd's *Memoir*, published with Radcliffe's *Posthumous Works* (Tompkins 221).

15. For a discussion of Radcliffe's valuation of sensibility, see Syndy M. Conger, who argues that Radcliffe reclaims sensibility for both women and "fellow-feeling." Its ethic is an "alternative to the ethic of the public world of passion and self-assertion in which eighteenth-century women played almost no role; it can 'sweeten' the 'austerities of confinement'" and can also be a means of personal fulfillment ("Sensibility" 137, 139).

CHAPTER 4. PUBLIC CENSORSHIP
AND PERSONAL REPRESSION: *THE MONK*

1. There is evidence to suggest that *The Monk* may have been published first in 1795 and "distributed with new title pages on 12 March 1796." See Howard Anderson's "Note on the Text" in the Oxford World Classics edition of *The Monk*, pp. xxii–xxiii. Anderson's edition has been set from the original manuscript that Lewis prepared for his printer, with the exception of the beginning of the first and the conclusion of the last chapters, which were in a different hand. These sections have been taken from the first 1796 edition. All parenthetical references to the text will be from Anderson's edition, which maintains most of Lewis's erratic punctuation and capitalization.

2. For a brief account of this social trend see André Parreaux, pp. 81–86.

3. *Emile* was still quite popular with artists and intellectuals during this period, and it is probably safe to assume that Lewis had second- if not firsthand knowledge of the ideas expressed in this work. Byron, and Percy and Mary Shelley (all of whom Lewis came to know after *The Monk* was published), were all familiar with Rousseau's writings.

4. J. H. Huizinga presents a lively discussion of Rousseau's many moral and intellectual inconsistencies, his "carelessness as a writer and lack of seriousness as a thinker" (225). Huizinga argues that Rousseau at other times seems to advocate "the need for thought-control, manipulation or brainwashing as it would nowadays be called" (224). "[T]he cumulative effect of Jean-Jacques's inability to commit himself, the 'chaos' of his ideas Diderot complained of, his highlighting of every side of every question, is that of a gathering darkness" (233).

5. See Erich Neumann's *The Great Mother*, plates 1 (Venus of Willendorf), 66 (Kali the Devourer), 67 (Kali).

6. This is Rudolf Otto's term for the absolute, intense conviction of mystery and awe that is part of the experience of the sacred.

CHAPTER 5. THE INDUSTRIAL DEMON: *FRANKENSTEIN*

1. Sir Walter Scott wrote favorably in *Blackwood's Edinburgh Magazine*, March 1818, that *Frankenstein* "'excites new reflections and untried sources of emotion'" (qtd. in Spark 140). A critic in the *Quarterly Review,* January 1818, however, complained that "'[o]ur taste and our judgement alike revolt at this kind of writing . . . it inculcates no lesson of conduct, manners, or morality'" (qtd. in Spark 140).

2. Steven Forry notes that the productions included both melodramas and burlesques, one of the latter being Peake's burlesque of his own original production, titled *Another Piece of Presumption* (see pp. 3–42). Forry's study includes the texts from seven *Frankenstein*-inspired plays, dating from 1823 to 1930.

3. For a listing of the various plays, films, television programs, novels, and comic books about Frankenstein that have appeared up until the early 1970s, see Donald F. Glut's *The Frankenstein Legend.* One of the more interesting items is the 1965 Japanese film *Furankenshutain tai Baragon,* released by American-International in the United States as *Frankenstein Conquers the World,* in which the "Frankenstein Monster" is apparently regenerated from his heart during the Hiroshima nuclear holocaust. "Frankenstein" saves some people, including one man who trusted the monster's benign intentions, by fighting and killing a prehistoric monster named Baragon; then a sudden earthquake swallows him up (213–14).

According to David Ketterer, the first-known attribution of Frankenstein's name to the monster, or more precisely to anything monstrous, occurred in 1838; *A Supplement to the Oxford English Dictionary* (1972) cites, "'1838 Gladstone in *Murrays Handbk. Sicily* (1864) p. xlvi, '[The mules] really seem like Frankensteins of the animal creation'" (Ketterer 118 n. 10).

There are, however, some earlier instances in which one can see the beginnings of a blurring of the scientist's and monster's identities. An 1833 political cartoon titled "Reform BILL's First Step Amongst his Political Frankensteins" conflates little William, the monster, and the 1832 Reform Bill; the "Frankensteins" are the political creators of the monster (see Michael Jones, *The Cartoon History of England,* 140). As well, Lee Sterrenburg has identified an 1830 article from *Fraser's Magazine* (Nov. 1830) that argues that a state without religion is as unnatural as "the Frankenstein monster" (qtd. in Sterrenburg 166).

4. References to the text will be to the revised edition where not otherwise indicated. My reasons for choosing this edition are first, that it includes the preface that Shelley wrote for this edition; second, that at the time I began this study it was still the one most publishers chose to print and so most readily available to the general reader; and third, that contrary to the opinion of some scholars, I believe that Shelley's revisions did not weaken *Frankenstein*'s social criticism, but rather strengthened it, as I hope to demonstrate further on in this chapter. As far

as my main argument is concerned, the textual debate is not a crucial issue, for much of the material selected for the purposes of this discussion is nearly identical in both versions. The fact that Shelley saw fit to alter so little of this material would seem to indicate that it does belong to the "core" of the story (Shelley's term, from her preface; 11).

5. Gay Clifford has shown that like *Caleb Williams, Frankenstein* employs psychological insight as a vehicle for social/political criticism. Clifford also demonstrates similarities between the narrative strategies of *Caleb Williams* and the framed structure of *Frankenstein*.

6. One notable exception is Martin Tropp, who stresses the relevance of *Frankenstein* to industrialism and its social ills.

7. Laura Crouch has argued persuasively that the particular work of Davy's which Shelley was reading in October 1816 when she working almost daily on *Frankenstein* was probably *Davy's Discourse, Introductory to A Course of Lectures on Chemistry* (1802). The editors of Shelley's *Journals,* however, cite Davy's *Elements of Chemical Philosophy* (1812 [142 n.2]).

8. A related issue to which Tim Marshall has drawn attention was the grave-robbing business that supplied anatomists with bodies to dissect for scientific research—research whose legitimacy was enhanced when the College of Surgeons became the Royal College of Surgeons in 1800. Over a thousand corpses a year disappeared from England's and Scotland's burial grounds during the first decade of the nineteenth century ("Chronology"). Scandal erupted later when measures to safeguard corpses had become more effective, and some enterprising individuals set about murdering vagrants and paupers to supply the anatomists with their needs: in one case at least, it was widely believed, with the scientist's knowledge and consent.

9. See Vasbinder's chapter, "Ceremonial Magic and Alchemy," where he distinguishes between the imitative practice of the necromancer and the contemplative practice of the alchemist (58). As well, see Fred Botting's chapter, "*Frankenstein* and the art of science," for a recent survey of critical opinions on the question of whether Frankenstein is working within the frame of the alchemical tradition or of modern science.

Marilyn Butler has drawn attention to the importance of the contemporary scientific debate about whether electricity, or some invisible substance analogous to it, could be equated with the "life-principle" or soul. Butler argues that *Frankenstein* is informed by the work of the well-known scientist William Lawrence, a friend of the Shelleys who championed the materialist view that science can be concerned only with the laws of the physical world. Butler further suggests that "Frankenstein, the blundering experimenter, still working with superseded notions, shadows the intellectual position of [John] Abernethy" (xix), Lawrence's chief opponent in the debate. In Butler's view, Mary Shelley's "detached, serio-comic" (xx) treatment of Frankenstein's efforts echoes Lawrence's scorn for Abernethy's attempt to reconcile science and religion. The idea that Shelley must have sided wholly with Lawrence's position is complicated, however, by the fact that in both the 1818 and 1831 editions Frankenstein stresses that his father took great care to prevent his son from imbibing superstitious beliefs of any kind; hence "a churchyard was to [Frankenstein] simply the receptacle of bodies deprived of life" (51; 1818 version 26). Thus, while it is certainly true that Frankenstein's belief in the possibility of discovering a fundamental, animating life principle can be connected with Abernethy, Frankenstein's irreverent attitude and his overestimation of the power of science to "explain life" (Lawrence 161) may also be connected with Lawrence.

10. The *OED* defines "tyro" (or "tiro") as "A beginner or learner in anything; one who is learning or who has mastered the rudiments only of any branch of knowledge; a novice."

11. Godwin shows keen insight in this section into the importance of free play for full development of a child's mental and physical faculties:

> Liberty is the school of understanding. . . . Liberty is the parent of strength. Nature teaches the child, by the play of the muscles, and pushing out his limbs in every direction, to give them scope to develop themselves. Hence it is that he is so fond of sports and tricks in the open air, and that these sports and tricks are so beneficial to him. . . . The mind of a child is no less vagrant than his steps; it pursues the gossamer, and flies from object to object, lawless and unconfined. (1: 247, 249)

12. In another edition of *The Wealth of Nations,* Smith enthuses about the enhanced efficiency of the division of labor, using the making of pins as an illustration: one man "draws out the wire, another straightens it, a third cuts it, a fourth points it, a fifth grinds it at the top for receiving the head," etc., so their combined efforts would result in the making of "four thousand eight hundred pins in a day" (5th ed., qtd. in Bowditch and Ramsland 13). The damaging physical and psychological effects of performing one of these tasks unceasingly through a long workday apparently never occurred to Smith.

13. Mary probably became pregnant in mid-July, midway through the trip. The baby girl was born prematurely on or about February 22, when Percy Shelley recorded that she was "not quite seven months" (M. Shelley, *Journals* 65). The most hostile journal entry cited by Mellor is dated August 28.

14. As Mary Shelley's letters, journals, and biographies attest, during her first pregnancy Percy and Jane developed the habit of going off on excursions together, leaving the frequently ill Mary at home alone.

15. Betty Bennett assigns the date of this letter to 1 June 1816. In the same letter, Shelley comments that the "temporary bloodshed and injustice" that "polluted" the French Revolution nevertheless "produced enduring benefits to mankind, which all the chicanery of statesmen, nor even the great conspiracy of kings, can entirely render vain" (*Letters* 1: 20).

16. Ketterer speculates that the relationship between Frankenstein and his monster may be one of suppressed homoerotic desire (as Sedgwick also has argued), but while it may be true that Frankenstein seems to express more passion toward men than toward women (Mellor, "Possessing" 225), it is also true that his double's erotic impulses are explicitly heterosexual; the monster wants a female mate.

17. Shelley's use of 'daemon' rather than 'demon' indicates the monster's originally neutral position, for the former term is more closely connected etymologically with the classical Greek 'daimon' ('kakadaimon' meaning a malevolent spirit and 'kaladaimon' meaning a benevolent one). Shelley's journals show that she began learning Greek shortly after eloping with Percy.

18. Mellor and others have noted the correlations between this scene and Henry Fuseli's painting *The Nightmare,* with which Shelley was familiar. This work is reproduced, along with other representations of incubus- and succubus-ridden women, in Twitchell (pl. 3–7).

19. Kernberg is quoted by Berman (62–63).

20. The antagonism between father and son, and between learning and commerce, is also strengthened in the later version. The 1818 version reads as follows:

> [Clerval] bitterly lamented that he was unable to accompany me; but his father could not be persuaded to part with him, intending that he should become a partner with him in business, in compliance with his favourite theory, that learning was superfluous in the commerce of ordinary life. Henry had a refined mind; he had no desire to be idle, and was well pleased to become his father's partner, but he believed that a man might become a very good trader, and yet possess a cultivated understanding. (22)

The 1831 version reads: "His father was a narrow-minded trader, and saw idleness and ruin in the aspirations and ambition of his son. Henry deeply felt the misfortune of being debarred from a liberal education. He said little; but when he spoke, I read in his kindling eye and in his animated glance a restrained but firm resolve, not to be chained to the miserable details of commerce" (44).

21. Political readings of *Frankenstein* have generally focused on gender relations and/or Shelley's use of political and social theory, especially in relation to the French Revolution. Johanna M. Smith's 1992 introduction to the Bedford / St. Martin's edition of *Frankenstein* (*Case Studies in Contemporary Criticism*) may

signal a shift in a new direction; Smith mentions "England's troubled industrial development" and the debate over enfranchisement as part of *Frankenstein's* historical context (13–15). Some Marxist critics besides Montag who have examined the theme of the process of production in *Frankenstein* include Elsie B. Michie, Franco Moretti, and Paul O'Flinn.

22. The episode does suggest, however, as Jeffrey Berman points out, that the child may be "thoroughly spoiled and obnoxious" and that the family's view of him as a darling angel might be just another symptom of their communal self-deception (67).

23. O'Rourke quotes liberally from Shelley's essay "Rousseau" because it "is not easily available outside of a few research libraries" (545). It appeared in the second volume of Lardner's *Cabinet Cyclopedia*, titled *Lives of the Most Eminent Literary And Scientific Men of France* (1839).

24. Merchant lists an impressive range of new technologies designed to directly alter the earth, developed after the 1600s: "lift and force pumps, cranes, windmills, geared wheels, flap valves, chains, pistons, treadmills, under- and over-shot watermills, fulling mills, flywheels, bellows, excavators, bucket chains, rollers, geared and wheeled bridges, cranks, elaborate block and tackle systems, worm, spur, crown, and lantern gears, cams and eccentrics, ratchets, wrenches, presses, and screws in magnificent variation and combination" (2–3).

25. For recent discussions of Shelley's interest in Rousseau's ideas about sociolinguistic development, see David Marshall and Christian Bök.

26. Volney's account is in turn indebted to Aeschylus's *Prometheus Bound*. Prometheus states that before he bestowed the gift of fire upon men, "like dream-shapes through the long years [they] confounded all things heedlessly . . . without judgement they did all things until the day I showed them" how to observe and measure nature, and transform it into culture (ll. 448–70).

27. Peter Dale Scott, who examines Shelley's relations with her father and her husband Percy, has argued that Mary Shelley may have been especially interested in the chapter where Volney attributes "cultural decay to political despotism, and despotism to paternal tyranny" and that she fuses allusions to "Dante's portrait of the sexually imbalanced psyche [in the *Inferno*] with Volney's portrait of a sexually imbalanced society" to form the "psychopolitical" feminist argument in *Frankenstein* (192, 193).

28. Ellen Moers was the first critic to draw attention (in 1976) to the significance of Shelley's traumatic personal history and her confrontations with birth and death before and during the writing of *Frankenstein*.

29. A parallel between conditions in early industrial England and the contemporary international economic situation has recently been drawn by Walter

Russell Mead, who argues that under the rules of a new GATT agreement, goods will be freer to circulate internationally, while the movement of labor will still be restricted. Mead points out that the legal barriers that prevent today's workers from moving to higher-wage from low-wage countries are similar to the English "poor laws dating back to the reign of Elizabeth I. . . . [which] made it virtually impossible for working people to move from the parish where they were born . . . to a parish where conditions were better" at the beginning of the Industrial Revolution (61).

CHAPTER 6. THE DESCENT OF MAN
AND THE ANXIETY OF UPWARD MOBILITY:
THE STRANGE CASE OF DR JEKYLL AND MR HYDE

1. An illustration from *Punch*, entitled "The Railway Juggernaut of 1845," shows top-hatted gentlemen throwing themselves under an oncoming train with their wives looking on, representing the disastrous financial and social consequences of unregulated speculation in railway stock (see a reproduction in Altick 157).

2. The age limit of thirteen had been established in 1875, when it was raised from twelve, which had been the legal age since the thirteenth century.

3. Bristow is quoting and translating one Hector France, *En 'Police Court'*, Paris 1891, ch. 3.

4. Gorham is quoting from *Hansard Parliamentary Debates* (Lords), 3d. ser., 289 (24 June 1884), col. 1219.

5. Nield is quoting from the *Lancet*, 7 November 1857 ([xix] n. 25). As his introduction is not paginated, I have supplied page numbers.

6. The *Pall Mall Gazette* special morning edition, 22 August 1885, printed one woman's address to the National Vigilance Association about the obligation of middle-class women to guard the virtue of their young female servants, because of the "appalling" things that went on while "we" were on vacation at the seaside or mountains. The woman recommended never leaving the girls alone with the footmen or butlers; but it is not quite clear whether "we" included the male head of the household, or whether he remained at home when the rest of the family took its extended vacations. Gorham, citing this speech, points out that the woman had clearly not thought about the facts that the young female servants were not entitled to go on such excursions themselves and that her own leisure was made possible by "the drudgery of servants" (377).

7. Calder is citing a letter from Stevenson to Will Low, from the collection of Stevenson material in the Beinecke Library, Yale University.

8. Maixner is citing the *Rock*, 2 April 1886.

9. Stevenson to John Paul Bocock, November 1887 (Huntington Library, HM 2414).

10. Andrew Lang, unsigned review, *Saturday Review*, 9 January 1886, lxi, 55–56.

11. E. T. Cook, unsigned notice, *Athenaeum*, 16 January 1886, 3038, 100.

12. Stevenson and Symonds met at a health resort in Switzerland. Their friendship was not an especially close one, and neither was entirely appreciative of the other's literary gifts.

13. J. A. Symonds to Stevenson, 3 March 1886.

14. Elaine Showalter examines the hints of homosexuality in *Dr Jekyll and Mr Hyde* and argues that the work "can most persuasively be read as a fable of fin-de-siècle homosexual panic, the discovery and resistance of the homosexual self" (107, 105–16). Showalter speculates that the homosexual subtext of *Dr Jekyll and Mr Hyde* may point to unresolved feelings of sexual ambiguity on Stevenson's part, and she offers the information that many men seemed to have been drawn physically to him. However, virtually all Stevenson's biographies attest to his extraordinary personal charm, to which both women and men responded. Showalter also mentions a confession made by Stevenson about dissatisfaction in the later years of his marriage to Fanny. Again, however, Stevenson's biographies make it clear that initially he was passionately devoted to Fanny. There is so much biographical and epistolary evidence of Stevenson's tolerant, balanced attitude that it is difficult to imagine him as homophobic or judgemental about what consenting adults do in private (see Bell, Calder, Furnas, Hennessy). I would argue that *Dr Jekyll and Mr Hyde* is concerned less with adult male homoerotic desire than with the abuse of male power in sexual violence and exploitation.

15. To Henry Graham Dakyns, 12 August 1866.

16. The more recent term *sexual abuse* is in my view preferable to the euphemistic *paedophilia*, because it emphasizes that an adult who becomes sexually involved with a child or youth, however mutual it may seem, can seriously damage the younger one's still-developing sense of personal boundaries (although as Gorham discusses, the idea of differentiating adolescence as a distinct stage of development only began to develop around this time; 369).

17. To Henry Graham Dakyns, 12 August 1866.

18. The first parliamentary ordinance imposing the death penalty for "the detestable and abominable vice of buggery committed with mankind or beast" was

enacted in 1533. Although 1836 was the last year anyone was executed for buggery or sodomy, the death penalty remained on the books until 1861, when it was replaced by life imprisonment. The act remained on the statute book until 1967 (Hyde 32, and frontispiece). The original wording of Labouchere's amendment shows that male prostitution was one of its main concerns:

> Any male person who, in public or private, commits, or is a party to the commission of, or *procures or attempts to procure* the commission by any male person, shall be guilty of a misdemeanour, and being convicted thereof, shall be liable, at the discretion of the court, to be imprisoned for any term not exceeding one year with or without hard labour. (qtd. in Hyde 134; my emphasis)

19. Stead's own motives in this enquiry were clearly mixed. One of his "research assistants," a regenerate prostitute, procured a young girl for him under false pretenses, telling the mother that the girl would be going into service. The girl was taken to a boarding house, where Stead, wearing "grotesque makeup that made him look like an old rake," entered her room and thoroughly terrified her before retreating. The girl underwent two gynaecological examinations, one before and one after her meeting with Stead, to confirm her virginity; then she was sent off to France. After her parents succeeded in reclaiming her, Stead was convicted of taking a child from its guardian without consent (E. Bristow 109).

20. Anne McClintock includes a reproduction of this advertisement in her study of race, gender, and sexuality in the British Empire (fig. 5.2, 215). McClintock shows that apes often were associated with socially inferior members of British society, such as women, immigrants, and colonized peoples.

21. The use of *shame* as a code word for sodomy was probably current in the mid-1880s. In 1894 the man who became Oscar Wilde's lover, Alfred Douglas, published a poem on same-sex passion titled "In Praise of Shame" in the first (and only) issue of an Oxford undergraduate magazine, the *Chameleon,* which featured poetry and fiction celebrating homosexual desire (J. Bristow 18).

22. See Paulo Medeiros for an account of how the ape was regarded as being particularly vigorous in this respect and thought by some to lust after human females.

23. Some of Stevenson's readers may have associated this reference with male prostitution. Private soldiers had a reputation for their casual attitude to sexual matters, and many supplemented their limited incomes by "obliging 'gentlemen' in this way." There was a male brothel near the Regent's Park soldiers' barracks, which Symonds visited with a friend in 1877 (Hyde 120, 106).

CHAPTER 7. THE REPTILIAN BRAIN
AT THE *FIN DE SIÈCLE: DRACULA*

1. The authorship of *Varney the Vampire* has not been definitively established. See E. F. Bleiler's introduction to "Rymer's" work. Margaret Carter lists *Varney the Vampire* under the name of Thomas P. Prest in her bibliography of vampire fiction, drama, and studies.

Another vampire story that influenced Stoker was Sheridan Le Fanu's *Carmilla.* In the opinion of Stoker's biographer, Harry Ludlam, Stoker had canceled a chapter in his own novel that was strongly reminiscent of Le Fanu's tale because it might have been "misconstrued" as a sign of indebtedness, when it had been intended simply as an "affectionate remembrance" (115). This excised chapter can be found under the title "Dracula's Guest" in *The Bram Stoker Bedside Companion,* ed. Charles Osborne. Phyllis A. Roth suggests that a comparison between "Carmilla" and *Dracula* illuminates Stoker's "shift in focus from the Promethean overreacher type of villain (or vampire) to the insidiously seductive female" (*Bram Stoker* 99; 148, n. 14).

2. James B. Twitchell has examined the vampire as a representation of the ways that "lovers, or artists, or parents, or the insane, or just ordinary people trade energy with those they contact" (38).

3. In his biography of Stoker, Daniel Farson suggests that the famous actor Henry Irving, who was Stoker's mentor and who owned the Lyceum Theatre, did not like the play and may have deliberately undermined it as a serious production by charging a prohibitive admission price of one guinea and having it performed at the odd time of 10:15 A.M. (163–64). Henry Ludlam contrastingly assumes that the responsibility for the limited staging of the work lay with Stoker, who wanted only to prevent unauthorized dramatizations, and thus was content that this production was the only one to be presented in his lifetime (109–14). When Stoker asked Irving's opinion after the four-hour performance, the actor replied, "Dreadful!" Farson thinks that Stoker may have felt hurt by his friend's comment, while Ludlam assumes that the author probably agreed.

4. One late Victorian issue that has interested critics for some time has been the question of whether or not *Dracula* endorses the expanded social role that women were beginning to assume during this period. More recently, critics have begun to examine *Dracula's* relevance to other contemporary sociopolitical and scientific issues. Kathleen Spencer for example stresses the modern urban setting of *Dracula* and shows that the *fin de siècle* was a period of destabilizing social and sexual categories, ruled by a scientific ethos. She utilizes the anthropological theories of Mary Douglas and René Girard to examine how *Dracula* enacts a ritual of purification and preservation of the community, while at the same time helping readers to acknowledge the unfamiliar. Rosemary Jann examines the tension between

religious and scientific/secular world views in *Dracula*. Other critics have focused on *Dracula*'s relation to the question of British imperial power: see Arata, Garnett, Wicke, and Stevenson. Nicholas Daly has shown how *Dracula* registers the rise of professionalism during the Victorian Era.

5. For a study of how Darwin's evolutionary vision affected Victorian thought and literary practice, see Gillian Beer.

6. Jennifer Wicke examines some of *Dracula*'s "cutting-edge technology" (470) with which, she suggests, the vampire is allied, as an avatar of the new, consumeristic mass culture.

7. Van Helsing makes no effort, however, to match blood types, "which in any event, [he] could not have known about until nearly three decades later" (Wolf 116 n. 5).

8. For information about the dates of these advancements I have relied on Bernard Grun, *The Timetables of History*, and Leonard Wolf's notes in his book *The Annotated Dracula*.

9. Barbara Belford's biography of Stoker includes reproductions of the covers of the 1901 Constable edition and the 1925 Rider edition (215, 273). An illustration of the 1901 edition also can be found in Frayling (214).

10. This is not to dispute Stephen D. Arata's point that Dracula possesses a definite capacity for planning, research, and organization. However, I would not agree with Arata's contention that no other character in the novel is as "receptive to new knowledge" as is the vampire (637), for as I hope to show, Dracula's resourcefulness is relatively limited, and his instinctual responses ultimately override his more "civilized" capabilities.

11. Demeter was the pagan goddess of agricultural fertility, whose daughter Persephone (or Kore) was abducted by Hades, god of the underworld. Demeter was prevented from effecting her daughter's complete release because Persephone had "tasted the food of the dead" (Graves 1:91) by eating some pomegranate seeds during her sojourn in the underworld. The mother goddess refused to lift the curse of barrenness she had inflicted on the earth until a compromise was reached; Persephone would spend three months in the underworld as Persephone, the consort of Hades, and the rest of the year above ground with her mother.

Additionally, the fact that Dracula enters England on a ship named after an ancient fertility goddess and leaves it on a ship named after the notorious, sexually voracious Czarina Catherine suggests the degradation of the feminine principle in the modern world.

Troy Boone notes the mythical allusion to "the mythological figure of rebirth and fruitfulness" (88) in arguing that *Dracula* presents a feminization of Victorian patriarchy. As well, Barbara Belford (among others) has pointed out the historical allusion to the *Dmitry*, "a Russian schooner out of Narva, [which] was beached near Whitby's Tate Hill Pier in October 1885." Belford adds that the actual vessel was from Varna, an anagram of Narva: "Stoker loved codes" (224).

12. Whitby was "founded as a monastic site in A.D. 657" and features the remains of an abbey described by Stoker as a "'most noble ruin'" (Belford 225). Stoker himself was Protestant but grew up in Ireland, a predominantly Catholic country.

13. For brief explanations of Stoker's allusions to current psychological and neurological research, see Wolf's notes: 71 n. 27; 74 nn. 31, 32; 172 n. 8.

14. Stephanie Moss has shown that Stoker's social circle included a number of prominent intellectuals involved in the emerging science of psychoanalysis. She argues persuasively that Stoker's presentation of conscious and unconscious states shows a familiarity not only with the work of Charcot which is mentioned in *Dracula*, but also with the work of Freud, and of Frederic W. H. Myers, a founder of the Society for Psychical Research, where the focus was mainly on extraordinary and extrasensory mental states, albeit with a somewhat scientific or systematic investigative approach. It appears that "in *Dracula* Stoker knowingly inscribes the historic moment that saw the birth of psychoanalysis" (90).

As well, although it may be impossible to determine definitively what Stoker may or may not have known of work in this field, it is worth considering that investigations into such areas as mesmerism and brain activity during sleep had been published as early as the 1830s, and that most nineteenth-century scholars had a fairly comprehensive knowledge of preceding research and theory (see Robinson).

15. Paul D. MacLean explains that he abandoned the term "visceral brain" in 1952, in favor of a modification of Broca's original term (*Triune* 266–67).

16. "[F]irst-hand researches included a trip to Regent's Park Zoo, where Stoker observed the behavior of certain animals" (Leatherdale, *Dracula* 86).

17. Ludlam writes that Stoker's nightmare "did not arise from an intense conversation, as did Mary Shelley's, nor from illness and worry, as did Stevenson's; but from a too generous helping of dressed crab at supper one night. At least, this was the story he persistently told" (99). Farson also mentions the rumor and suggests that it may have arisen from a popular confusion between *Frankenstein*, whose author did "dream up" the tale, and *Dracula*. Farson does note, however, that Whitby, which Stoker had visited and which is the locale of the vampire's first attack and entry into England, was famous for its crab (152). Stoker's working notes, discovered in the 1970s, reveal that *Dracula* was in fact carefully researched and planned, probably beginning in 1890 (Leatherdale, *Dracula* 85–86). Nevertheless, it is difficult to imagine anyone writing such a novel without some vivid dreaming.

18. Van Helsing apparently uses masculine pronouns because he is thinking of Dracula in particular, but I have changed them to neutral in order to emphasize the fact that the vampire in general can be either male or female.

19. Ernest Fontana discusses the way that Cesare Lombroso's late-nineteenth-century "pseudoscientific conception of the criminal personality" informs Stoker's presentation of Dracula. Fontana argues that Mina and Lucy as well exhibit symptoms of degenerative tendencies identified by Lombroso as characteristic of the atavistic criminal mind.

20. The ambiguous mixture of humor and horror is caught brilliantly by Bella Lugosi in the 1931 film *Dracula,* particularly in the scene where Dracula barely manages to restrain himself from feeding on Jonathan Harker, who must be allowed to live if he is going to help Dracula fulfill his plan to conquer the modern world. To my mind, Lugosi's suggestion of the vampire's reptilian quality shows greater insight into the original text than does Francis Ford Coppola's sentimentalized romance, which makes much of Dracula's response to the female vampires' accusation that he "never loved": "I too can love; you yourselves can tell it from the past" (53). In Coppola's version, Dracula enters the nineteenth century in order to reclaim his original, long-lost true love.

21. According to Phyllis A. Roth, Mina's comment that the "New Woman" will one day make the marriage proposal herself constitutes one of the novel's typical verbal assaults against the New Woman ("Suddenly Sexual Women" 58). Judith Weissman takes the above statement by Mina, along with her frank acceptance of her own "appetite," as a reflection of Stoker's own unconscious "anxieties about women's sexuality" (74).

22. In Gail B. Griffen's opinion the "ideal [of stainless womanhood] and its underlying misogyny are the real heart of *Dracula* . . . . the worst horror [Stoker's Victorian gothic] can imagine is not Dracula at all but the released, transforming sexuality of the Good Woman" (148). Judith Weissman states that *Dracula* is a "man's version of a noble band of men restoring a woman to purity and passivity. . . . an extreme version of the stereotypically Victorian attitudes toward sexual roles" (69). Weissman argues that the men's fight against Dracula is actually about "control over women" (77). Anne Cranny-Francis goes so far as to accuse Stoker of participating in the "fun" or "titillation" of patriarchal "assertion of male dominance [in] the taming/destruction of the female," in his division of women into pure (Mina) and alluring (Lucy) types who respectively are tamed and punished (69).

23. To illustrate the point, Neumann includes reproductions of a sixth-century B.C. Greek marble relief of the Gorgon, a modern Balinese painting of Rangda stealing children, a medieval wood sculpture of souls in the jaws of Hell, and a seventeenth–eighteenth-century copper sculpture from India of Kali the Devourer (see pl. 70, 71, 81, 66).

Phyllis A. Roth also notes "the fear of the devouring woman," which she sees as the "central anxiety" of *Dracula*, but she employs a Freudian psycho-analytical perspective, arguing that a "hostility toward the mother" and a "fantasy of matricide" are "[c]entral to the structure and unconscious theme of *Dracula*" ("Suddenly Sexual Women" 64, 57, 61, 65).

24. Stephanie Moss has noted significant correspondences between Pierre Janet's description of the stages of hysteria and Stoker's description of Lucy's sinking into the life of the undead.

25. Franco Moretti makes the intriguing suggestion that Quincey himself may be a vampire; as an agent of American capitalism, whose source of wealth is never revealed, Quincey is in secret alliance with Dracula (94–96).

26. During this period, Vlad's penchant for savage torture in warfare was not unique, although he was also noted for torturing his own citizens, including women and children and even animals when no humans were available. See Raymond McNally and Radu Florescu, as well as Gabriel Ronay.

27. "Min" in some Scandinavian languages means "my."

CHAPTER 8. AMERICAN GOTHIC: HISTORICAL AND PSYCHOLOGICAL CRITIQUE IN STEPHEN KING'S *THE SHINING*

1. King had already begun to establish a name for himself as a master of American horror with two earlier works, *Carrie* (1974) and *'Salem's Lot* (1975), the latter being King's reworking of the Dracula myth into the American landscape. For discussions of the relation between *'Salem's Lot* and Stoker's *Dracula*, see Gregory Waller, James E. Hicks, and Carol A. Senf ("Blood").

2. These include, besides the introductory epigraph from Edgar Allan Poe, "The Masque of the Red Death"; references to Horace Walpole (168); movie versions of *Frankenstein* (111, 327); Algernon Blackwood (264); and Shirley Jackson's *Haunting of Hill House* (281). "Bluebeard" is also mentioned more than once (88, 169–70, 215). There are as well many other references to American and British writers and literary works that are not part of the Gothic tradition; the most frequent allusions are to Lewis Carroll's *Alice's Adventures in Wonderland* and *Through the Looking Glass and What Alice Found There*.

3. One may note the repetition of history in the Bush administration's American invasion of Panama to apprehend Manuel Noriega, in which there was considerable (and in the opinion of many, unnecessary) bloodshed.

4. See Richard Slotkin's second chapter, "Cannibals and Christians," in his *Regeneration Through Violence;* see also his third chapter, "A Home in the Heart of

Darkness," where he describes the conflicts between the people of Rhode Island, who generally adopted a conciliatory approach to the aboriginal peoples, and those of Massachusetts, who tended to characterize the Indian as the devil incarnate who must be vanquished.

5. See Linda C. Badley's discussion of the "motif of automotive horror" in King's work where "moving down the road really means *going back:* devolution or reversion" (84).

6. Sand Creek is located about one hundred miles (as the crow flies) from the elegant old Stanley Hotel in Estes Park, Colorado, where King first conceived of *The Shining.* As Douglas E. Winter records, King and his family were, like the Torrance family at the Overlook, the only guests left in the Stanley Hotel. King has stated that the Stanley struck him as "the perfect—maybe the archetypal—setting for a ghost story" (Winter 45). Winter is quoting from King's "On Becoming a Brand Name" (*Adelina,* February 1980 [45]) and adds that the Stanley Hotel "has since been converted into luxury condominiums" (199 n. 2).

7. In the Pequot slaughter, Captain John Mason, with ninety Englishmen and hundreds of Naragansett allies, "marched to one of the Pequot villages on the Mystic River, which he put to the torch, slaughtering all the inhabitants," including several hundred women and children. "As Captain John Underhill wrote . . . the Naragansetts . . . 'cried . . . it is too furious, and slaies too many men'" (Washburn, "Seventeenth" 90; qtg. John Underhill, *Newes from America* [London 1638; 42–43]). Richard Slotkin records Underhill's uneasy justification of the event:

> Many were burnt in the fort, both men, women, and children. Others forced out . . . which our soldiers received and entertained with the sword. Down fell men, women, and children. . . . Great and doleful was the bloudy sight to the view of young soldiers that never had been in war, to see so many souls lie gasping on the ground, so thick, in some places, that you could hardly pass along. . . . Sometimes the Scripture declareth women and children must perish with their parents. Sometimes the case alters; but we will not dispute it now. We had sufficient light from the word of God for our proceedings. (76; quoting Underhill, *Newes* 25).

In the Great Swamp Fight forty years later, English troops broke into the Naragansett fort, which only women, children, and the wounded were occupying, and burned it to the ground (Slotkin 85).

8. The rising up of ghosts from Indian burial grounds recently has become another less complex but more popular topos in horror fiction and films, from King's *Pet Sematary* to Steven Speilberg's *Poltergeist.*

9. This phrase was taken up by Perry Miller in his influential study of the Puritan apocalyptic imagination as a crucial factor in the formation of American national identity.

10. Wendy is paraphrasing Emerson's statement that Nature "pardons no mistakes. Her yea is yea, and her nay, nay" (38).

11. It is debatable whether or not King subscribed to the theory that Kennedy's assassination was a plot engineered by American interest groups who opposed the president's planned withdrawal of American troops from Vietnam, although King's inclusion of a gangland murder in the Presidential Suite of the Overlook Hotel does suggest that possibility. The speculation that Kennedy was planning a withdrawal has only recently been proved correct; see John M. Newman.

12. Miller (n. 9 above) concludes his study by citing a military report about the bombing of Hiroshima: "The authors of the highly official *United States Bombing Survey* are not, I am persuaded, theologians or poets, and they probably did not know that they were falling into the pattern of a literary form more ancient, and more rigid, than the sonnet" (238).

13. Tony Magistrale has shown how a later story of King's "Children of the Corn" deals with the American destruction of Vietnamese land with toxic chemicals such as Agent Orange; see "Stephen King's Vietnam Allegory."

14. Brown has been called the "father of American fiction" by Donald Ringe (36) and the "father of American gothic" by Leslie Fiedler; Fiedler declares that Brown's work inaugurates the moment at which "our serious literature began" (*Love and Death* 80, 148).

15. See Jean Hagstrum, pl. LIb.

16. Jung's memoirs record the following conversation, which he recalls having with a local chief during his visit to the Taos pueblos in New Mexico:

> "See, Ochwiay Biano said, "how cruel the whites look. Their lips are thin, their noses sharp, their faces furrowed and distorted by folds. Their eyes have a staring expression; they are always seeking something. What are they seeking? The whites always want something; they are always uneasy and restless. We do not know what they want. We do not understand them. We think that they are mad."
> I asked him why he thought the whites were all mad.
> "They say that they think with their heads," he replied.
> "Why of course. What do you think with?" I asked him in surprise.
> "We think here," he said, indicating his heart.

In Jung's account, the exchange provoked in him "a long meditation," in which he saw a series of vivid visions of European invasions, including the Roman conquest of Gaul, the "pillaging and murdering bands of the Crusading armies," the colonization of the Americas with "fire, sword, torture, and Christianity," and "the peoples of the Pacific islands decimated by firewater, syphilis, and scarlet fever." He realized that "the spread of civilization" had another face, "the face of a bird of prey, seeking with cruel intentness for distant quarry" (*Memories* 247–48).

Jung also visited Africa, where, he says, looking down upon a broad expanse of savanna from the vantage of a low hill, he felt as if he had witnessed the beginning of creation (*Memories* 255–56).

EPILOGUE: *ALIEN* AND THE FUTURE OF GOTHIC

1. Generically speaking, science fiction is Gothic's nearest relation, although some critics would include within the Gothic canon other forms of literature that show a strong Gothic influence, such as detective novels, twentieth-century "southern Gothic," and works by writers such as the Brontës, Hardy, Hawthorne, James, and even Thomas Pynchon (William Patrick Day argues that *Wuthering Heights* is not a Gothic novel, but Sherlock Holmes is a Gothic character, while David Punter includes in his study the works of Pynchon and Robert Coover). My reason for excluding such works is that they do not possess a number of the characteristic components of Gothic narratives.

Detective novels, for example, employ the Gothic plot of bringing some hidden knowledge to light, usually a murder; but the detective novel is primarily an intellectual puzzle, lacking the emotive and imagistic power of the Gothic novel. The tension of reading detective novels develops through the process of gradually piecing together the puzzle, whereas the tension in Gothic novels grows as the reader registers the discrepancy between his or her own perception of the menace awaiting a protagonist, and the protagonist's continued resistance to the truth of the situation.

It is also important to clarify that not all science fiction conforms to the Gothic model, especially that branch of science fiction that combines a celebration of scientific and technological advancement with a conservative sociopolitical outlook.

2. One science fiction film that successfully takes up the cultural concerns addressed in *Frankenstein* is *Blade Runner*, although it also demonstrates the distance that science fiction can place between itself and its Gothic origins. The plot of *Blade Runner* does not follow the narrative pattern usual to Gothic, of gradual hints followed by sudden revelation, nor does it evoke "superstitious dread." The audience learns almost immediately who the "alien" is that must be vanquished, and there are no characters who are resistant to recognizing the threat. However, there is a "castle" of corporate power, the enormous ziggurat of the Tyrell corporation; yet although the "king" is killed, the edifice remains standing. *Blade Runner* does employ the Gothic device of displaced setting—the earth after environmental collapse, when people are emigrating to off-world "colonies"—to examine

social, moral, and spiritual issues raised almost two hundred years earlier in *Frankenstein:* poverty and privilege; division of labor; the power of commerce; irresponsible research and technology; the degradation and disempowerment of women; the usurpation of female biology in the "workshop of filthy creation" (specifically, the production of eyeballs); the problem of perspective; and the question of the soul (suggested in the last scene when the dying "replicant" releases a dove he has been holding, which flies skyward).

3. The last two films in the *Alien* series cannot be said to belong to the Gothic tradition, partly because they lack the power of archetypal imagery that is so strong in the first two. Although there is still a sense of menace in these later films, the message seems to be one of pessimism rather than admonition. One of the problems with *Alien 3* (1992) is that the monster is not ancient enough, in evolutionary terms. Presumably intended to resemble a prehistoric therapod dinosaur, it looks a bit like a long-beaked ostrich. In this film, doors are closed more often than they are opened. The heroine's suicidal self-sacrifice at the end of the movie, when she dives into a vat of molten lead so that the monster within her cannot "hatch," is a gesture of personal, but not archetypal, heroism. In the archetypal fight with the dragon, there is both descent *and* return.

Alien Resurrection (1997) suffers from similar problems. The critique of corporate power is abandoned in favor of a more simplistic version of governmental-military-scientific conspiracy. The film features a number of elements clearly derived from *Frankenstein,* but they are presented in a rather heavy-handed manner: a roomful of grotesque homunculi preserved in jars, misbegotten monsters cloned by mad scientists; a humanoid who is more humane than the humans; a great deal of explicit birth imagery, including forceps; and a "hideous progeny" in the part-human alien that has been "born" from Ripley (who herself is now part alien, having been cloned back to life). This particular alien has the head of a human skull, and there are ludicrous moments of maternal/filial affection between Ripley and her progeny before she blasts (or aborts) the thing back into outer space. The self-parody on which this film is always verging becomes most apparent when a character who is host to an alien manages to hold back its eruption from his body, burping in what looks like a case of severe indigestion, until the group is on board the escape ship.

WORKS CITED

PRIMARY SOURCES

Major Works

Alien. Dir. Ridley Scott. Story Dan O'Bannon and Ronald Shusett. Screenplay Dan O'Bannon. Twentieth Century Fox, 1979.

Kelly, Isabella. *The Abbey of St. Asaph.* 1795. Intro. Devendra P. Varma. 3 vols. New York: Arno, 1977.

King, Stephen. *The Shining.* 1977. New York: Signet-NAL, 1980.

Lewis, Matthew. *The Monk.* 1796. Ed. Howard Anderson. Oxford: Oxford UP, 1986.

Radcliffe, Ann. *A Sicilian Romance.* 1790. 1821 ed. Intro. Devendra P. Varma. New York: Arno-McGrath, 1972.

Shelley, Mary Wollstonecraft. *Frankenstein: The 1818 Text.* Ed. J. Paul Hunter. New York: Norton, 1996.

———. *Frankenstein, or the Modern Prometheus.* 1831 ed. Ed. James Kinsley and M. K. Joseph. Oxford: Oxford UP, 1980.

Stevenson, Robert Louis. *The Strange Case of Dr Jekyll and Mr Hyde. The Strange Case of Dr Jekyll and Mr Hyde and Other Stories.* 1886. Ed. Jenni Calder. London: Penguin, 1987.

Stoker, Bram. *Dracula.* 1897. London: Puffin-Penguin, 1986.

Walpole, Horace. *The Castle of Otranto.* 1764. 1765 ed. *The Castle of Otranto, The Mysteries of Udolpho, Northanger Abbey.* Ed. Andrew Wright. New York: Holt, 1963.

Peripheral Works

2001: A Space Odyssey. Dir. Stanley Kubrick. MGM, 1968.

Aeschylus. *Prometheus Bound.* Trans. Janet Case. London: Dent, 1922.

Alien 3. Dir. David Fincher. Story Vincent Ward. Screenplay David Giler, Walter Hill, and Larry Ferguson. Twentieth Century Fox, 1992.

Alien Resurrection. Dir. Jean-Pierre Jeunet. Story by Joss Whedon. Brandywine-Twentieth Century Fox, 1997.

Aliens. Dir. James Cameron. Story James Cameron, Walter Hill, and David Giler. Screenplay James Cameron. Twentieth Century Fox, 1986.

Blade Runner. Dir. Ridley Scott. Screenplay Hampton Fancher and David Peoples. Warner, 1982.

Blake, William. *The Marriage of Heaven and Hell.* 1790–93. *English Romantic Writers.* Ed. David Perkins. New York: Harcourt, 1967. 69–75.

Bram Stoker's Dracula. Dir. Francis Ford Coppola. Screenplay James V. Hart. Columbia, 1992.

Brown, Charles Brockden. *Wieland, or The Transformation.* 1798. Port Washington, NY: Kennikat, 1963.

Carroll, Lewis. *Alice's Adventures in Wonderland and Through the Looking-Glass.* Great Britain: Winston, 1923.

Conrad, Joseph. *Nostromo: A Tale of the Seaboard.* 1904. Garden City, NY: Doubleday, 1931.

Dickens, Charles. *Bleak House.* 1853. Boston: Riverside-Houghton, 1956.

Disraeli, Benjamin. *Sybil, or The Two Nations.* 1845. Harmondsworth, Middlesex, Eng.: Penguin, 1980.

d'Israeli, Isaac. *Vaurien.* 1797.

Dracula. Dir. Tod Browning. Screenplay Garret Fort. Universal, 1931.

Godwin, William. *Fleetwood, or, The New Man of Feeling.* 1805. 3 vols. New York: Garland, 1979.

———. *Caleb Williams.* 1794. Ed. David McCracken. London: Oxford UP, 1970.

Hardy, Thomas. *Tess of the d'Urbervilles.* 1891. New York: Bantam, 1981.

———. *The Return of the Native.* 1878. New York: Bantam, 1981.

Hogg, James. *The Private Memoirs and Confessions of a Justified Sinner.* 1824. Ed. John Carey. London: Oxford UP, 1969.

Homer. *The Odyssey*. Trans. E. V. Rieu. Harmondsworth, Middlesex, Eng.: Penguin, 1977.

Jackson, Shirley. *The Haunting of Hill House*. New York: Viking, 1959.

James, Henry. *The Turn of the Screw*. 1898. *The Turn of the Screw and Daisy Miller*. New York: Dell, 1956.

King, Stephen. *Pet Sematary*. Garden City, NY: Doubleday, 1983.

———. "Children of the Corn." *Night Shift*. New York: Signet-NAL, 1979.

———. *The Dead Zone*. New York: Viking, 1979.

———. *Salem's Lot*. 1975. New York: Signet-NAL, 1976.

———. *Carrie*. 1974. New York: Signet-NAL, 1975.

Lawrence, D. H. *St. Mawr and The Man Who Died*. 1925, 1928. New York: Random-Vintage, 1953.

Le Fanu, Sheridan. "Carmilla." *Through a Glass Darkly*. 1872. New York: Warner, 1974. 358–471.

Marlowe, Christopher. *The Tragical History of Doctor Faustus*. *A Treasury of the Theatre: Volume One: World Drama from Aeschylus to Ostrovsky*. Ed. John Gassner. New York: Simon, 1967. 221–37.

Maturin, Charles Robert. *Melmoth the Wanderer*. 1820. Lincoln: U of Nebraska P, 1961.

Parsons, Eliza. *The Mysterious Warning*. 1796. Intro. Devendra P. Varma. London: Folio, 1967.

Perrault, Charles. "Blue Beard." *Perrault's Complete Fairy Tales*. Trans. A. E. Johnson et al. Harmondsworth, Middlesex, Eng.: Penguin, 1961. 78–87.

Pet Sematary. Dir. Mary Lambert. Screenplay Stephen King. Paramount, 1989.

Poe, Edgar Allan. "The Masque of the Red Death." *The Fall of the House of Usher and Other Tales*. New York: Signet-NAL, 1963.

Polidori, John. "The Vampyre." 1819. *Vampyres: Lord Byron to Count Dracula*. Christopher Frayling. London: Faber, 1991. 107–25.

Poltergeist. Dir. Tobe Hooper. Prod. Steven Speilberg. MGM, 1982.

Radcliffe, Ann. *The Italian*. 1797. London: Oxford UP, 1986.

———. *The Mysteries of Udolpho*. 1794. London: Oxford UP, 1970.

Richardson, Samuel. *Clarissa*. 1748–49. 4 vols. London: Dent, 1932.

————. *Pamela, or Virtue Rewarded.* 1740–41. Intro. William M. Sale, Jr. New York: Norton, 1958.

Rymer, James Malcolm (or Thomas Peckett Prest). *Varney the Vampyre or, The Feast of Blood.* 1847. Intro. E. F. Bleiler. 2 vols. New York: Dover, 1972.

Scott, Sir Walter. *The Bride of Lammermoor.* 1819. London: Dent, 1988.

————. *The Heart of Midlothian.* 1818. London: Dent, 1932.

Shakespeare, William. *The Complete Works of Shakespeare.* Ed. Hardin Craig and David Bevington. Brighton, Eng.: Scott, 1973.

Smith, Charlotte. *The Old Manor House.* 1793. Ed. intro. Anne Henry Ehrenpreis. London: Oxford UP, 1969.

Trollope, Anthony. *The Way We Live Now.* 1875. New York: Knopf, 1950.

Walpole, Horace. *The Castle of Otranto.* (Abridged). *The Universal Magazine* 36 (April 1765): 202–8, 235–42.

Webster, John. *The Duchess of Malfi. A Treasury of the Theatre: Volume One: World Drama from Aeschylus to Ostrovsky.* Ed. John Gassner. New York: Simon, 1967. 326–60.

Wolf, Leonard, ed. *The Annotated Dracula by Bram Stoker.* New York: Potter, 1975.

SECONDARY SOURCES

Pre-Twentieth Century

Aiken, John, and Anna Laetitia Aiken. *Miscellaneous Pieces in Prose.* London: J. Johnson, 1773.

Bacon, Sir Francis. *Novum Organum.* 1620. Ed. Joseph Devey. New York: Collier, 1901.

Bennett, E. T. *The Gardens and Menagerie of the Zoological Society Delineated.* London: Tilt, 1831.

Boswell, James. *Journal of a Tour to the Hebrides.* 1785. Ed. Allan Wendt. Boston: Mifflin-Riverside, 1965.

Burke, Edmund. *A Philosophical Enquiry into the Origin of our Ideas of the Sublime and Beautiful.* 2nd ed., 1759. Ed. & intro. J. T. Boulton. London: Routledge, 1958.

Byron, George Gordon. *Lord Byron: The Complete Miscellaneous Prose.* Ed. Andrew Nicholson. Oxford: Clarendon, 1991.

Coleridge, Samuel Taylor. *Coleridge's Miscellaneous Criticism.* Ed. Thomas Middleton Raysor. London: Constable, 1936.

———. *Biographia Literaria.* 1817. Ed. George Watson. Rev. ed. London: Dent, 1982.

Darwin, Charles. *The Origin of Species by Means of Natural Selection or The Preservation of Favored Races in the Struggle for Life* and *The Descent of Man and Selection in Relation to Sex.* 1859, 1871. New York: Modern Library, 1900.

Davy, Sir Humphrey. *Elements of Chemical Philosophy.* Vol. 4 of *The Collected Works Sir Humphrey Davy.* Ed. John Davy. London: Smith, Elder, 1840.

———. *A discourse, Introductory to A Course of Lectures on Chemistry, Delivered in the Theatre of the Royal Institution on the 21st of January, 1802.* London: Sold at the House of the Royal Institution, 1802.

Emerson, Ralph Waldo. *Nature.* 1836. *Selections from Ralph Waldo Emerson.* Ed. Stephen E. Whicher. Boston: Riverside-Houghton, 1960. 21–56.

Ferrier, David. *The Functions of the Brain.* Rev. enl. ed. 1886. Washington, DC: U Publications of America, 1978. *Significant Contributions to the History of Psychology 1750–1920.* Vol. 3 of Ser. E, *Physiological Psychology.* Ed. Daniel N. Robinson. 4 vols.

Godwin, William. *Enquiry Concerning Political Justice and Its Influence on Modern Morals and Happiness.* 1798 ed. Harmondsworth, Middlesex, Eng.: Penguin, 1976.

———. *Memoirs of the Author of A Vindication of the Rights of Woman.* 2nd. ed. London, 1798.

Hughes, John. "Remarks on *The Faerie Queene* and *The Shepheardes' Calender.*" *Edmund Spenser's Poetry.* Ed. Hugh MacLean. New York: Norton, 1968. 511–18.

Hunt, Leigh. "On the Employment of Children in Manufactories." *The Examiner* [London] 5 Apr. 1818. *Shelley—Leigh Hunt: How Friendship Made History.* Ed. R. Brimly Johnson. 2nd ed. London: Ingpen, 1929. 249–53.

Hurd, Richard. *Letters on Chivalry and Romance.* 1762. New York: Garland, 1971.

Lawrence, William. *An Introduction to Comparative Anatomy, being two introductory lectures delivered at the Royal College of Surgeons.* London, 1816.

Lee, Sarah (Mrs. T. Bowdich). *Anecdotes of Habits and Instincts of Birds, Reptiles and Fishes.* Philadelphia: Lindsay and Blakiston, 1853.

———. *Anecdotes of Habits and Instincts of Animals.* 2nd ed. London: Griffith, Farran, Okeden and Welsh, 1852.

Locke, John. *Essay on Human Understanding.* 1690. 2 vols. New York: Dover, 1959.

Longinus. *On the Sublime. Critical Theory Since Plato.* Ed. Hazard Adams. New York: Harcourt, 1971. 77–102.

Mayhew, Henry. *London Labour and the London Poor: A Cyclopedia of the Condition and Earnings of Those That Will Work, Those That Cannot Work, and Those That Will Not Work.* 3 vols. New York: Harper, 1851.

Milton, John. *Areopagitica. John Milton: Complete Poems and Major Prose.* Ed. Merritt Y. Hughes. Indianapolis: Odyssey-Bobbs, 1981. 716–49.

Ovid. *Metamorphoses.* Trans. Mary M. Innis. Harmondsworth, Middlesex, Eng.: Penguin, 1979.

Paine, Thomas. *The Rights of Man.* 1790. Harmondsworth, Middlesex, Eng.: Penguin, 1969.

Pettigrew, Thomas. *On Superstitions connected with the History and Practice of Medicine and Surgery.* London: John Churchill, 1844.

Radcliffe, Ann. "On the Supernatural in Poetry." *New Monthly Magazine* 16 (1826). 145–53.

———. *A Journey Made in the Summer of 1794, through Holland and the Western Frontier of Germany, With a Return Down the Rhine: to Which are added Observations During a Tour to the Lakes of Lancashire, Westmoreland, and Cumberland.* 2nd ed. 2 vols. London, 1796.

Rousseau, Jean-Jacques. *Emile or On Education.* 1762. Trans. Allan Bloom. New York: Basic, 1979.

Scott, Sir Walter. "Introduction to *The Castle of Otranto.*" 1811. *Horace Walpole: The Critical Heritage.* Ed. Peter Sabor. London: Routledge, 1987.

Shaftesbury, Anthony Ashley Cooper. *Characteristics of Men, Manners, Opinions, and Times.* 1714 ed. Ed. J. M. Robertson. London, 1900.

Shelley, Percy Bysshe. "A Philosophical View of Reform." 1819–20. *Political Tracts of Wordsworth, Coleridge and Shelley.* Ed. R. J. White. Cambridge, Eng.: Cambridge UP, 1953. 209–62.

Smith, Adam. *An Inquiry into the Nature and Causes of the Wealth of Nations.* 1776. Vol. 1. New York: Dutton, 1910.

Stead, William T. "The Maiden Tribute of Modern Babylon." *Pall Mall Gazette* 6 July 1885: 1–9.

Stevenson, Robert Louis. "A Chapter on Dreams." *Scribner's* January 1888.

Volney, Count Constantin François. *Volney's Ruins, or Meditation on the Revolutions of Empires.* 1791. Trans. Count Daru. Boston: Mendum, 1883.

Walpole, Horace. *The Works of Horace Walpole, Earl of Orford.* 5 vols. London: Robinson & Edwards, 1798.

———. *Historic Doubts on the Life and Reign of King Richard the Third.* London, 1768.

Warton, Thomas. *Observations on the Fairy Queen of Spenser.* 1762. 2 vols. New York: Garland, 1970.

Wollstonecraft, Mary. *Political Writings: Rights of Men, Rights of Woman, French Revolution.* Ed. Janet Todd. Toronto: U of Toronto P, 1993.

Twentieth Century

Abbott, C. C. *The Letters of Gerard Manly Hopkins to Robert Bridges.* London: Oxford UP, 1935.

Aldiss, Brian W. *Billion Year Spree: The True History of Science Fiction.* New York: Schocken, 1975.

Altick, Richard D. *Victorian People and Ideas.* New York: Norton, 1973.

Apter, T. E. *Fantasy Literature: An Approach to Reality.* Bloomington: Indiana UP, 1982.

Arata, Stephen D. "The Occidental Tourist: *Dracula* and the Anxiety of Reverse Colonization." *Victorian Studies* 33 (1990): 621–45.

Auerbach, Nina. *Woman and the Demon: The Life of a Victorian Myth.* Cambridge, MA: Harvard UP, 1982.

Badley, Linda C. "Love and Death in the American Car: Stephen King's Auto-Erotic Horror." *The Gothic World of Stephen King: Landscape of Nightmares.* Ed. Gary Hoppenstand and Ray B. Browne. Bowling Green, OH: Bowling Green State UP, 1987. 84–94.

Bakhtin, Mikhail. *Rabelais and His World.* Trans. Hélène Iswolsky. Bloomington: Indiana UP, 1984.

Baldick, Chris. *In Frankenstein's Shadow: Myth, Monstrosity, and Nineteenth-Century Writing.* Oxford: Clarendon, 1987.

Beer, Gillian. *Darwin's Plots: Evolutionary Narrative in Darwin, George Eliot and Nineteenth-Century Fiction.* London and Boston: Routledge, 1983.

Belford, Barbara. *Bram Stoker: A Biography of the Author of Dracula.* New York: Knopf, 1996.

Bell, Ian. *Dreams of Exile: Robert Louis Stevenson: A Biography.* New York: Holt, 1993.

Bercovitch, Sacvan. *The American Jeremiad.* Madison: U of Wisconsin P, 1978.

Bergson, Henri. *Laughter: An Essay on the Meaning of the Comic.* Trans. Cloudesley Brereton and Fred Rothwell. London: MacMillan, 1911.

Berman, Jeffrey. *Narcissism and the Novel.* New York: New York UP, 1990.

Birkhead, Edith. *The Tale of Terror: A Study of the Gothic Romance.* London: Constable, 1921.

Blakey, Dorothy. *The Minerva Press, 1790–1820.* London: Oxford UP, 1939.

Bök, Christian. "The Monstrosity of Representation: *Frankenstein* and Rousseau." *English Studies in Canada* 18 (1992): 415–32.

Boone, Troy. "'He Is English and Therefore Adventurous': Politics, Decadence, and *Dracula.*" *Studies in the Novel* 25 (1993): 76–89.

Bosky, Bernadette Lynn. "The Mind's a Monkey: Character and Psychology in Stephen King's Recent Fiction." *Kingdom of Fear: The World of Stephen King.* Ed. Tim Underwood and Chuck Miller. San Francisco: Underwood-Miller, 1986. 209–38.

Botting, Fred. *Making monstrous: Frankenstein, criticism, theory.* Manchester: Manchester UP. New York: St. Martin's, 1991.

Bowditch, John, and Clement Ramsland. *Voices of the Industrial Revolution: Selected Readings from the Liberal Economists and Their Critics.* U of Michigan P, 1968.

Brantlinger, Patrick, and Richard Boyle. "The Education of Edward Hyde: Stevenson's 'Gothic Gnome' and the Mass Readership of Late-Victorian England." *Dr Jekyll and Mr Hyde after One Hundred Years.* Ed. William Veeder and Gordon Hirsch. Chicago: U of Chicago P, 1988. 265–82.

Bredvold, Louis I. *The Natural History of Sensibility.* Detroit: Wayne State UP, 1962.

Briggs, Asa. *The Age of Improvement.* London: Longmans, 1959.

Briggs, Julia. *Night Visitors: The Rise and Fall of the English Ghost Story.* London: Faber, 1977.

Bristow, Edward J. *Vice and Vigilance: Purity Movements in Britain since 1700.* Dublin: Gill, 1977.

Bristow, Joseph. Intro. to *The Importance of Being Earnest and Related Writings.* Oscar Wilde. London: Routledge, 1992. 1–26.

Brooks, Peter. "Virtue and Terror: *The Monk.*" *ELH* 40 (1973): 249–63.

Brown, Roger Lee. "The Rise and Fall of the Fleet Marriages." *Marriage and Society: Studies in the Social History of Marriage.* Ed. R. B. Outhwaite. New York: St. Martin's, 1981. 117–36.

Burke, Kenneth. "Literature as Equipment for Living." *The Philosophy of Literary Form: Studies in Symbolic Action.* 1941. New York: Vintage-Random, 1957. 253–62.

Butler, Marilyn. Introduction. *Mary Shelley: Frankenstein: 1818 Text.* Oxford: Oxford UP, 1994. ix-li.

Calder, Jenni. *Robert Louis Stevenson: A Life Study.* New York: Oxford UP, 1980.

Carter, Margaret, ed. *The Vampire in Literature: A Critical Bibliography.* Ann Arbor: UMI Research P, 1989.

———. *Specter or Delusion? The Supernatural in Gothic Fiction.* Ann Arbor: UMI Research P, 1987.

Chesterton, G. K. *Robert Louis Stevenson.* London: Hodder, 1927.

Clark, Kenneth. *The Gothic Revival: An Essay in the History of Taste.* 4th ed. London: Murray, 1974.

Clery, E. J. *The Rise of Supernatural Fiction, 1762–1800.* Cambridge, Eng.: Cambridge UP, 1995.

Clifford, Gay. "*Caleb Williams* and *Frankenstein*: First-Person Narratives and 'Things as They Are.'" *Genre* 10 (1977): 601–17.

Conger, Syndy McMillen. "Sensibility Restored: Radcliffe's Answer to Lewis's *The Monk*." *Gothic Fictions: Prohibition/Transgression.* Ed. Kenneth W. Graham. New York: AMS, 1989. 113–49.

———. "Faith and Doubt in *The Castle of Otranto*." *Gothic: The Review of Supernatural Fiction* 1 (1979): 51–59.

Coleman, William Emmet. *On the Discrimination of Gothicisms.* New York: Arno, 1980.

Cox, Stephen D. "*The Stranger within Thee*": Concepts of Self in Late Eighteenth-Century Literature.* Pittsburgh: U of Pittsburgh P, 1980.

Cranny-Francis, Anne. "Sexual Politics and Political Repression in Bram Stoker's *Dracula*." *Nineteenth-Century Suspense: From Poe to Conan Doyle.* Ed. Clive Bloom et al. New York: St. Martin's, 1988. 64–79.

Crouch, Laura. "Davy's *A Discourse, Introductory to A Course of Lectures on Chemistry*. A Possible Scientific Source of *Frankenstein*." *Keats-Shelley Journal* 27 (1978): 35–44.

Daly, Nicholas. "*Dracula* and the Rise of Professionalsim." *Texas Studies in Literature and Language* 39 (1997): 181–203.

Darvall, Frank Ongley. *Popular Disturbances and Public Order in Regency England.* 1934. New York: Kelley, 1969.

Day, William Patrick. *In the Circles of Fear and Desire: A Study of Gothic Fantasy.* U of Chicago P, 1985.

DeLamotte, Eugenia C. *Perils of the Night: A Feminist Study of Nineteenth-Century Gothic.* New York: Oxford UP, 1990.

Docherty, Brian, ed. *American Horror Fiction: From Brockden Brown to Stephen King.* New York: St. Martin's, 1990.

Dole, Carol M. "Three Tyrants in *The Castle of Otranto.*" *English Language Notes* 26 (Sept. 1988): 26–35.

Donatelli, Joseph M. P. "The Medieval Fictions of Thomas Warton and Thomas Percy." *University of Toronto Quarterly* 60 (1991): 435–51.

Doody, Margaret Anne. "Deserts, Ruins and Troubled Waters: Female Dreams in Fiction and the Development of the Gothic Novel." *Genre* 10 (1977): 529–72.

———. *A Natural Passion: A Study of the Novels of Samuel Richardson.* Oxford: Clarendon, 1974.

Dunn, Richard J. "Narrative Distance in *Frankenstein.*" *Studies in the Novel* 6 (1974): 408–17.

Egan, James. "Sacral Parody in the Fiction of Stephen King." *Journal of Popular Culture* 23:3 (1989): 125–41.

Eliade, Mircea. *The Myth of the Eternal Return: or, Cosmos and History.* 1954. Trans. Willard R. Trask. New York: Harper Torchbooks, 1974.

Eliot, T. S. "Tradition and the Individual Talent." 1917. *Critical Theory Since Plato.* Ed. Hazard Adams. New York: Harcourt, 1971. 784–87.

Ellis, Kate Ferguson. *The Contested Castle: Gothic Novels and the Subversion of Domestic Ideology.* Urbana: U of Illinois P, 1989.

Ellis-Fermor, U. M. *The Jacobean Drama: An Interpretation.* London: Methuen, 1936.

Faraday, Ann. *Dream Power.* 1972. New York: Berkley, 1986.

Farson, Daniel. *The Man Who Wrote Dracula: A Biography of Bram Stoker.* London: Joseph, 1975.

Fiedler, Leslie. *Love and Death in the American Novel.* Cleveland: World, 1962.

———. "Archetype and Signature." 1952. *Art and Psychoanalysis: Studies in the Application of Psychoanalytic Theory to the Creative Process.* Ed. William Phillips. Cleveland: Meridian, 1963. 452–72.

Florescu, Radu. *In Search of Frankenstein.* Boston: New York Graphic Soc., 1975.

Fontana, Ernest. "Lombroso's Criminal Man and Stoker's *Dracula.*" 1984. *Dracula: The Vampire and the Critics.* Ed. Margaret Carter. Forward William Veeder. Ann Arbor: UMI Research P, 1988. 159–65.

Forry, Steven Earl. *Hideous Progenies: Dramatizations of Frankenstein from Mary Shelley to the Present.* Philadelphia: U of Pennsylvania P, 1990.

Frank, Frederick S. "From Boudoir to Castle Crypt: Richardson and the Gothic Novel." *Revue des Langues Vivantes* 41 (1975): 49–59.

Frankl, Paul. *The Gothic: Literary Sources and Interpretations through Eight Centuries.* Princeton, NJ: Princeton UP, 1960.

Frayling, Christopher. *Vampyres: Lord Byron to Count Dracula.* London: Faber, 1991.

Freud, Sigmund. *The Standard Edition of the Complete Psychological Works.* Trans. ed. James Strachy et al. 24 vols. London: Hogarth, 1953–1958.

———. *Sigmund Freud: The Interpretation of Dreams.* Trans. James Strachey. 1953. New York: Avon, 1965.

———. "The Origin and Development of Psychoanalysis." 1910. *A General Selection from the Works of Sigmund Freud.* E. John Rickman. 1937. New York: Anchor-Doubleday, 1957. 3–36.

Frye, Northrop. "Towards Defining an Age of Sensibility." *Fables of Identity: Studies in Poetic Mythology.* New York: Harcourt, 1963. 130–37.

Furnas, J. C. *Voyage to Windward: The Life of Robert Louis Stevenson.* 1951. London: Faber, 1952.

Garnett, Rhys. "*Dracula* and *The Beetle:* Imperial and Sexual Guilt and Fear in Late Victorian Fantasy." *Science Fiction Roots and Branches: Contemporary Critical Approaches.* Ed. Rhys Garnett and R. J. Ellis. Houndmills, Basingstoke, Hampshire, Eng.: MacMillan, 1990. 30–54.

Gassner, John, ed. *A Treasury of the Theatre: Volume One: World Drama from Aeschylus to Ostrovsky.* Ed. John Gassner. New York: Simon, 1967.

Gilbert, Sandra M., and Susan Gubar. *The Madwoman in the Attic: The Woman Writer and the Nineteenth-Century Literary Imagination.* New Haven: Yale UP, 1979.

Glut, Donald F. *The Frankenstein Legend: A Tribute to Mary Shelley and Boris Karloff.* Metuchen, NJ: Scarecrow, 1973.

Gorham, Deborah. "The 'Maiden Tribute of Modern Babylon' Re-examined: Child Prostitution and the Idea of Childhood in Late-Victorian England." *Victorian Studies* 21 (1978): 353–79.

Grant, D. *The Cock Lane Ghost.* London: Macmillan, 1965.

Graves, Robert. *The Greek Myths.* 2 vols. Rev. ed. 1960. Harmondsworth, Middlesex, Eng.: Penguin, 1983.

Griffen, Gail B. "'Your Girls That You Love are Mine': *Dracula* and the Victorian Sexual Imagination." 1980. *Dracula: The Vampire and the Critics.* Ed. Margaret Carter. Forward William Veeder. Ann Arbor: UMI Research P, 1988. 137–48.

Grosskurth, Phyllis. *John Addington Symonds.* London: Longman's, 1964.

Grudin, Peter. "*The Monk:* Matilda and the Rhetoric of Deceit." *Journal of Narrative Technique* 5.2 (1975): 136–46.

Grun, Bernard. *The Timetables of History.* New York: Touchstone-Simon, 1982.

Gurevich, Aron. *Medieval popular culture: Problems of belief and perception.* 1988. Trans. János M. Bak and Paul A. Hollingsworth. Cambridge: Cambridge UP, 1990.

Gwynn, Stephen. *The Life of Horace Walpole.* New York: Haskell House, 1971.

Haggerty, George E. "The Gothic Form of *Wuthering Heights.*" *Victorian Newsletter* 74 (1988): 1–6.

Hagstrum, Jean H. *William Blake: Poet and Painter: An Introduction to the Illuminated Verse.* Chicago: U of Chicago P, 1978.

Harth, Erica. "The Virtue of Love: Lord Hardwicke's Marriage Act." *Cultural Critique* 9 (Spring 1988): 123–54.

Heath, Stephen. "Psychopathia Sexualis: Stevenson's *Strange Case.*" *Critical Quaterly* 28 (1986): 93–108.

Heller, Terry. *The Delights of Terror: An Aesthetics of the Tale of Terror.* Urbana: U of Illinois P, 1987.

Hennessy, James Pope. *Robert Louis Stevenson.* London: Cape, 1974.

Hicks, James E. "Stephen King's Creation of Horror in *'Salem's Lot:* A Prolegomenon Towards a New Hermeneutic of the Gothic Novel." *The Gothic World of Stephen King: Landscape of Nightmares.* Ed. Gary Hoppenstand and Ray B. Browne. Bowling Green, OH: Bowling Green State UP, 1987. 75–83.

Hillman, James. *Archetypal Psychology: A Brief Account.* Dallas, TX: Spring, 1985.

Hoxie, Frederick E., ed. *Indians in American History: An Introduction.* Arlington Heights, IL: Davidson, 1988.

Huizinga, J. *The Waning of the Middle Ages.* 1924. Garden City, NY: Doubleday-Anchor, 1954.

Huizinga, J. H. *Rousseau: The Self-Made Saint.* New York: Viking-Grossman, 1976.

Hunter, J. Paul. *Before Novels: The Cultural Contexts of Eighteenth-Century English Fiction.* New York: Norton, 1990.

Hyde, J. Montgomery. *The Love That Dared Not Speak Its Name.* Boston: Little, 1970.

Isaacson, Robert L. *The Limbic System.* New York: Plenum, 1974.

Jackson, Rosemary. *Fantasy, the Literature of Subversion.* London: Methuen, 1981.

Jann, Rosemary. "Saved by Science? The Mixed Messages of Stoker's *Dracula.*" *Texas Studies in Literature and Language* 31 (1989): 273–87.

Jones, Michael W. *The Cartoon History of Britain.* New York: MacMillan, 1971.

Jones, Wendy. "Stories of Desire in *The Monk.*" *ELH* 57 (1990): 129–50.

Jung, C. G. *The Archetypes and the Collective Unconscious.* Trans. R. F. C. Hull. 2nd. ed. Princeton, NJ: Princeton UP, 1980.

———. *Memories, Dreams, Reflections.* Ed. Aniela Jaffé. Trans. Richard and Clara Wilson. New York: Vintage-Random, 1965.

———. "The Psychology of the Child Archetype." *Essays on a Science of Mythology; The Myth of the Divine Child and the Mysteries of Eleusis.* C. G. Jung and C. Kerényi. 1963. Trans. R. F. C. Hull. Princeton, NJ: Princeton UP, 1969. 70–100.

———. *The Structure and Dynamics of the Psyche.* Vol. 8 of *The Collected Works.* Trans. R. F. C. Hull. London: Routledge, 1960.

Kahane, Claire. "The Gothic Mirror." *The (M)other Tongue: Essays in Feminist Psychoanalytic Interpretation.* Ed. Shirley Nelson Garner et al. Ithaca: Cornell UP, 1985. 334–51.

———. "The Maternal Legacy: The Grotesque Tradition in Flannery O'Connor's Female Gothic." *The Female Gothic.* Ed. Julian E. Fleenor. Montreal: Eden, 1983. 242–56.

Kallich, Martin. *Horace Walpole.* New York: Twayne, 1971.

Keily, Robert. *The Romantic Novel in England.* Cambridge, MA: Harvard UP, 1972.

Kennedy, Paul. *The Rise and Fall of the Great Powers: Economic Change and Military Conflict from 1500 to 2000.* New York: Random, 1987.

Kernberg, Otto. *Borderline Conditions and Pathological Narcissism.* New York: Jason Aronson, 1975.

Ketterer, David. "Frankenstein's 'Conversion' from Natural Magic to Modern Science—and a *Shifted* (and Converted) Last Draft Insert." *Science-Fiction Studies* 24 (1997): 57–78.

———. *Frankenstein's Creation: The Book, the Monster, and Human Reality.* Victoria, BC, Canada: U of Victoria P, 1979.

Ketton-Cremer, R. W. *Horace Walpole: A Biography.* 3rd ed. Ithaca, NY: Cornell UP, 1964.

Kiessling, Nicolas K. "Demonic Dread: The Incubus Figure in British Literature." *The Gothic Imagination: Essays in Dark Romanticism.* Ed. G. R. Thompson. Pullman, WA: Washington State UP, 1974. 22–41.

King, Stephen. "The *Playboy* Interview." With Eric Norden. 1983. *The Stephen King Companion.* Ed. George Beahm. Kansas City: Andrews, 1989. 19–45.

———. *Stephen King's Danse Macabre.* New York: Everest, 1981.

Kliger, Samuel. *The Goths in England: A Study in Seventeenth and Eighteenth Century Thought.* New York: Octagon, 1972.

Leatherdale, Clive. *The Origins of Dracula.* London: Kimber, 1987.

———. *Dracula: The Novel and the Legend.* Wellingborough, Northamptonshire: Aquarian, 1985.

Leavis, F. R. *The Great Tradition.* New York: New York UP, 1969.

Leites, Edmund. *The Puritan Conscience and Modern Sexuality.* New Haven: Yale UP, 1986.

Lewis, W. S. *Selected Letters of Horace Walpole.* New Haven: Yale UP, 1973.

Longueil, Alfred E. "The Word 'Gothic' in Eighteenth-Century Criticism." *Modern Language Notes* 38 (1923): 453–60.

Lovell, Terry. *Consuming Fiction.* London: Verso, 1987.

Lyndenberg, Robin. "Gothic Architecture and Fiction: A Survey of Critical Responses." *Centennial Review* 22 (1978): 95–109.

Ludlam, Harry. *A Biography of Dracula: The Life Story of Bram Stoker.* London: Foulsham, 1962.

MacAndrew, Elizabeth. *The Gothic Tradition in Fiction.* New York: Columbia UP, 1979.

MacLean, Paul. *The Triune Brain in Evolution: Role in Paleocerebral Functions.* New York: Plenum, 1990.

———. "Cerebral Evolution and Emotional Processes: New Findings on the Striatal Complex." *Annals New York Academy of Sciences* 193 (1972).

Magistrale, Tony. *Landscape of Fear: Stephen King's American Gothic.* Bowling Green: Bowling Green State U Popular P, 1988.

———. "Stephen King's Vietnam Allegory: An Interpretation of 'Children of the Corn.'" *Cuyahoga Review* 2 (1984): 61–66.

Maixner, Paul, ed. *Robert Louis Stevenson: The Critical Heritage.* London: Routledge, 1981.

Marcus, Steven. *The Other Victorians: A Study of Sexuality and Pornography in Mid-nineteenth-century England.* Toronto: Basic-Bantam, 1967.

Marshall, David. *The Surprising Effects of Sympathy: Marivaux, Diderot, Rousseau and Mary Shelley.* Chicago: U of Chicago P, 1988.

Marshall, Peter H. *William Godwin.* New Haven: Yale UP, 1984.

Marshall, Tim. *Murdering to Dissect: Grave-robbing, Frankenstein and the Anatomy Literature.* Manchester: Manchester UP, 1995.

Masson, Jeffrey M. "Freud and the Seduction Theory: A challenge to the foundations of psychoanalysis." *The Atlantic* February 1984: 33–60.

Mayo, Robert D. "How Long Was Gothic Fiction in Vogue?" *Modern Language Notes* (58) 1943: 58–64.

McClintock, Anne. *Imperial Leather: Race, Gender and Sexuality in the Colonial Contest.* New York: Routledge, 1995.

McDonald, Michael. *Witchcraft and Hysteria in Elizabethan London: Edward Jorden and the Mary Glover Case.* London: Tavistock-Routledge, 1991.

McIntyre, Clara F. "The Later Career of the Elizabethan Villain-Hero." *PMLA* 40 (1925): 874–80.

———. "Were the 'Gothic Novels' Gothic?" *PMLA* 36 (1921): 644–67.

McKeon, Michael. *The Origins of the English Novel 1600–1740.* Baltimore: Johns Hopkins UP, 1987.

McNally, Raymond T., and Radu Florescu. *In Search of Dracula.* New York: Warner, 1972.

Mead, Walter Russell. "Why the Deficit Is a Godsend: And Five Other Economic Heresies." *Harper's* May 1993: 56–63.

Medeiros, Paulo. "Simian Narratives and the Intersection of Science and Literature." *Modern Language Quarterly* 23.2 (1993): 59–73.

Mehrota, K. K. *Horace Walpole and the English Novel: A Study of "The Castle of Otranto": 1764–1820.* Oxford: Blackwell, 1934.

Mellor, Anne K. *Mary Shelley: Her Life, Her Fiction, Her Monsters.* New York: Methuen, 1988.

———. "Possessing Nature: The Female in *Frankenstein.*" *Romanticism and Feminism.* Ed. Anne K. Mellor. Bloomington: Indiana UP, 1988. 220–32.

Merchant, Carolyn. *The Death of Nature: Women, Ecology, and the Scientific Revolution.* San Francisco: Harper, 1980.

Michasiw, Kim Ian. "Ann Radcliffe and the Terrors of Power." *Eighteenth-Century Fiction* 6 (1994): 327–46.

Michie, Elsie. "*Frankenstein* and Marx's Theories of Alienated Labor." *Approaches to Teaching Shelley's Frankenstein.* Ed. Stephen C. Behrendt. New York: MLA, 1990. 93–98.

———. "Production Replaces Creation: Market Forces and *Frankenstein* as Critique of Romanticism." *Nineteenth-Century Contexts* 12.1 (1988): 27–33.

Miller, Perry. *Errand into the Wilderness.* Cambridge, MA: Harvard UP, Belknap, 1956.

Mise, Raymond W. *The Gothic Heroine and the Nature of the Gothic Novel.* New York: Arno, 1980.

Moers, Ellen. "Female Gothic." 1976. *The Endurance of* Frankenstein: *Essays on Mary Shelley's Novel.* Ed. George Levine and U. C. Knoepflmacher. Berkeley: U of California P, 1979. 77–87.

Montag, Warren. "The Workshop of Filthy Creation: A Marxist Reading of *Frankenstein.*" *Mary Shelley: Frankenstein.* Ed. Johanna M. Smith. Boston: Bedord-St. Martin's, 1992. 300–11.

Moretti, Franco. *Signs Taken for Wonders: Essays in the Sociology of Literary Forms.* Trans. Susan Fischer et al. London: Verso, 1983.

Moss, Stephanie. "Bram Stoker and the Society for Psychical Research." *Dracula: The Shade and the Shadow.* Ed. Elizabeth Miller. Westcliff-on-Sea, UK: Desert Island, 1998. 82–92.

Musson, A. E. "The Diffusion of Technology in Great Britain during the Industrial Revolution." 1969. *Science, Technology, and Economic Growth in the Eighteenth Century.* Ed. intro. A. E. Musson. London: Methuen, 1972. 97–114.

Napier, Elizabeth R. *The Failure of Gothic: Problems of Disjunction in Eighteenth-Century Literary Form.* Oxford: Clarendon, 1987.

Neumann, Erich. *The Great Mother: An Analysis of the Archetype.* 1963. Trans. Ralph Manheim. Princeton, NJ: Princeton UP, 1972.

———. *The Origins and History of Consciousness.* 1954. Trans. R. F. C. Hull. Princeton, NJ: Princeton UP, 1970.

Newman, John M. *JFK and Vietnam: Deception, Intrigue, and the Struggle for Power.* New York: Warner, 1992.

Nevins, Allan, and Henry Steele Commager. *A Pocket History of the United States.* New York: Washington Square, 1981.

Nichols, Nina da Vinci. "Place and Eros in Radcliffe, Lewis, and Brontë." *The Female Gothic.* Ed. Juliann E. Fleenor. Montreal: Eden, 1983. 187–206.

Nield, Keith, ed. *Prostitution in the Victorian Age: Debates on the Issue From 19th Century Critical Journals.* Westmead, Farnborough, Hants, Eng.: Gregg, 1973.

Nitchie, Elizabeth. "The Stage History of *Frankenstein.*" *South Atlantic Quarterly* 41 (1942): 384–98.

Norton, Rictor. "Aesthetic Gothic Horror." *Yearbook of Comparative and General Literature* 21 (1972): 31–40.

O'Flinn, Paul. "Production and Reproduction: The Case of *Frankenstein.*" *Literature and History* 9.2 (1983): 194–213.

O'Rourke, James. "'Nothing More Unnatural': Mary Shelley's Revision of Rousseau." *ELH* 56 (1989): 543–69.

Osborne, Charles, ed. *The Bram Stoker Bedside Companion: 10 Stories by the Author of Dracula.* New York, 1973.

Otto, Rudolf. *The Idea of the Holy: An Inquiry into the non-rational factor in the idea of the divine and its relation to the rational.* Trans. John W. Harvey. London: Oxford UP, 1950. 2nd ed.

Paglia, Camille. *Sexual Personae: Art and Decadence from Nefertiti to Emily Dickinson.* London: Yale UP, 1990.

Parreaux, André. *The Publication of* The Monk*: A Literary Event 1796–1798.* Paris: Librairie Marcel Didier, 1960.

Peck, Louis F. *A Life of Matthew G. Lewis.* Cambridge, MA: Harvard UP, 1961.

Peithmann, Irwin M. *Broken Peace Pipes: A Four-Hundred-Year History of the American Indian.* Springfield, IL: Thomas, 1964.

Pike, E. Royston. *Human Documents of the Industrial Revolution.* London: Allen, 1966.

Poovey, Mary. *The Proper Lady and the Woman Writer: Ideology as Style in the Works of Mary Wollstonecraft, Mary Shelley, and Jane Austen.* Chicago: U of Chicago P, 1984.

Porte, Joel. "In the Hands of an Angry God: Religious Terror in Gothic Fiction." *The Gothic Imagination: Essays in Dark Romanticism.* Ed. G. R. Thompson. Pullman, WA: Washington State UP, 1974. 42–64.

Punter, David. *The Literature of Terror: A History of Gothic Fictions from 1765 to the Present Day.* London: Longman, 1980.

Railo, Eino. *The Haunted Castle: A Study of the Elements of English Romanticism.* 1927. New York: Humanities, 1964.

Rank, Otto. *The Double: A Psychoanalytic Study.* Trans. Harry Tucker, Jr. Chapel Hill, NC: U of North Carolina P, 1971.

Richardson, Maurice. "The Psychoanalysis of Ghost Stories." *Twentieth Century* 166 (1959): 419–31.

Ringe, Donald A. *American Gothic: Imagination and Reason in Nineteenth-Century Fiction.* Lexington, KY: UP of Kentucky, 1982.

Roberts, Bette B. *The Gothic Romance: Its Appeal to Women Writers and Readers in Late Eighteenth-Century England.* New York: Arno, 1980.

Robinson, Daniel N., ed. *Significant Contributions to the History of Psychology 1750–1920.* Vol. 10 of Ser. A, *Orientations.* Washington, DC: U Publications of America, 1977. 11 vols.

Ronald, Ann. "Terror-Gothic: Nightmare and Dream in Ann Radcliffe and Charlotte Brontë." *The Female Gothic.* Ed. Juliann E. Fleenor. Montreal: Eden, 1983. 177–86.

Ronay, Gabriel. *The Truth about Dracula.* New York: Stein, 1972.

Roth, Phyllis A. *Bram Stoker.* Boston: Twayne-Hall, 1982.

———. "Suddenly Sexual Women in *Dracula.*" 1977. *Dracula: The Vampire and the Critics.* Ed. Margaret Carter. Forward William Veeder. Ann Arbor: UMI Research P, 1988. 57–67.

Sabor, Peter. *Horace Walpole: The Critical Heritage.* London: Routledge, 1987.

St. Clair, William. *The Godwins and the Shelleys: The Biography of a Family.* New York: Norton, 1989.

Samson, John. "Politics Gothicized: The Conway Incident and *The Castle of Otranto.*" *Eighteenth-Century Life* 10.3 (1986): 145–58.

Scarborough, Dorothy. *The Supernatural in Modern English Fiction.* New York: Putnam's, 1917.

Scherren, Henry. *The Zoological Society of London.* London: Cassell, 1905.

Scott, Peter Dale. "Vital Artifice: Mary, Percy, and the Psychopolitical Integrity of *Frankenstein.*" *The Endurance of* Frankenstein: *Essays on Mary Shelley's Novel.* Ed. George Levine and U. C. Knoepflmacher. Berkeley: U of California P, 1979. 172–202.

Sedgwick, Eve Kosofsky. *The Coherence of Gothic Conventions.* 1980. New York: Methuen, 1986.

Seed, David. "The Narrative Method of *Dracula.*" 1985. *Dracula: The Vampire and the Critics.* Ed. Margaret Carter. Forward William Veeder. Ann Arbor: UMI Research P, 1988. 195–206.

Senf, Carol A. "*Dracula:* The Unseen Face in the Mirror." 1979. *Dracula: The Vampire and the Critics.* Ed. Margaret Carter. Forward William Veeder. Ann Arbor: UMI Research P, 1988. 93–103.

———. "Blood, Eroticism, and the Vampire in Twentieth-Century Popular Literature." *The Gothic World of Stephen King: Landscape of Nightmares.* Ed. Gary Hoppenstand and Ray B. Browne. Bowling Green, OH: Bowling Green State UP, 1987. 20–30.

Shelley, Mary Wollstonecraft. *The Journals of Mary Shelley: 1814–1844.* Vol 1. Ed. Paula R. Feldman and Diana Scott-Kilvert. Oxford: Clarendon, 1987.

———. *The Letters of Mary Wollstonecraft Shelley.* Ed. Betty T. Bennett. 2 vols. Baltimore: Johns Hopkins, 1980.

Showalter, Elaine. *Sexual Anarchy: Gender and Culture at the Fin de Siècle.* New York: Viking, 1990.

Slotkin, Richard. *Regeneration Through Violence: The Mythology of the American Frontier, 1600–1860.* Middletown, CT: Wesleyan UP, 1973.

Smith, Johanna M. "Introduction: Biographical and Historical Contexts." *Frankenstein: Mary Shelley.* 1831. Ed. Johanna M. Smith. *Case Studies in Contemporary Criticism.* Ed. Ross C. Murfin. Boston: Bedford-St. Martin's, 1992. 3–18.

Spark, Muriel. *Child of Light: A Reassessment of Mary Wollstonecraft Shelley.* Hadleigh, Essex, Gt. Brit.: Tower Bridge, 1951.

Spector, Robert Donald. *The English Gothic: A Bibliographical Guide to Writers from Horace Walpole to Mary Shelley.* Westport, CT: Greenwood, 1984.

Spencer, Kathleen L. "Purity and Danger: *Dracula,* the Urban Gothic, and the Late Victorian Degeneracy Crisis." *ELH* 59 (1992): 197–225.

Steiner, Arpad. "The Faust Legend and the Christian Tradition." *PMLA* 54 (1939): 391–404.

Stern, Paul J. *C. G. Jung: The Haunted Prophet.* New York: Brazilier, 1976.

Sterrenburg, Lee. "Mary Shelley's Monster: Politics and Psyche in *Frankenstein.*" *The Endurance of* Frankenstein: *Essays on Mary Shelley's Novel.* Ed. George Levine and U. C. Knoepflmacher. Berkeley: U of California P, 1979. 143–71.

Stevenson, John Allen. "A Vampire in the Mirror: The Sexuality of *Dracula.*" *PMLA* 103 (1988): 139–47.

Stone, Lawrence. *Road to Divorce: England 1530–1987.* Oxford: Oxford UP, 1990.

———. *The Family, Sex and Marriage in England, 1500–1800.* New York: Harper, 1977.

———. "Literacy and Education in England 1640–1900." *Past and Present* 42 (1969): 69–139.

Sugg, Richard P., ed. *Jungian Literary Criticism* Evanston, IL: Northwestern UP, 1992.

Sullivan, Jack. *Elegant Nightmares: The English Ghost Story from Le Fanu to Blackwood.* Athens, OH: Ohio UP, 1978.

Summers, Montague. *The Gothic Quest: A History of the Gothic Novel.* 1938. New York: Russell, 1964.

Sunstein, Emily. *Mary Shelley: Romance and Reality.* London: Little, 1989.

Symonds, John Addington. *The Letters of John Addington Symonds.* Ed. Herbert M. Schueller and Robert L. Peters. Vol. 1. Detroit: Wayne State UP, 1967.

Tames, Richard L., ed. *Documents of the Industrial Revolution 1750–1850.* London: Hutchinson, 1971.

Thomas, Keith. *Religion and the Decline of Magic.* 1971. London: Penguin, 1988.

Todd, Janet. *The Sign of Angelica: Women, Writing and Fiction, 1660–1800.* London: Virago, 1989.

Todorov, Tzvetan. *The Fantastic: A Structural Approach to a Literary Genre.* Trans. Richard Howard. Cleveland: P of Case Western Reserve U, 1973.

Tompkins, Jane. *Sensational Designs: The Cultural Work of American Fiction, 1790–1860.* New York: Oxford UP, 1985.

Tompkins, J. M. S. *The Popular Novel in England: 1770–1800.* 1932. Westport, CT: Greenwood, 1976.

Tropp, Martin. *Images of Fear: How Horror Stories Helped Shape Modern Culture (1818–1919).* Jefferson, NC: McFarland, 1990.

Twitchell, James B. *The Living Dead: A Study of the Vampire in Romantic Literature.* Durham, NC: Duke UP, 1981.

Varma, Devendra P. *The Gothic Flame: Being a History of the Gothic Novel in England: Its Origins, Efflorescence, Disintegration, and Residuary Influences.* London: Barker, 1957.

Varnado, S. L. *Haunted Presence: The Numinous in Gothic Fiction.* Tuscaloosa and London: U of Alamaba P, 1987.

Vasbinder, Samuel Holmes. *Scientific Attitudes in Mary Shelley's* Frankenstein. Ann Arbor: UMI Research P, 1984.

Veeder, William. "Children of the Night: Stevenson and Patriarchy." *Dr Jekyll and Mr Hyde after One Hundred Years.* Ed. William Veeder and Gordon Hirsch. Chicago: U of Chicago P, 1988. 107–60.

———. *Mary Shelley and* Frankenstein: *The Fate of Androgyny.* Chicago: U of Chicago P, 1986.

Wagner, Peter. "Trial Reports as a Genre of Eighteenth-Century Erotica." *British Journal of Eighteenth-Century Studies* 5 (1983): 117–21.

Walkowitz, Judith R. *City of Dreadful Delight: Narratives of Sexual Danger in Late-Victorian London.* Chicago: U of Chicago P, 1992.

Waller, Gregory A. *The Living and the Undead: From Stoker's* Dracula *to Romero's* Dawn of the Dead. Urbana, IL: U of Illinois P, 1986.

Washburn, Wilcomb E. "The Seventeenth-Century Indian Wars." Vol. 15 of *Handbook of North American Indians.* Gen. ed. William C. Sturtevant. Vol. ed. Bruce G. Trigger. 20 vols. Washington: Smithsonian, 1978. 89–100.

———, vol. ed. Vol. 4 of *Handbook of North American Indians.* Gen. ed. William C. Sturtevant. 20 vols. Washington: Smithsonian, 1988.

Wasson, Richard. "The Politics of *Dracula*." 1979. *Dracula: The Vampire and the Critics.* Ed. Margaret Carter. Forward William Veeder. Ann Arbor: UMI Research P, 1988. 19–23.

Watt, Ian. *The Rise of the Novel: Studies in Defoe, Richardson and Fielding.* Berkeley: U of California P, 1957.

Weil, Judith. *Christopher Marlowe: Merlin's Prophet.* Chatham, Eng.: Mackay, 1977.

Weeks, Jeffrey. *Sex, Politics and Society: The regulation of sexuality since 1800.* 2nd ed. London: Longman, 1989.

Weissman, Judith. "Women and Vampires: *Dracula* as a Victorian Novel." 1977. *Dracula: The Vampire and the Critics.* Ed. Margaret Carter. Forward William Veeder. Ann Arbor: UMI Research P, 1988. 69–77.

Whyte, Lancelot Law. *The Unconscious Before Freud.* New York: Basic, 1960.

Wicke, Jennifer. "Vampiric Typewriting: *Dracula* and Its Media." *ELH* 59 (1992): 467-93.

Williams, Ioan, ed. *Novel and Romance 1700–1800: A Documentary Record.* London: Routledge, 1970.

Wilt, Judith. *Ghosts of the Gothic: Austen, Eliot, & Lawrence.* Princeton, NJ: Princeton UP, 1980.

Winter, Douglas E. *Stephen King: The Art of Darkness.* New York: Signet-NAL, 1984.

Wolff, Cynthia Griffin. "The Radcliffean Gothic Model: A Form for Feminine Sexuality." *The Female Gothic.* Ed. Juliann E. Fleenor. Montreal: Eden, 1983. 207–23.

Wood, James Playsted. *The Lantern Bearer: A Life of Robert Louis Stevenson.* New York: Pantheon-Random, 1965.

Worringer, Wilhelm. *Form in Gothic.* 1927. Trans. ed. intro. Sir Herbert Read. London: Tiranti, 1957.

INDEX